THE SUPER SPIDER-MAN
A TROUBLED MIND

W9-DGE-497

WRITER
DAN SLOTT

PENCILER, #6-8
HUMBERTO RAMOS

PENCILER, #9-10
RYAN STEGMAN

INKER, #6-8
VICTOR OLAZABA

INKER, #9-10
RYAN STEGMAN
WITH CAM SMITH (#10)

COLORIST
EDGAR DELGADO

LETTERER
CHRIS ELIOPOULOS

COVER ART
HUMBERTO RAMOS & EDGAR DELGADO (#6-8) AND MARCOS MARTIN (#9-10)

ASSISTANT EDITOR
ELLIE PYLE

EDITOR
STEPHEN WACKER

Collection Editor: **Jennifer Grünwald** • Assistant Editors: **Alex Starbuck & Nelson Ribeiro** • Editor, Special Projects: **Mark D. Beazley**
Senior Editor, Special Projects: **Jeff Youngquist** • SVP of Print & Digital Publishing Sales: **David Gabriel** • Book Design: **Jeff Powell**

Editor in Chief: **Axel Alonso** • Chief Creative Officer: **Joe Quesada** • Publisher: **Dan Buckley** • Executive Producer: **Alan Fine**

Jefferson Twp. Public Library
1031 Weldon Road
Oak Ridge, NJ 07438
973-208-6244
www.jeffersonlibrary.net

PERIOR SPIDER-MAN VOL. 2: A TROUBLED MIND. Contains material originally published in magazine form as SUPERIOR SPIDER-MAN #6-10. First printing 2013. ISBN# 978-0-7851-6705-1. Published by MARVEL
RLDWIDE, INC., a subsidiary of MARVEL ENTERTAINMENT, LLC. OFFICE OF PUBLICATION: 135 West 50th Street, New York, NY 10020. Copyright © 2013 Marvel Characters, Inc. All rights reserved. All characters featured
his issue and the distinctive names and likenesses thereof, and all related indicia are trademarks of Marvel Characters, Inc. No similarity between any of the names, characters, persons, and/or institutions in this
gazine with those of any living or dead person or institution is intended, and any such similarity which may exist is purely coincidental. **Printed in the U.S.A.** ALAN FINE, EVP - Office of the President, Marvel Worldwide,
. and EVP & CMO Marvel Characters B.V.; DAN BUCKLEY, Publisher & President - Print, Animation & Digital Divisions; JOE QUESADA, Chief Creative Officer; TOM BREVOORT, SVP of Publishing; DAVID BOGART, SVP of
erations & Procurement, Publishing; C.B. CEBULSKI, SVP of Creator & Content Development; DAVID GABRIEL, SVP of Print & Digital Publishing Sales; JIM O'KEEFE, VP of Operations & Logistics; DAN CARR, Executive
ctor of Publishing Technology; SUSAN CRESPI, Editorial Operations Manager; ALEX MORALES, Publishing Operations Manager; STAN LEE, Chairman Emeritus. For information regarding advertising in Marvel Comics
n Marvel.com, please contact Niza Disla, Director of Marvel Partnerships, at ndisla@marvel.com. For Marvel subscription inquiries, please call 800-217-9158. **Manufactured between 6/28/2013 and 8/5/2013 by**
AD/GRAPHICS ST. CLOUD, ST. CLOUD, MN, USA.

987654321

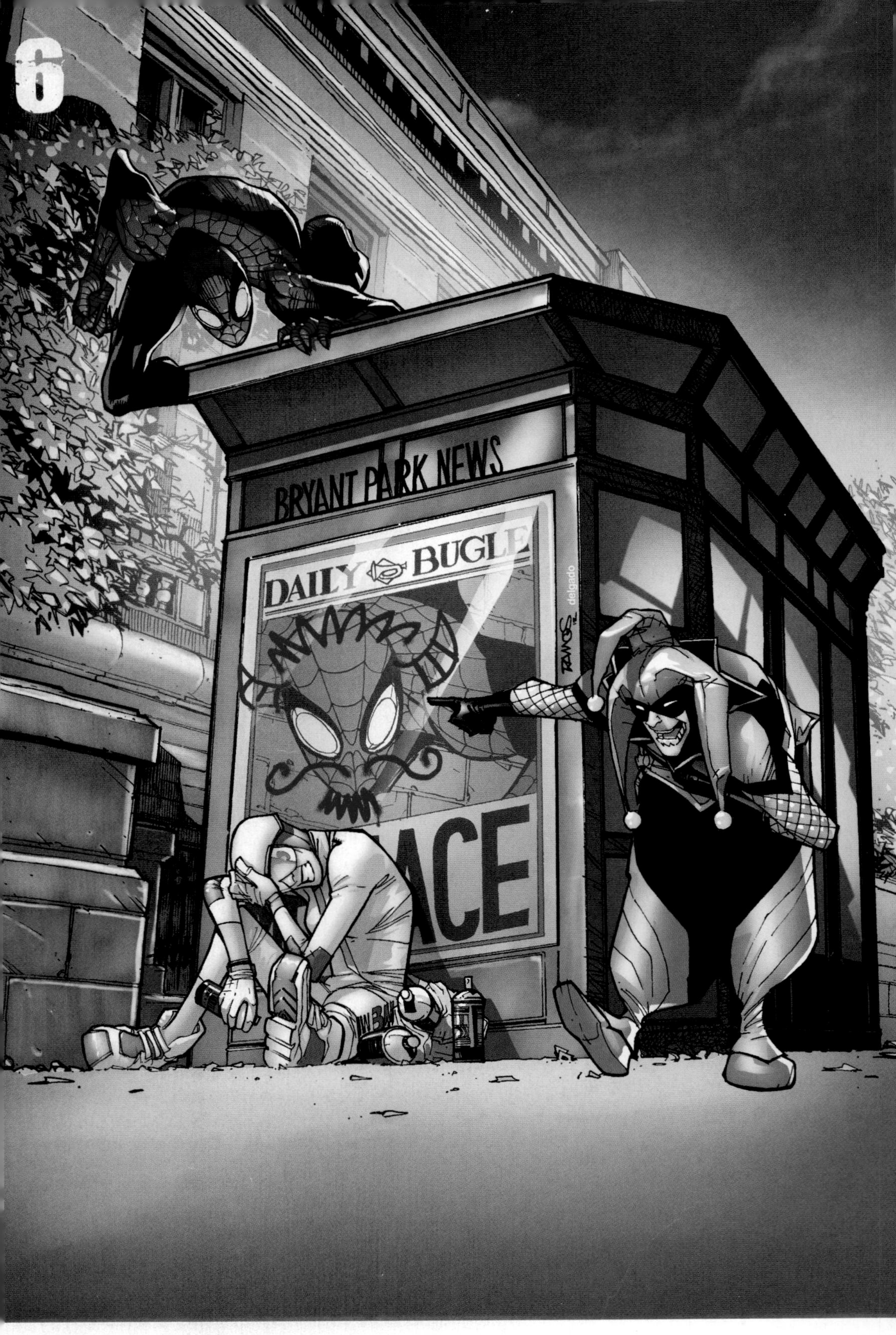
6
BRYANT PARK NEWS
DAILY BUGLE
ACE

JOKING HAZARD

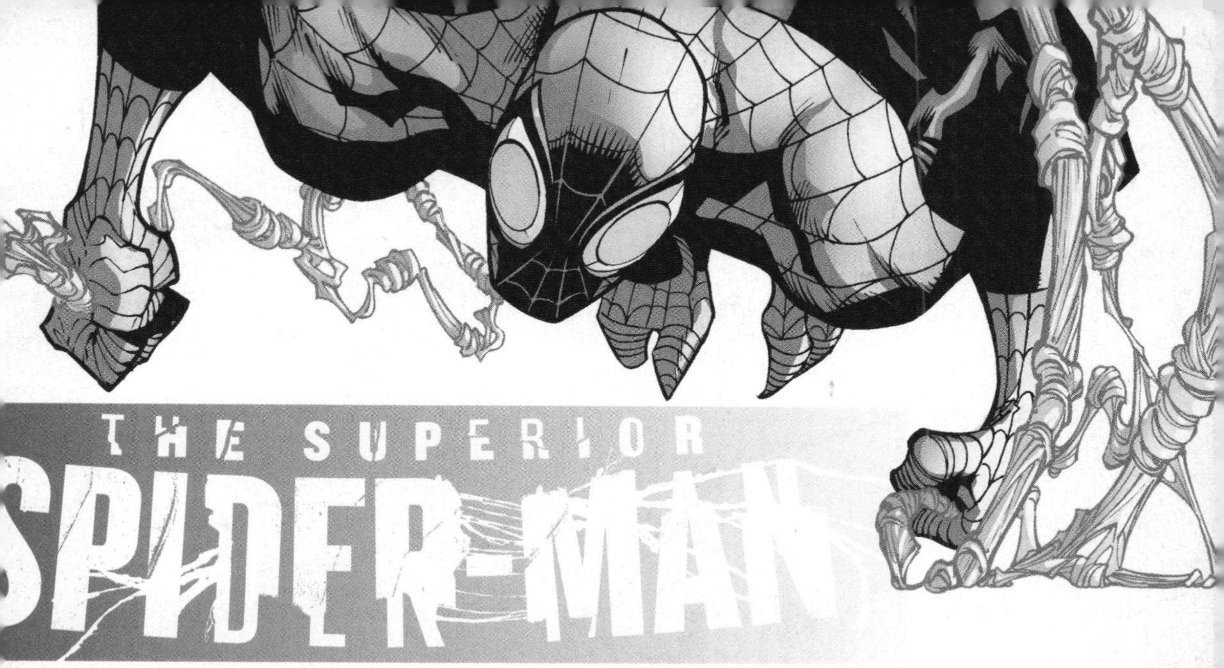
THE SUPERIOR
SPIDER-MAN

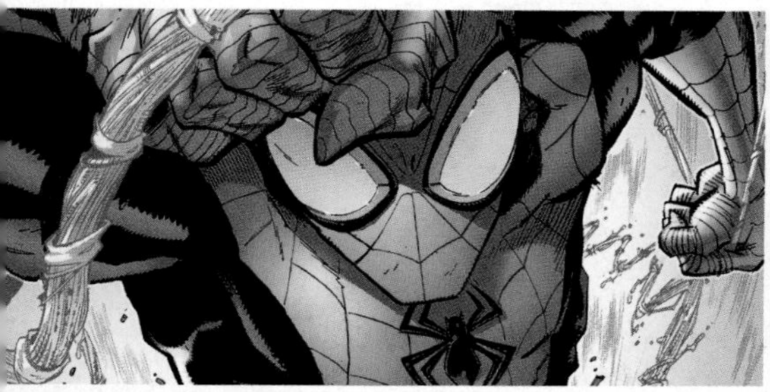

TTO OCTAVIUS IS A MAN WHO CHEATED DEATH, BUT AT A RICE. WHEN HE EXCHANGED BODIES WITH **PETER PARKER,** E GAINED THE AMAZING SKILLS OF SPIDER-MAN — AND L OF PETER'S MEMORIES. OTTO FINALLY UNDERSTANDS PETER'S MISSION OF GREAT RESPONSIBILITY.

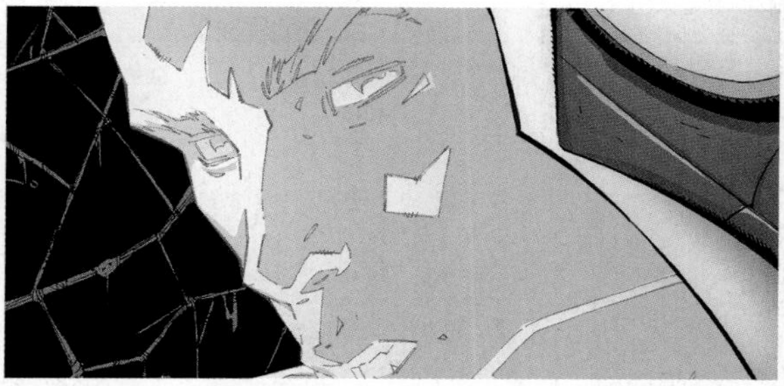

BUT A TINY PIECE OF PETER PARKER IS STILL THERE IN THE SUPERIOR SPIDER-MAN'S BRAIN, WATCHING OTTO LIVE OUT HIS LIFE AND TRYING TO KEEP THE REFORMED VILLAIN IN CHECK.

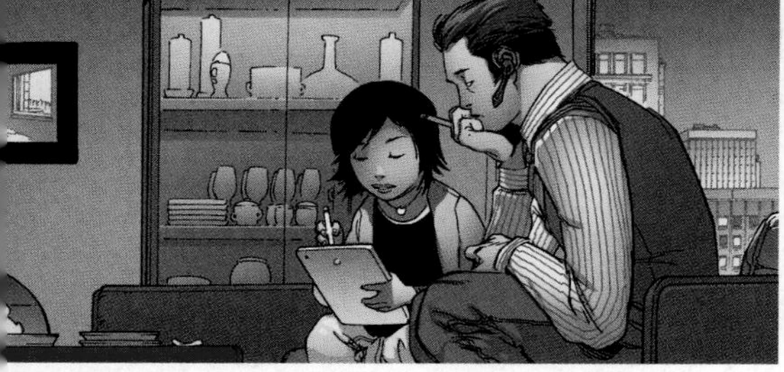

ID OCK HAS BEEN MAKING SOME IMPROVEMENTS ON ETER'S LIFE, SUCH AS GOING BACK TO SCHOOL TO GET HIS PHD.

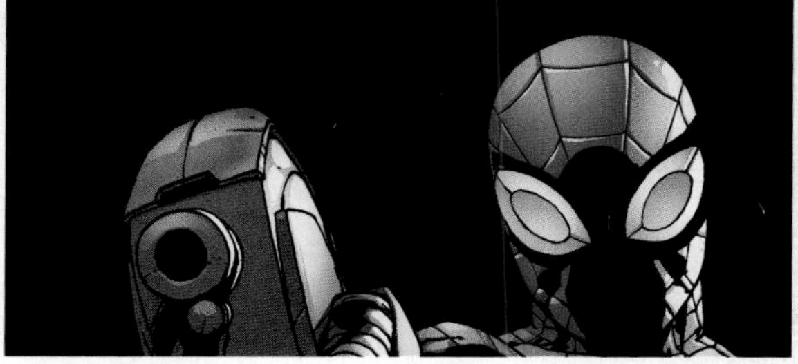

BUT WHEN ONE OF SPIDER-MAN'S ENEMIES, MASSACRE, WENT ON A SHOOTING SPREE IN GRAND CENTRAL STATION, PETER PARKER WAS UNABLE TO STOP DOC OCK FROM USING DEADLY FORCE TO END THE THREAT ONCE AND FOR ALL.

When you see this: AR, open up the MARVEL AR APP (available on applicable Apple ® iOS or Android TM devices) and use your camera-enabled device to unlock extra-special exclusive features!*

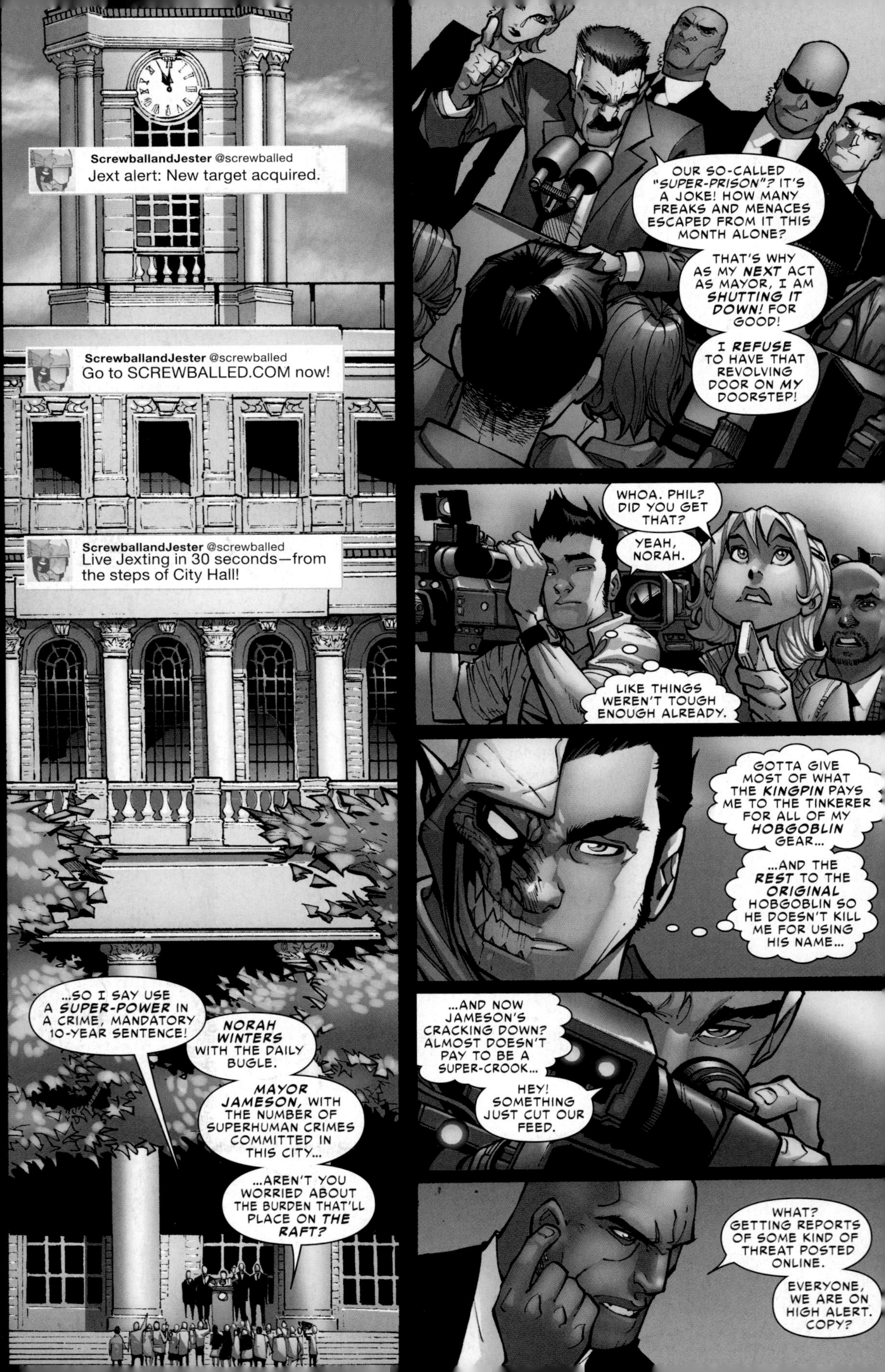
ScrewballandJester @screwballed
Jext alert: New target acquired.
ScrewballandJester @screwballed
Go to SCREWBALLED.COM now!
ScrewballandJester @screwballed
Live Jexting in 30 seconds—from the steps of City Hall!
...SO I SAY USE A SUPER-POWER IN A CRIME, MANDATORY 10-YEAR SENTENCE!
NORAH WINTERS WITH THE DAILY BUGLE.
MAYOR JAMESON, WITH THE NUMBER OF SUPERHUMAN CRIMES COMMITTED IN THIS CITY...
...AREN'T YOU WORRIED ABOUT THE BURDEN THAT'LL PLACE ON THE RAFT?
OUR SO-CALLED "SUPER-PRISON"? IT'S A JOKE! HOW MANY FREAKS AND MENACES ESCAPED FROM IT THIS MONTH ALONE?
THAT'S WHY AS MY NEXT ACT AS MAYOR, I AM SHUTTING IT DOWN! FOR GOOD!
I REFUSE TO HAVE THAT REVOLVING DOOR ON MY DOORSTEP!
WHOA. PHIL? DID YOU GET THAT?
YEAH, NORAH.
LIKE THINGS WEREN'T TOUGH ENOUGH ALREADY.
GOTTA GIVE MOST OF WHAT THE KINGPIN PAYS ME TO THE TINKERER FOR ALL OF MY HOBGOBLIN GEAR...
...AND THE REST TO THE ORIGINAL HOBGOBLIN SO HE DOESN'T KILL ME FOR USING HIS NAME...
...AND NOW JAMESON'S CRACKING DOWN? ALMOST DOESN'T PAY TO BE A SUPER-CROOK...
HEY! SOMETHING JUST CUT OUR FEED.
WHAT? GETTING REPORTS OF SOME KIND OF THREAT POSTED ONLINE.
EVERYONE, WE ARE ON HIGH ALERT. COPY?

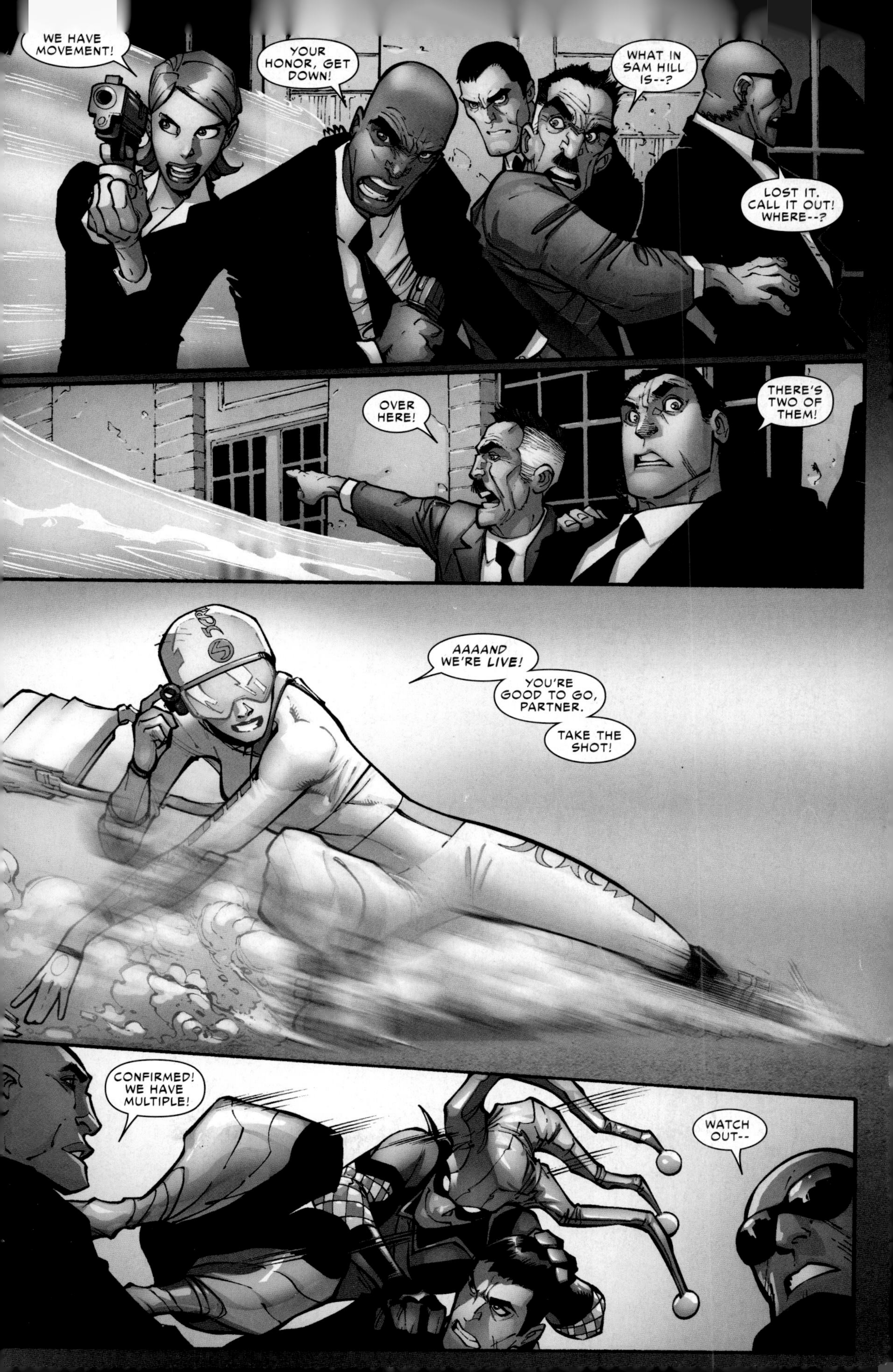
WE HAVE MOVEMENT!
YOUR HONOR, GET DOWN!
WHAT IN SAM HILL IS--?
LOST IT. CALL IT OUT! WHERE--?
OVER HERE!
THERE'S TWO OF THEM!
AAAAND WE'RE LIVE!
YOU'RE GOOD TO GO, PARTNER.
TAKE THE SHOT!
CONFIRMED! WE HAVE MULTIPLE!
WATCH OUT--

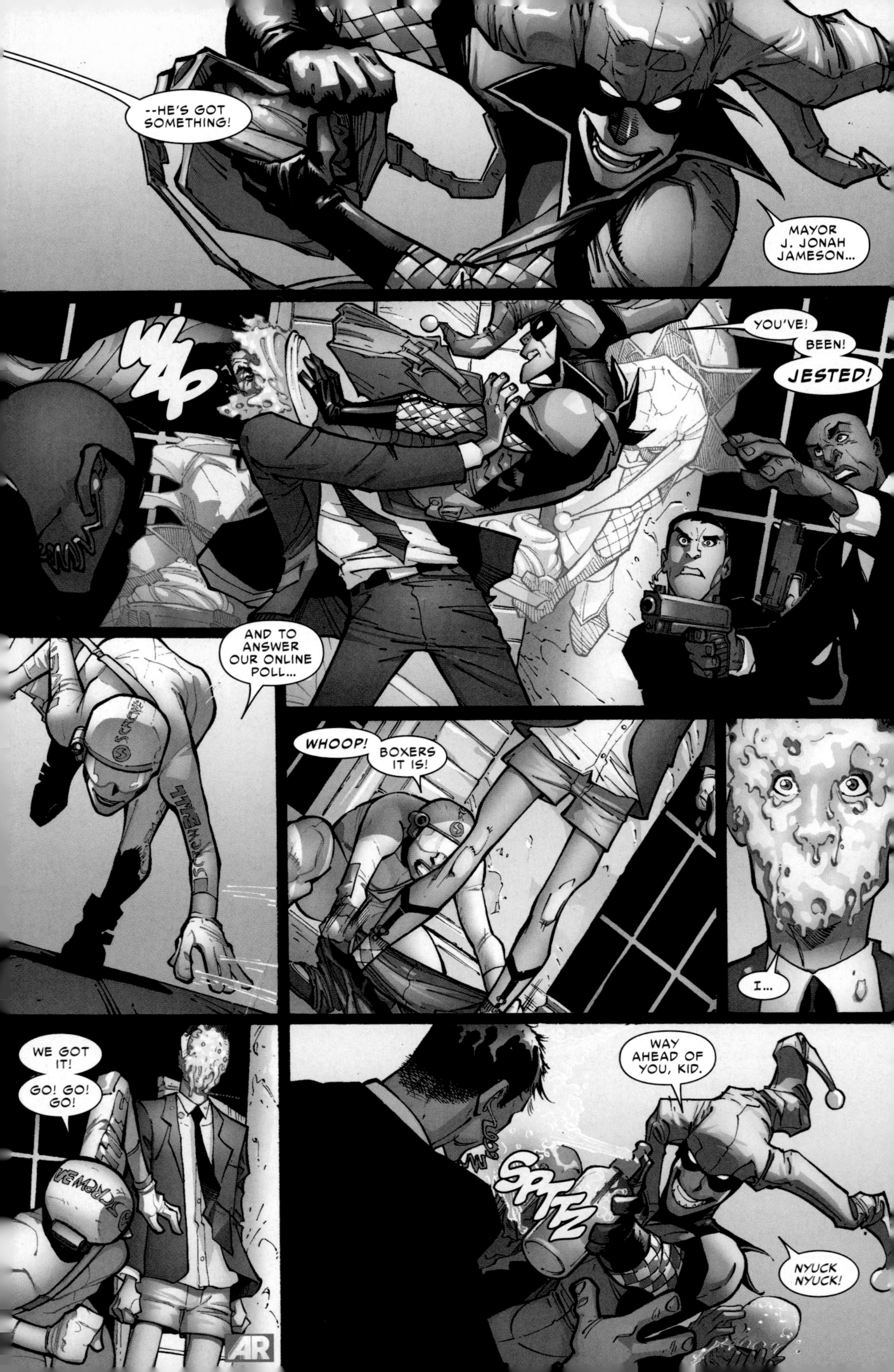
--HE'S GOT SOMETHING!
MAYOR J. JONAH JAMESON...
WAP
YOU'VE!
BEEN!
JESTED!
AND TO ANSWER OUR ONLINE POLL...
WHOOP!
BOXERS IT IS!
I...
WE GOT IT!
GO! GO! GO!
WAY AHEAD OF YOU, KID.
SPTZ
NYUCK NYUCK!

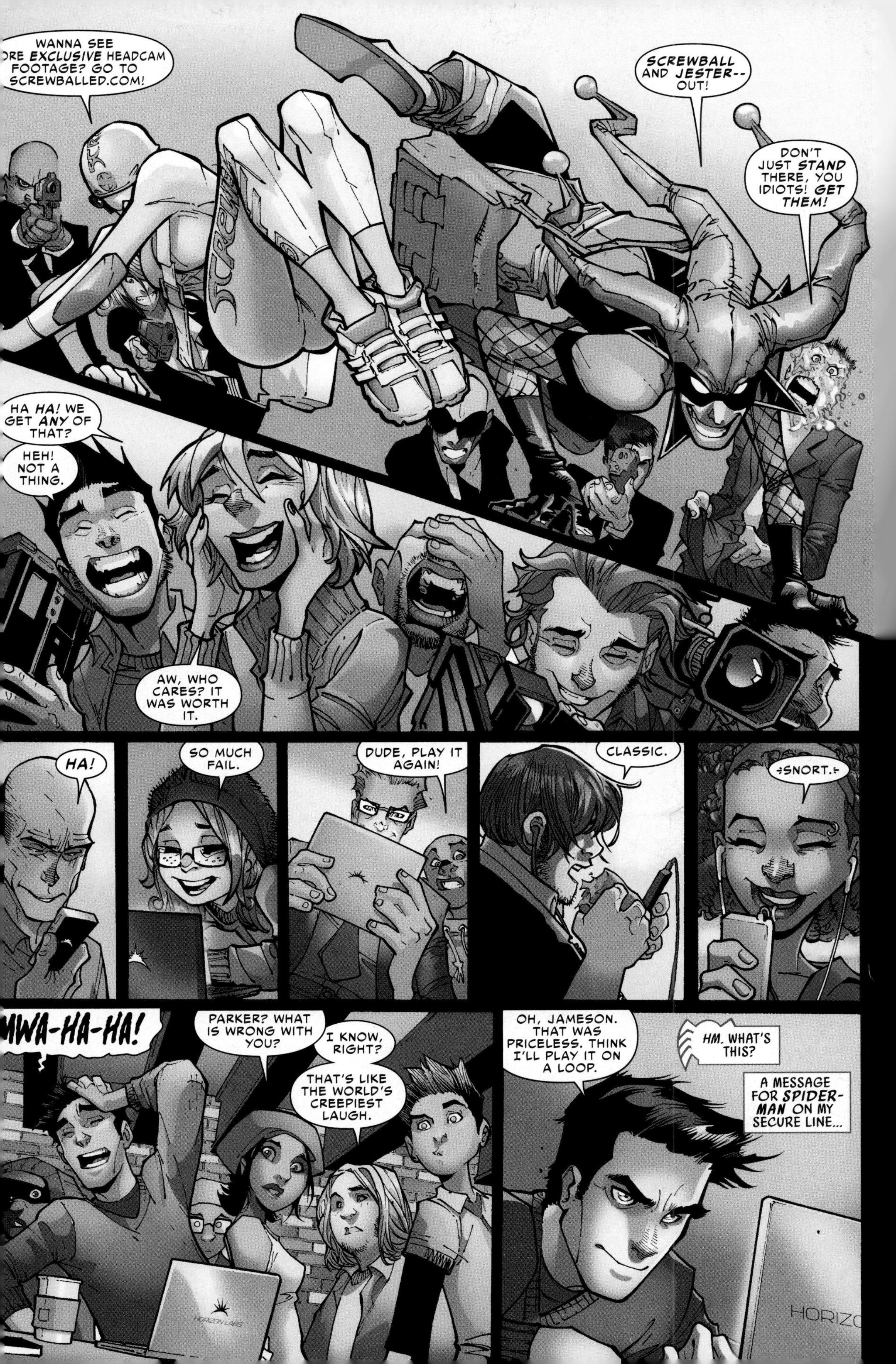

WANNA SEE ORE EXCLUSIVE HEADCAM FOOTAGE? GO TO SCREWBALLED.COM!
SCREWBALL AND JESTER-- OUT!
DON'T JUST STAND THERE, YOU IDIOTS! GET THEM!
HA HA! WE GET ANY OF THAT?
HEH! NOT A THING.
AW, WHO CARES? IT WAS WORTH IT.
HA!
SO MUCH FAIL.
DUDE, PLAY IT AGAIN!
CLASSIC.
SNORT.
MWA-HA-HA!
PARKER? WHAT IS WRONG WITH YOU?
I KNOW, RIGHT?
THAT'S LIKE THE WORLD'S CREEPIEST LAUGH.
OH, JAMESON. THAT WAS PRICELESS. THINK I'LL PLAY IT ON A LOOP.
HM. WHAT'S THIS?
A MESSAGE FOR SPIDER-MAN ON MY SECURE LINE...
HORIZON LABS
HORIZ

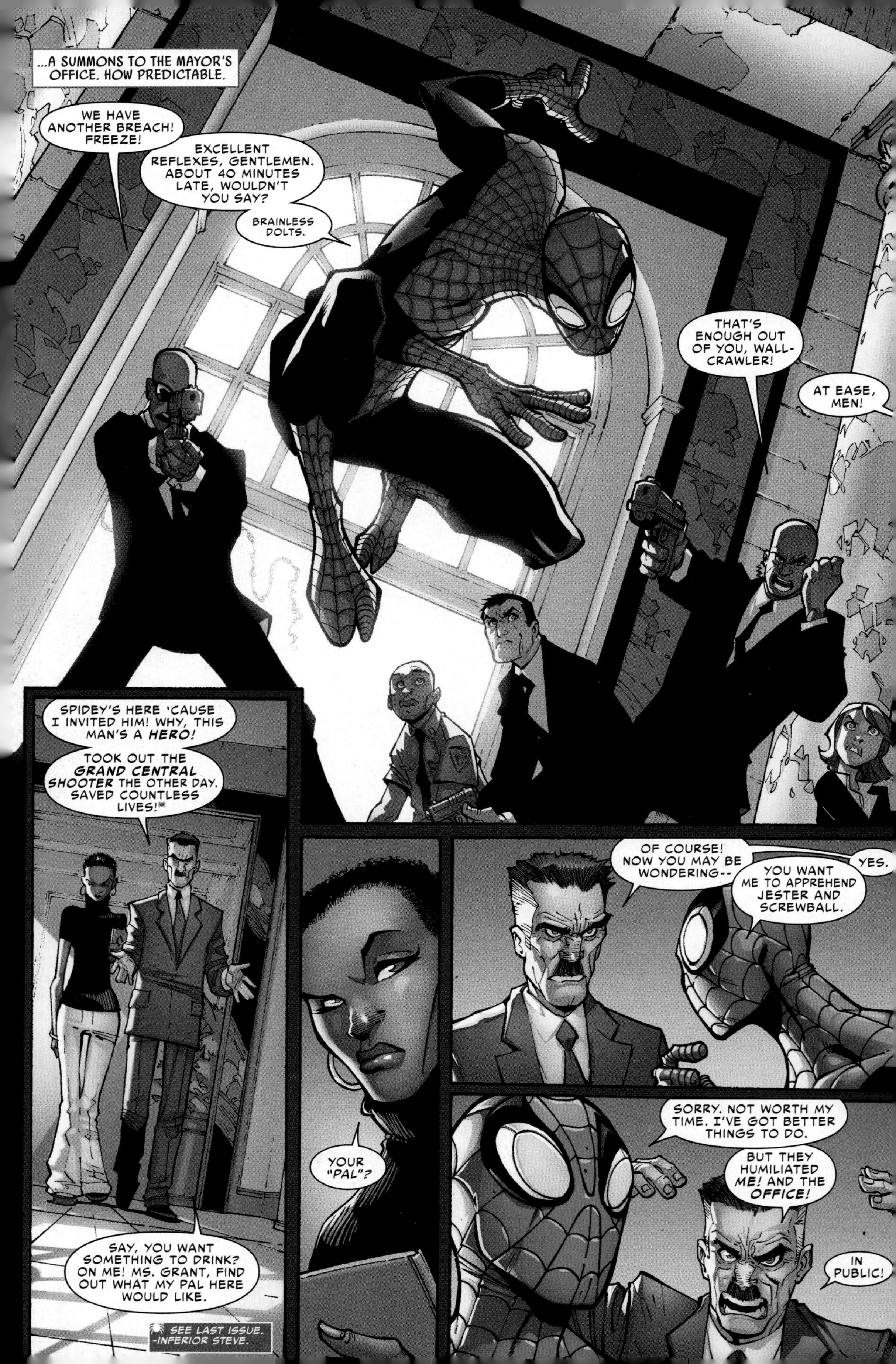
...A SUMMONS TO THE MAYOR'S OFFICE. HOW PREDICTABLE.
WE HAVE ANOTHER BREACH! FREEZE!
EXCELLENT REFLEXES, GENTLEMEN. ABOUT 40 MINUTES LATE, WOULDN'T YOU SAY?
BRAINLESS DOLTS.
THAT'S ENOUGH OUT OF YOU, WALL-CRAWLER!
AT EASE, MEN!
SPIDEY'S HERE 'CAUSE I INVITED HIM! WHY, THIS MAN'S A HERO!
TOOK OUT THE GRAND CENTRAL SHOOTER THE OTHER DAY. SAVED COUNTLESS LIVES!*
SAY, YOU WANT SOMETHING TO DRINK? ON ME! MS. GRANT, FIND OUT WHAT MY PAL HERE WOULD LIKE.
*SEE LAST ISSUE. -INFERIOR STEVE.
YOUR "PAL"?
OF COURSE! NOW YOU MAY BE WONDERING--
YOU WANT ME TO APPREHEND JESTER AND SCREWBALL.
YES.
SORRY. NOT WORTH MY TIME. I'VE GOT BETTER THINGS TO DO.
BUT THEY HUMILIATED ME! AND THE OFFICE!
IN PUBLIC!

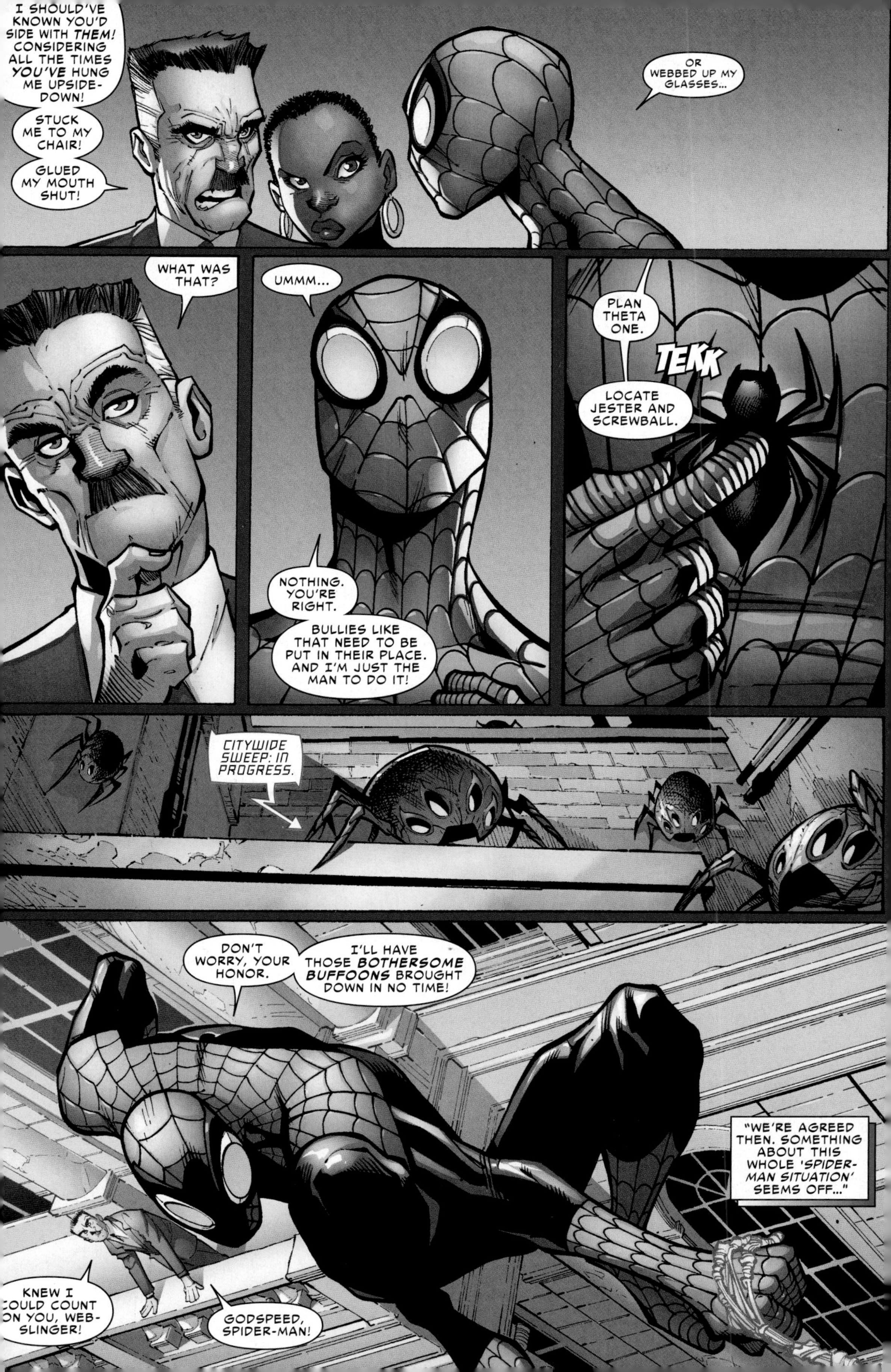
I SHOULD'VE KNOWN YOU'D SIDE WITH THEM! CONSIDERING ALL THE TIMES YOU'VE HUNG ME UPSIDE-DOWN!
STUCK ME TO MY CHAIR!
GLUED MY MOUTH SHUT!
OR WEBBED UP MY GLASSES...
WHAT WAS THAT?
UMMM...
NOTHING. YOU'RE RIGHT.
BULLIES LIKE THAT NEED TO BE PUT IN THEIR PLACE. AND I'M JUST THE MAN TO DO IT!
PLAN THETA ONE.
TEKK
LOCATE JESTER AND SCREWBALL.
CITYWIDE SWEEP: IN PROGRESS.
DON'T WORRY, YOUR HONOR.
I'LL HAVE THOSE BOTHERSOME BUFFOONS BROUGHT DOWN IN NO TIME!
"WE'RE AGREED THEN. SOMETHING ABOUT THIS WHOLE 'SPIDER-MAN SITUATION' SEEMS OFF..."
KNEW I COULD COUNT ON YOU, WEB-SLINGER!
GODSPEED, SPIDER-MAN!

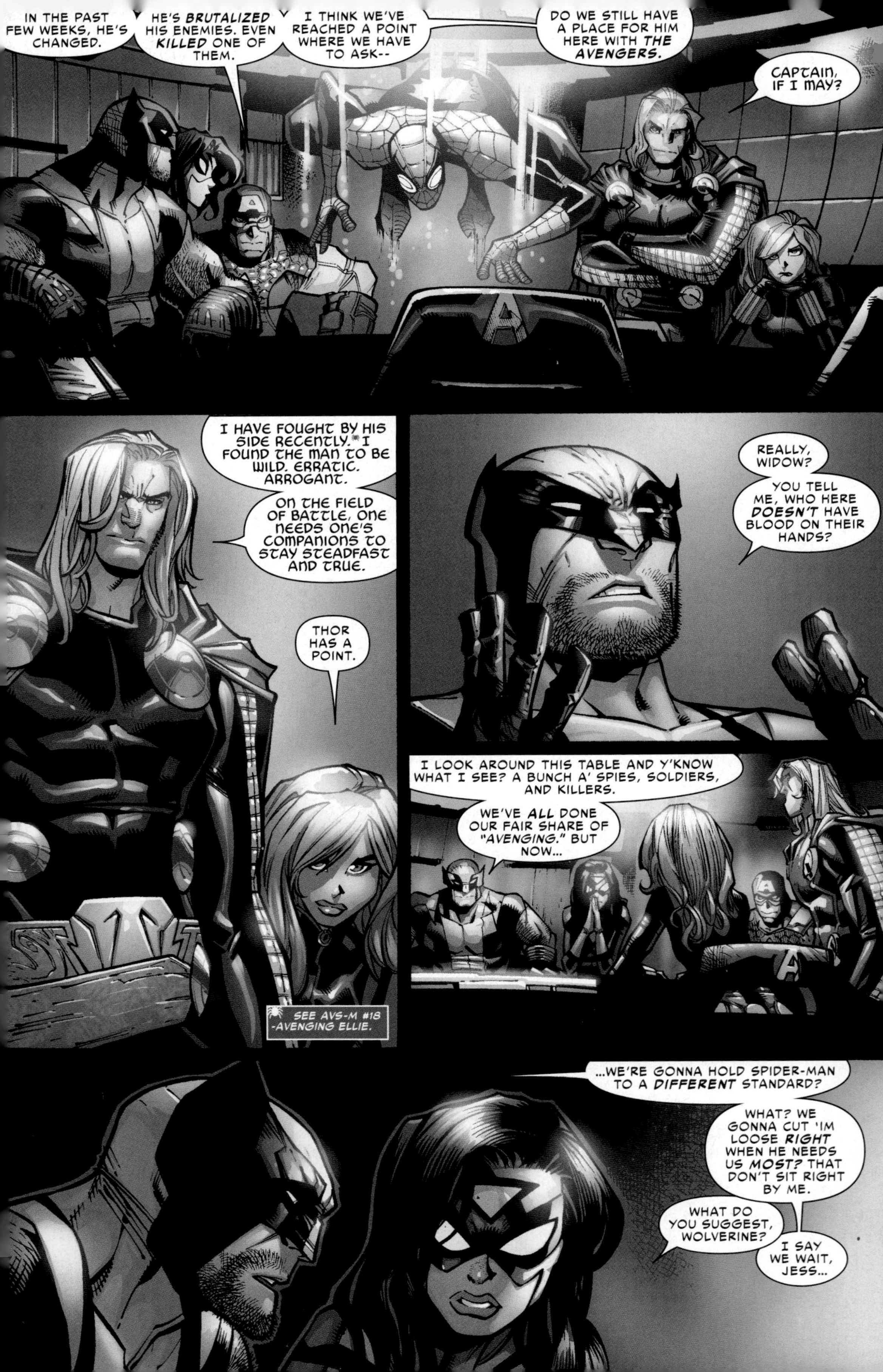
IN THE PAST FEW WEEKS, HE'S CHANGED.
HE'S BRUTALIZED HIS ENEMIES. EVEN KILLED ONE OF THEM.
I THINK WE'VE REACHED A POINT WHERE WE HAVE TO ASK--
DO WE STILL HAVE A PLACE FOR HIM HERE WITH THE AVENGERS.
CAPTAIN, IF I MAY?
I HAVE FOUGHT BY HIS SIDE RECENTLY.* I FOUND THE MAN TO BE WILD. ERRATIC. ARROGANT.
ON THE FIELD OF BATTLE, ONE NEEDS ONE'S COMPANIONS TO STAY STEADFAST AND TRUE.
THOR HAS A POINT.
* SEE AVS-M #18 -AVENGING ELLIE.
REALLY, WIDOW?
YOU TELL ME, WHO HERE DOESN'T HAVE BLOOD ON THEIR HANDS?
I LOOK AROUND THIS TABLE AND Y'KNOW WHAT I SEE? A BUNCH A' SPIES, SOLDIERS, AND KILLERS.
WE'VE ALL DONE OUR FAIR SHARE OF "AVENGING." BUT NOW...
...WE'RE GONNA HOLD SPIDER-MAN TO A DIFFERENT STANDARD?
WHAT? WE GONNA CUT 'IM LOOSE RIGHT WHEN HE NEEDS US MOST? THAT DON'T SIT RIGHT BY ME.
WHAT DO YOU SUGGEST, WOLVERINE?
I SAY WE WAIT, JESS...

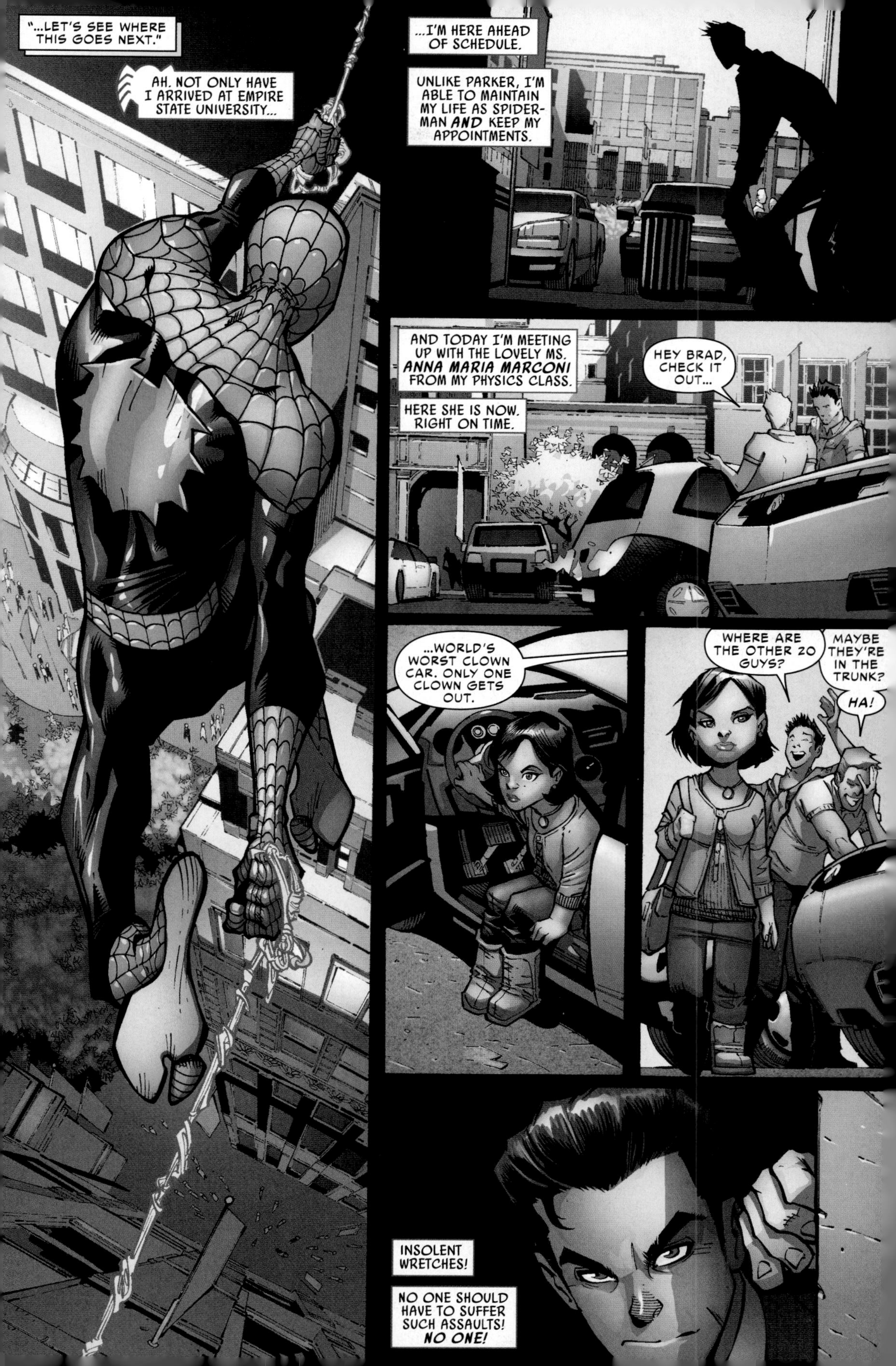
"...LET'S SEE WHERE THIS GOES NEXT."
AH. NOT ONLY HAVE I ARRIVED AT EMPIRE STATE UNIVERSITY...
...I'M HERE AHEAD OF SCHEDULE.
UNLIKE PARKER, I'M ABLE TO MAINTAIN MY LIFE AS SPIDER-MAN AND KEEP MY APPOINTMENTS.
AND TODAY I'M MEETING UP WITH THE LOVELY MS. ANNA MARIA MARCONI FROM MY PHYSICS CLASS.
HERE SHE IS NOW. RIGHT ON TIME.
HEY BRAD, CHECK IT OUT...
...WORLD'S WORST CLOWN CAR. ONLY ONE CLOWN GETS OUT.
WHERE ARE THE OTHER 20 GUYS?
MAYBE THEY'RE IN THE TRUNK?
HA!
INSOLENT WRETCHES!
NO ONE SHOULD HAVE TO SUFFER SUCH ASSAULTS! NO ONE!

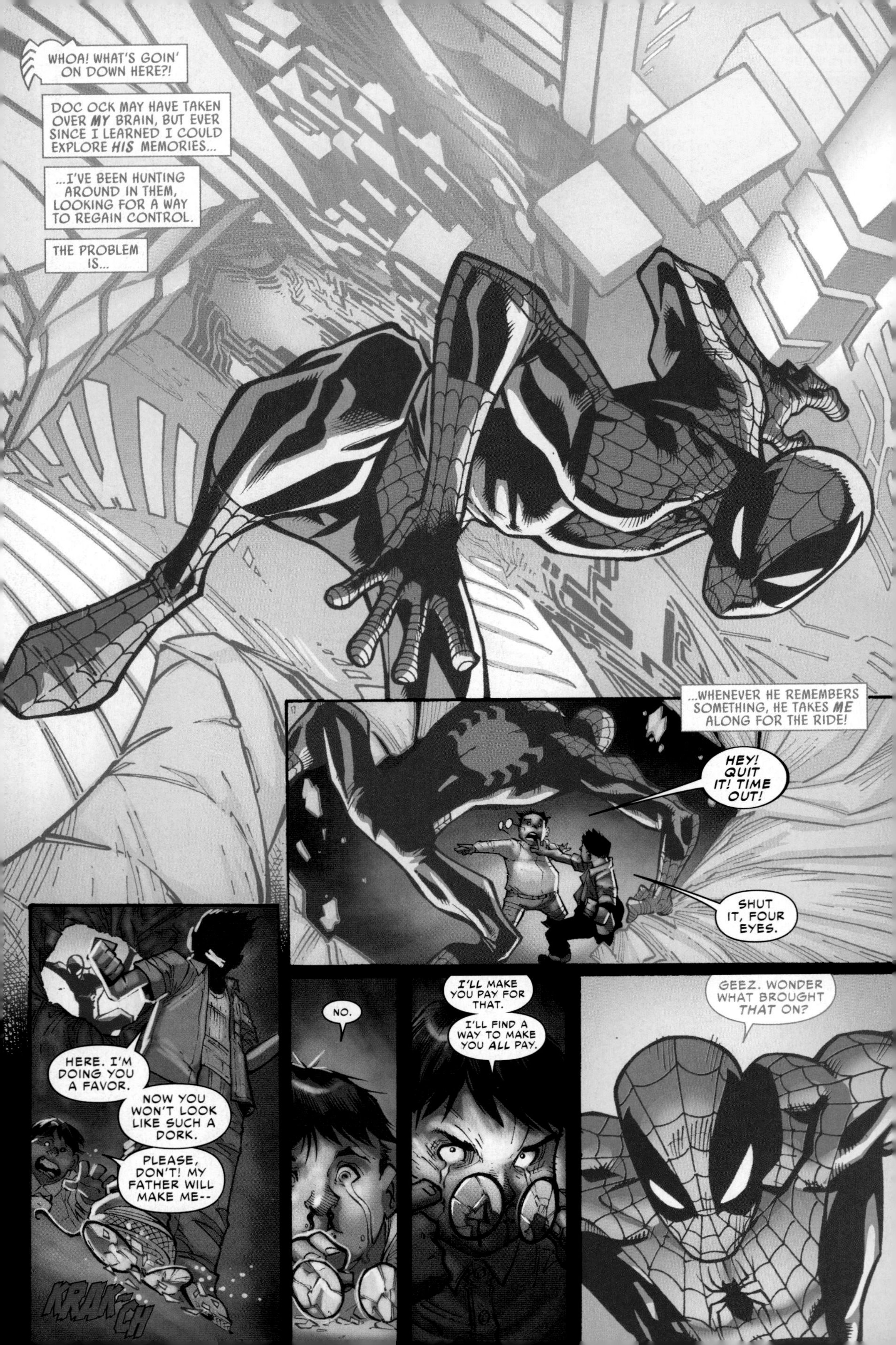
WHOA! WHAT'S GOIN' ON DOWN HERE?!
DOC OCK MAY HAVE TAKEN OVER *MY* BRAIN, BUT EVER SINCE I LEARNED I COULD EXPLORE *HIS* MEMORIES...
...I'VE BEEN HUNTING AROUND IN THEM, LOOKING FOR A WAY TO REGAIN CONTROL.
THE PROBLEM IS...
...WHENEVER HE REMEMBERS SOMETHING, HE TAKES *ME* ALONG FOR THE RIDE!
HEY! QUIT IT! TIME OUT!
SHUT IT, FOUR EYES.
HERE. I'M DOING YOU A FAVOR.
NOW YOU WON'T LOOK LIKE SUCH A DORK.
PLEASE, DON'T! MY FATHER WILL MAKE ME--
KRAK-CH
NO.
I'LL MAKE YOU PAY FOR THAT.
I'LL FIND A WAY TO MAKE YOU *ALL* PAY.
GEEZ. WONDER WHAT BROUGHT *THAT* ON?

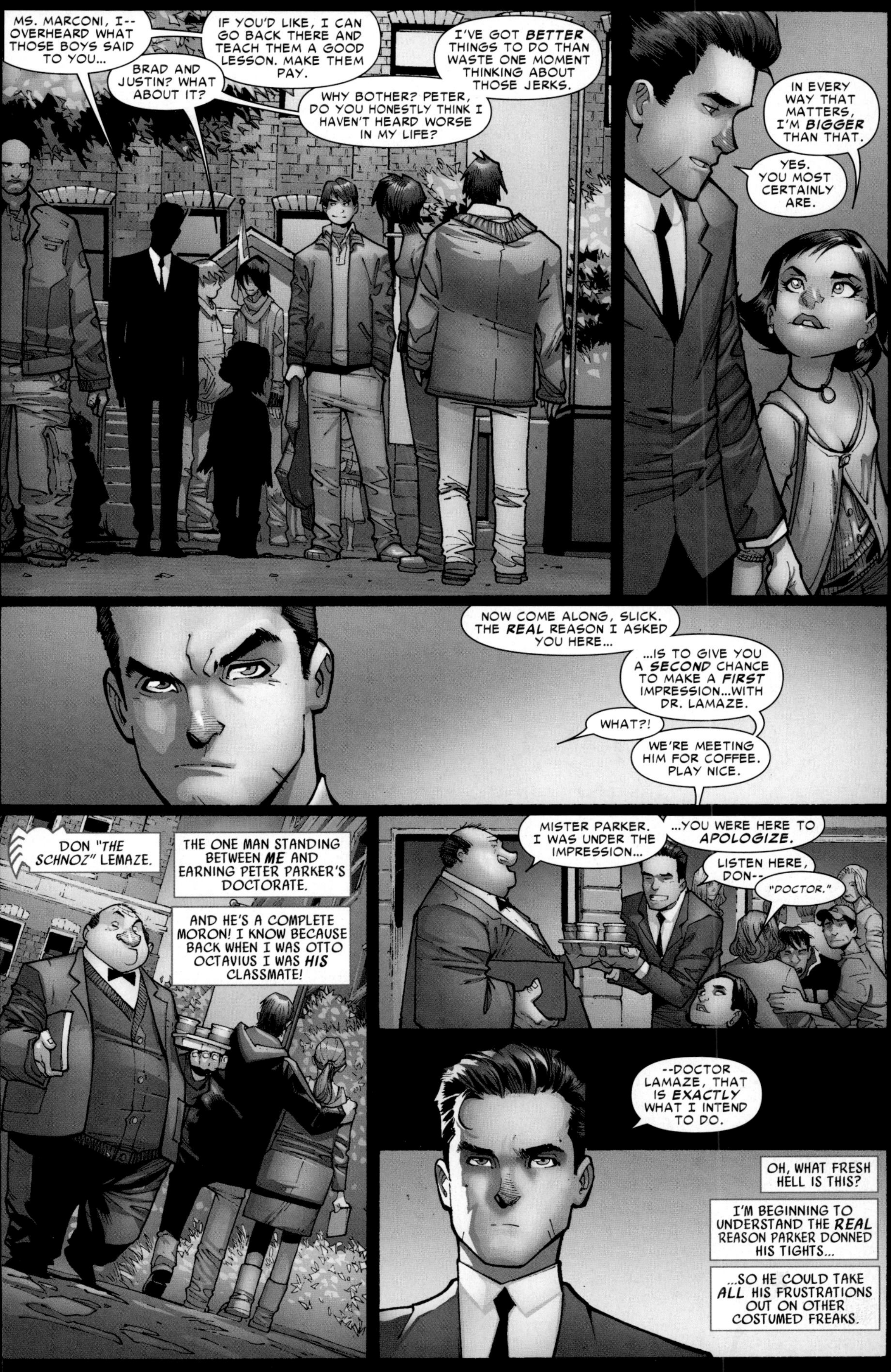
MS. MARCONI, I-- OVERHEARD WHAT THOSE BOYS SAID TO YOU...
BRAD AND JUSTIN? WHAT ABOUT IT?
IF YOU'D LIKE, I CAN GO BACK THERE AND TEACH THEM A GOOD LESSON. MAKE THEM PAY.
WHY BOTHER? PETER, DO YOU HONESTLY THINK I HAVEN'T HEARD WORSE IN MY LIFE?
I'VE GOT BETTER THINGS TO DO THAN WASTE ONE MOMENT THINKING ABOUT THOSE JERKS.
IN EVERY WAY THAT MATTERS, I'M BIGGER THAN THAT.
YES. YOU MOST CERTAINLY ARE.
NOW COME ALONG, SLICK. THE REAL REASON I ASKED YOU HERE...
...IS TO GIVE YOU A SECOND CHANCE TO MAKE A FIRST IMPRESSION...WITH DR. LAMAZE.
WHAT?!
WE'RE MEETING HIM FOR COFFEE. PLAY NICE.
DON "THE SCHNOZ" LEMAZE.
THE ONE MAN STANDING BETWEEN ME AND EARNING PETER PARKER'S DOCTORATE.
AND HE'S A COMPLETE MORON! I KNOW BECAUSE BACK WHEN I WAS OTTO OCTAVIUS I WAS HIS CLASSMATE!
MISTER PARKER. I WAS UNDER THE IMPRESSION...
...YOU WERE HERE TO APOLOGIZE.
LISTEN HERE, DON--
"DOCTOR."
--DOCTOR LAMAZE, THAT IS EXACTLY WHAT I INTEND TO DO.
OH, WHAT FRESH HELL IS THIS?
I'M BEGINNING TO UNDERSTAND THE REAL REASON PARKER DONNED HIS TIGHTS...
...SO HE COULD TAKE ALL HIS FRUSTRATIONS OUT ON OTHER COSTUMED FREAKS.

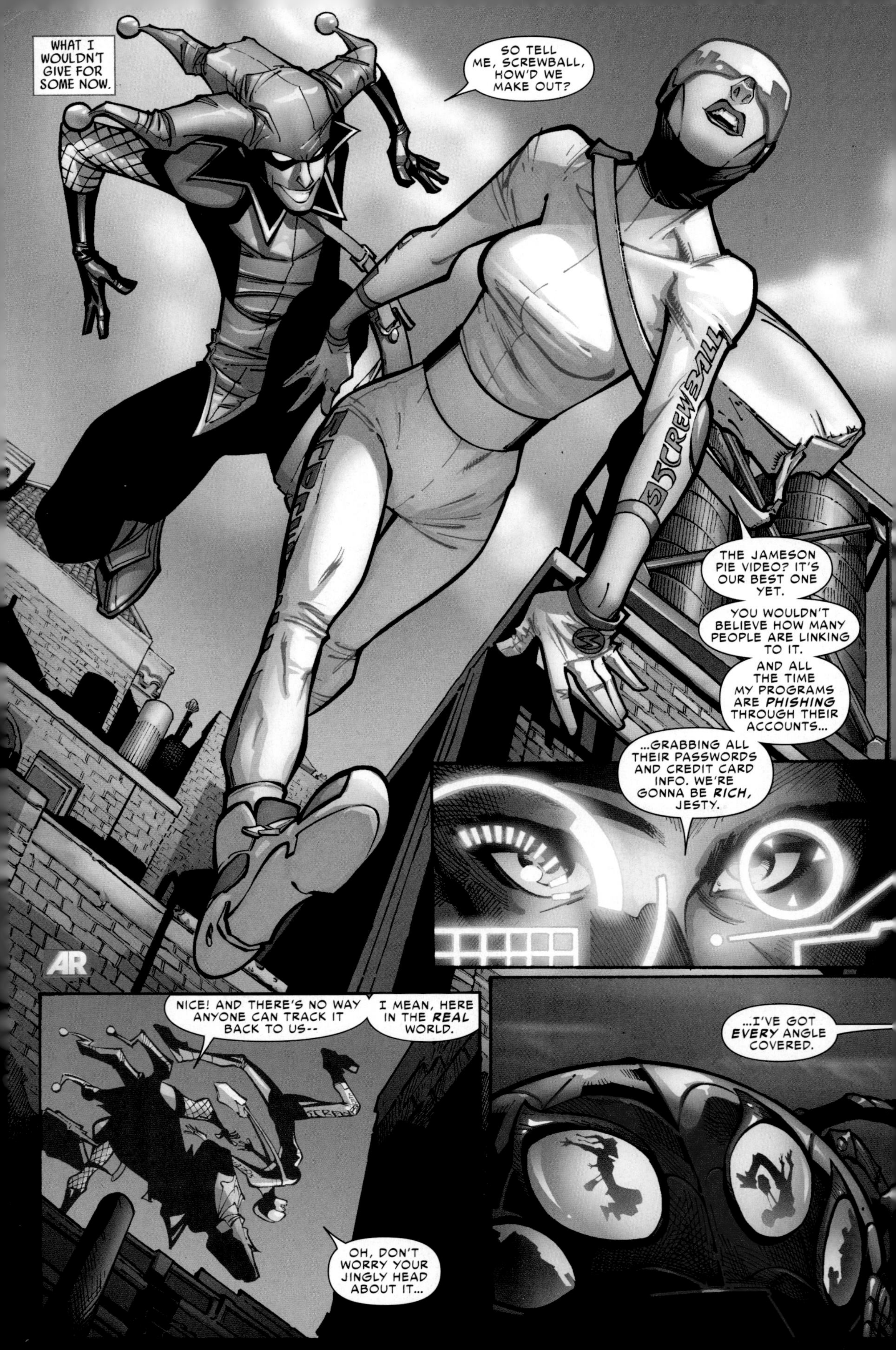
WHAT I WOULDN'T GIVE FOR SOME NOW.
SO TELL ME, SCREWBALL, HOW'D WE MAKE OUT?
THE JAMESON PIE VIDEO? IT'S OUR BEST ONE YET.
YOU WOULDN'T BELIEVE HOW MANY PEOPLE ARE LINKING TO IT.
AND ALL THE TIME MY PROGRAMS ARE PHISHING THROUGH THEIR ACCOUNTS...
...GRABBING ALL THEIR PASSWORDS AND CREDIT CARD INFO. WE'RE GONNA BE RICH, JESTY.
NICE! AND THERE'S NO WAY ANYONE CAN TRACK IT BACK TO US--
I MEAN, HERE IN THE REAL WORLD.
OH, DON'T WORRY YOUR JINGLY HEAD ABOUT IT...
...I'VE GOT EVERY ANGLE COVERED.

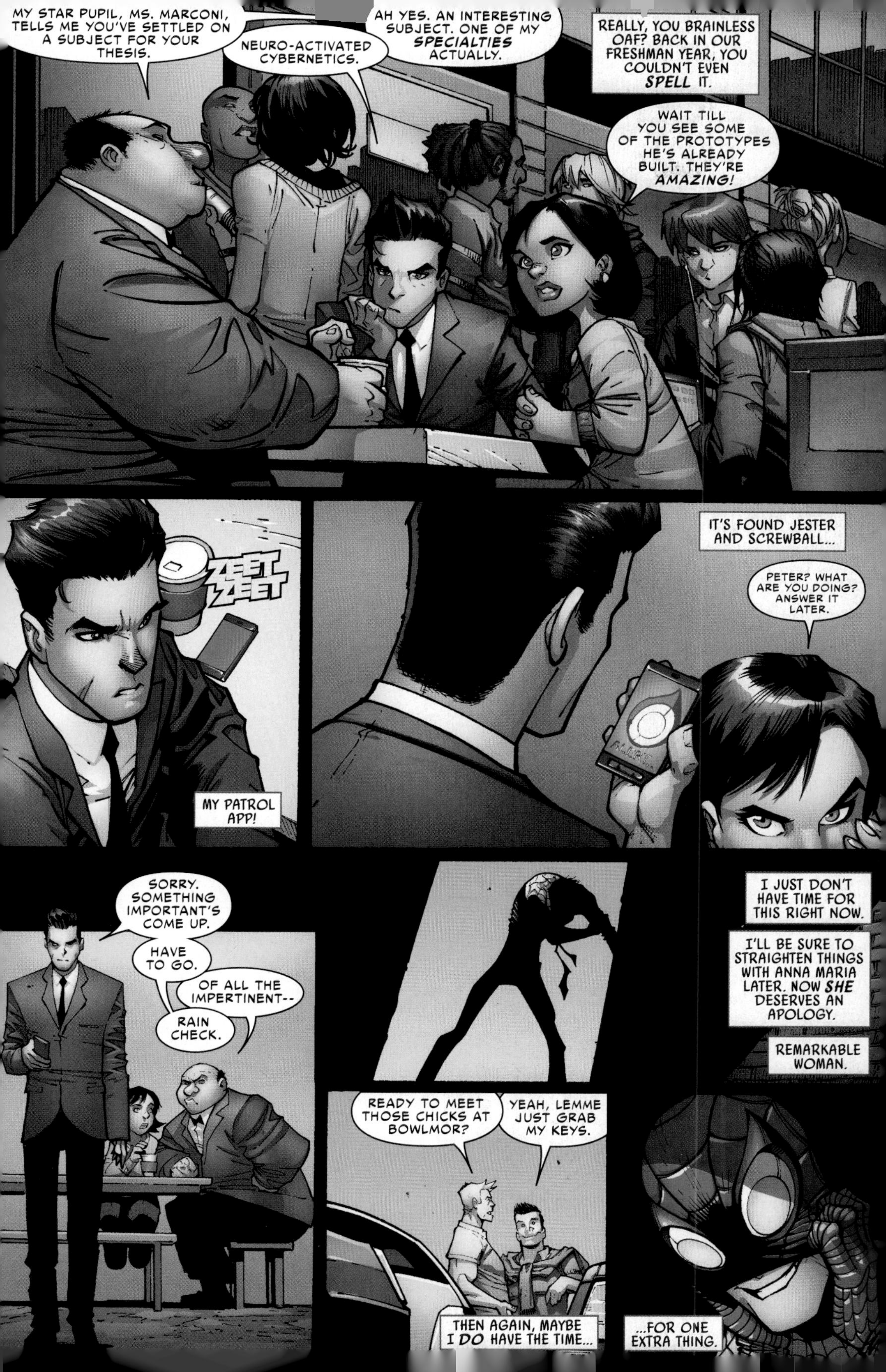
MY STAR PUPIL, MS. MARCONI, TELLS ME YOU'VE SETTLED ON A SUBJECT FOR YOUR THESIS.
NEURO-ACTIVATED CYBERNETICS.
AH YES. AN INTERESTING SUBJECT. ONE OF MY SPECIALTIES ACTUALLY.
REALLY, YOU BRAINLESS OAF? BACK IN OUR FRESHMAN YEAR, YOU COULDN'T EVEN SPELL IT.
WAIT TILL YOU SEE SOME OF THE PROTOTYPES HE'S ALREADY BUILT. THEY'RE AMAZING!
ZEET ZEET
MY PATROL APP!
IT'S FOUND JESTER AND SCREWBALL...
PETER? WHAT ARE YOU DOING? ANSWER IT LATER.
ALERT.
SORRY. SOMETHING IMPORTANT'S COME UP.
HAVE TO GO.
OF ALL THE IMPERTINENT--
RAIN CHECK.
I JUST DON'T HAVE TIME FOR THIS RIGHT NOW.
I'LL BE SURE TO STRAIGHTEN THINGS WITH ANNA MARIA LATER. NOW SHE DESERVES AN APOLOGY.
REMARKABLE WOMAN.
READY TO MEET THOSE CHICKS AT BOWLMOR?
YEAH, LEMME JUST GRAB MY KEYS.
THEN AGAIN, MAYBE I DO HAVE THE TIME...
...FOR ONE EXTRA THING.

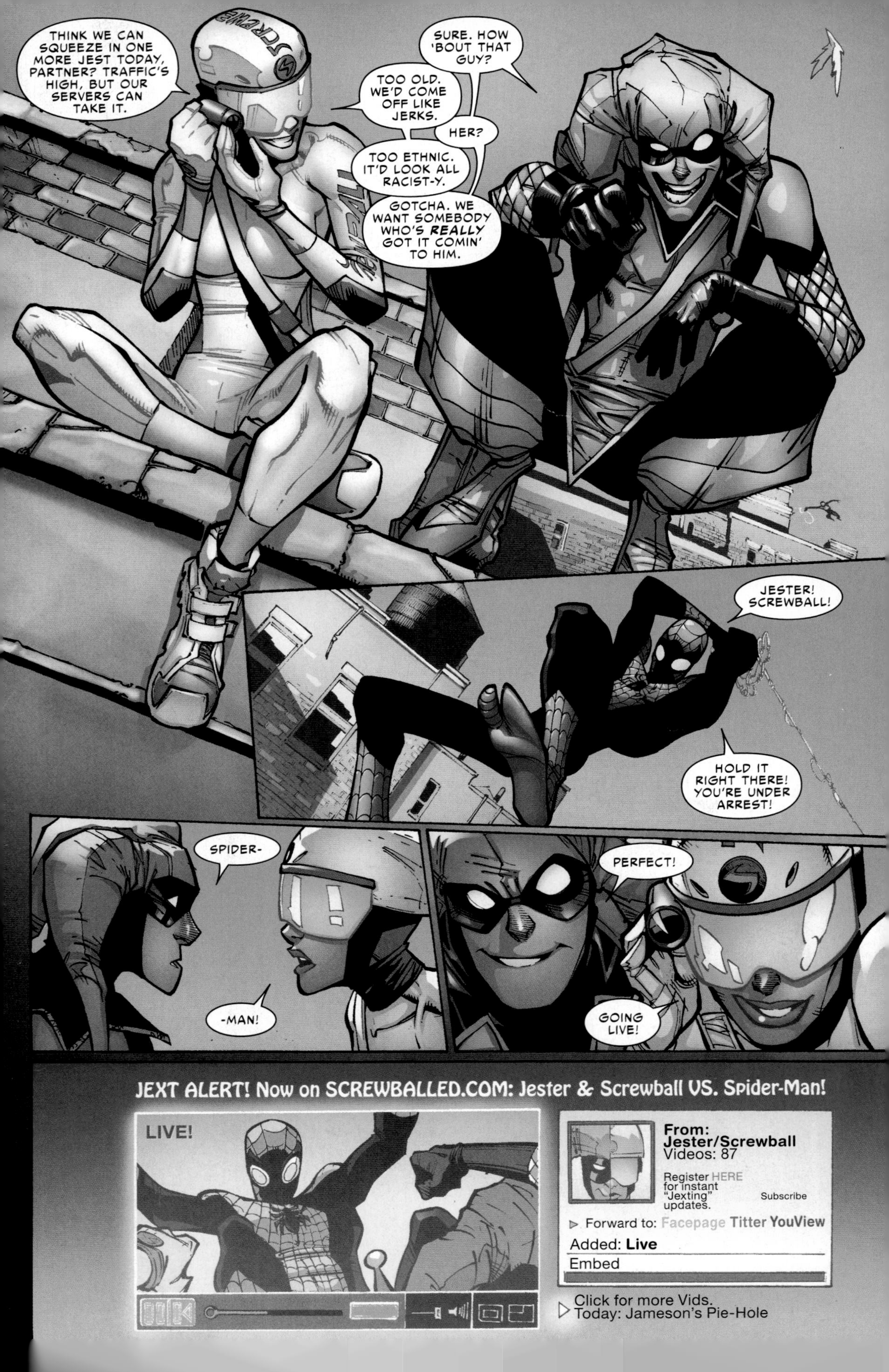
THINK WE CAN SQUEEZE IN ONE MORE JEST TODAY, PARTNER? TRAFFIC'S HIGH, BUT OUR SERVERS CAN TAKE IT.
SURE. HOW 'BOUT THAT GUY?
TOO OLD. WE'D COME OFF LIKE JERKS.
HER?
TOO ETHNIC. IT'D LOOK ALL RACIST-Y.
GOTCHA. WE WANT SOMEBODY WHO'S *REALLY* GOT IT COMIN' TO HIM.
JESTER! SCREWBALL!
HOLD IT RIGHT THERE! YOU'RE UNDER ARREST!
SPIDER-
-MAN!
PERFECT!
GOING LIVE!
JEXT ALERT! Now on SCREWBALLED.COM: Jester & Screwball VS. Spider-Man!
LIVE!
From: Jester/Screwball
Videos: 87
Register HERE for instant "Jexting" updates.
Subscribe
Forward to: Facepage Titter YouView
Added: Live
Embed
Click for more Vids.
Today: Jameson's Pie-Hole

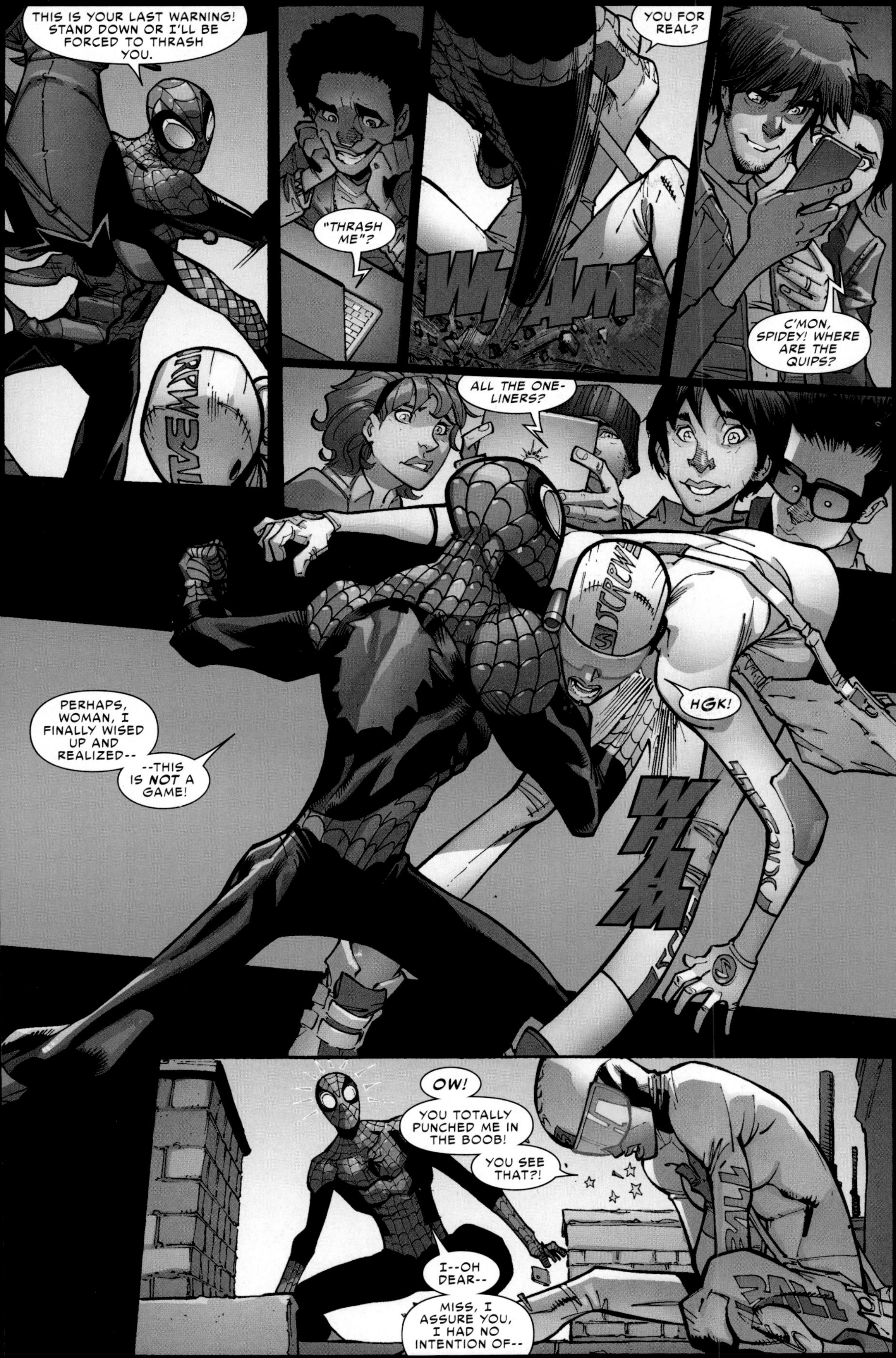
THIS IS YOUR LAST WARNING! STAND DOWN OR I'LL BE FORCED TO THRASH YOU.
"THRASH ME"?
WHAM
YOU FOR REAL?
C'MON, SPIDEY! WHERE ARE THE QUIPS?
ALL THE ONE-LINERS?
HGK!
PERHAPS, WOMAN, I FINALLY WISED UP AND REALIZED--
--THIS IS NOT A GAME!
WHAM
OW!
YOU TOTALLY PUNCHED ME IN THE BOOB!
YOU SEE THAT?!
I--OH DEAR--
MISS, I ASSURE YOU, I HAD NO INTENTION OF--

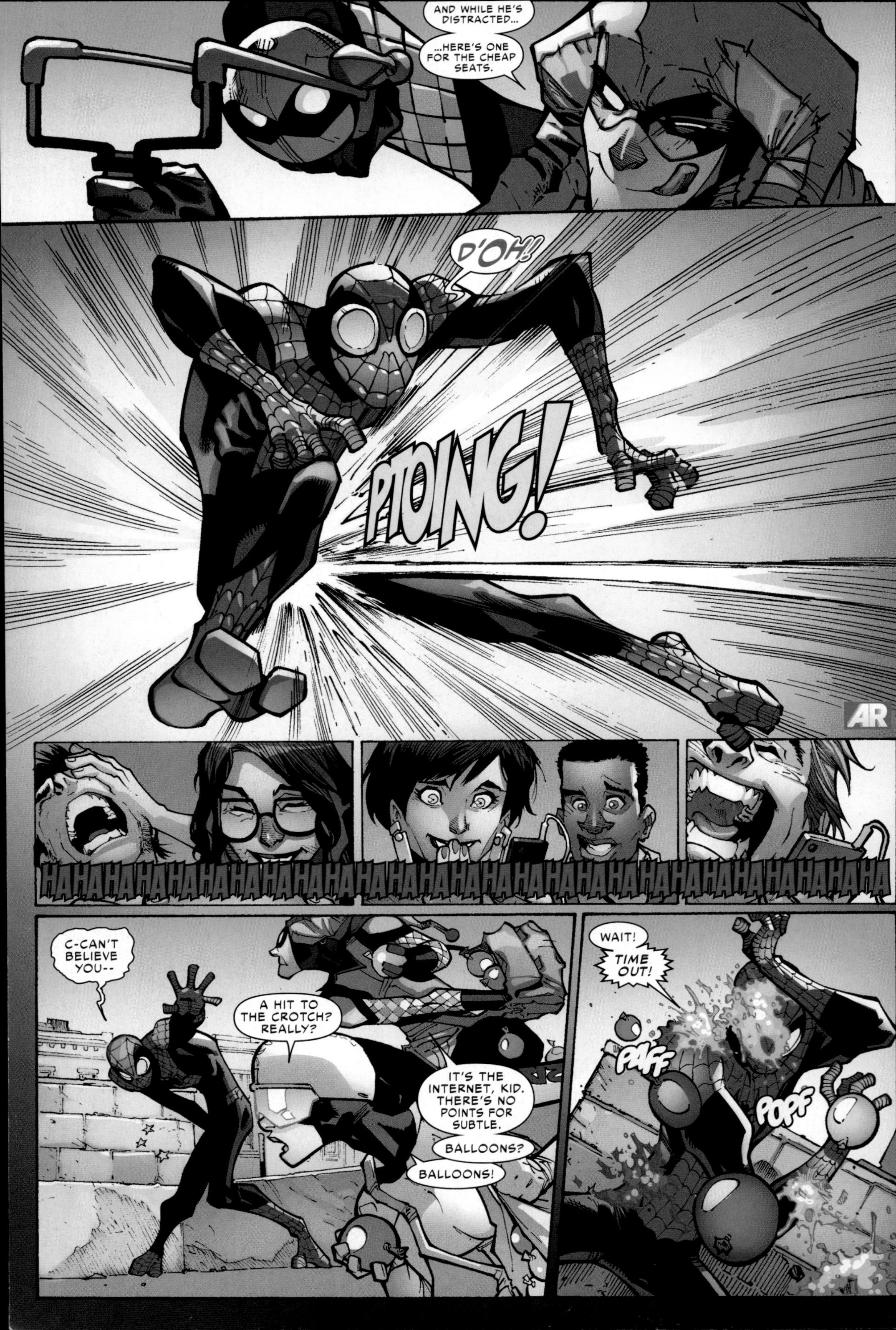

AND WHILE HE'S DISTRACTED...
...HERE'S ONE FOR THE CHEAP SEATS.
D'OH!!
PTOING!
AR
HAHAHAHAHAHAHAHAHAHAHAHAHAHAHAHAHAHAHAHAHAHAHAHAHAHAHAHA
C-CAN'T BELIEVE YOU--
A HIT TO THE CROTCH? REALLY?
IT'S THE INTERNET, KID. THERE'S NO POINTS FOR SUBTLE.
BALLOONS?
BALLOONS!
WAIT!
TIME OUT!
PAFF
POPF

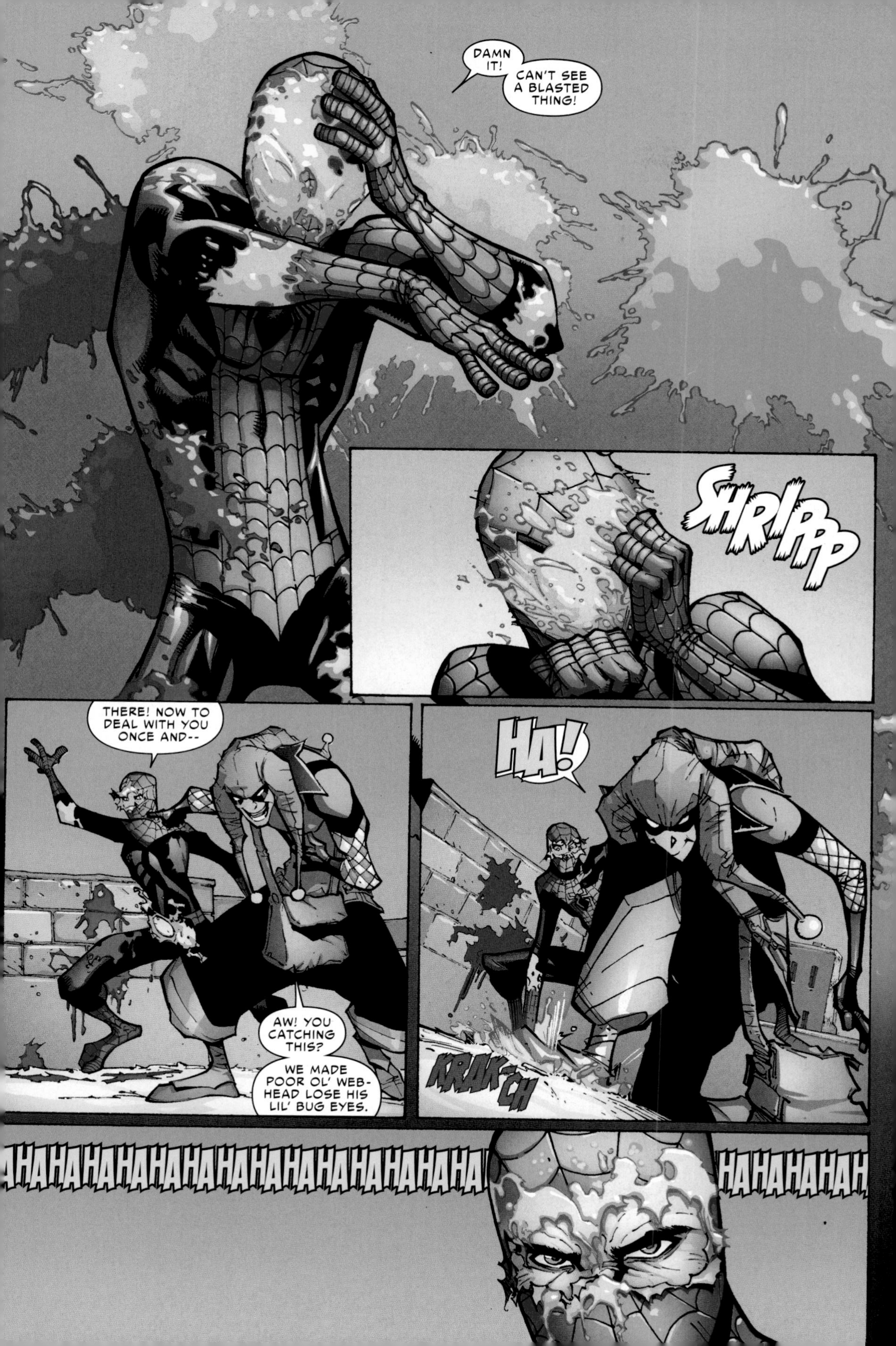
DAMN IT!
CAN'T SEE A BLASTED THING!
SHRIPPP
THERE! NOW TO DEAL WITH YOU ONCE AND--
AW! YOU CATCHING THIS?
WE MADE POOR OL' WEB-HEAD LOSE HIS LIL' BUG EYES.
HA!
KRAK-CH
HAHAHAHAHAHAHAHAHAHAHAHAHAHAHA
HAHAHAHAH

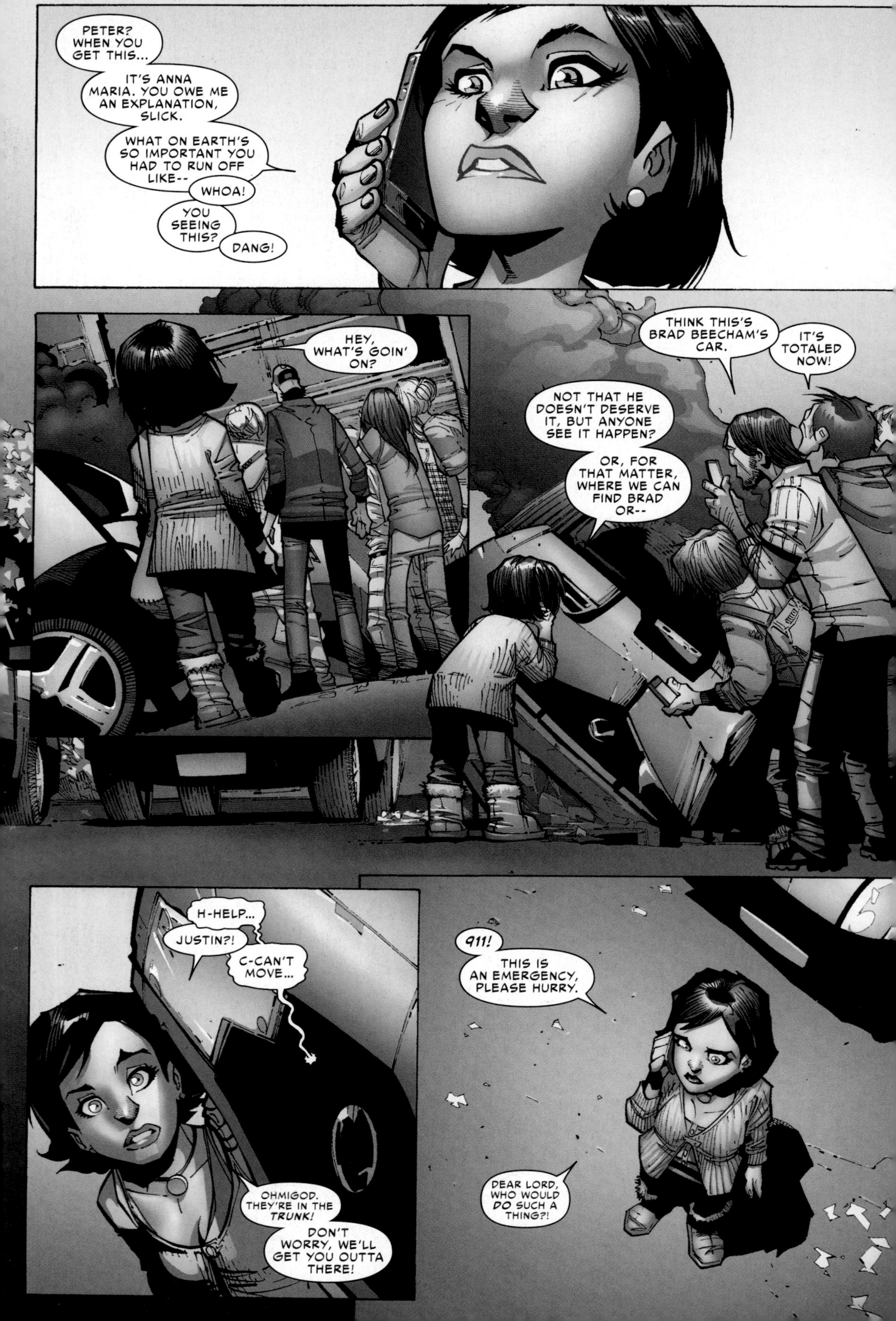
PETER? WHEN YOU GET THIS...
IT'S ANNA MARIA. YOU OWE ME AN EXPLANATION, SLICK.
WHAT ON EARTH'S SO IMPORTANT YOU HAD TO RUN OFF LIKE--
WHOA!
YOU SEEING THIS?
DANG!
HEY, WHAT'S GOIN' ON?
THINK THIS'S BRAD BEECHAM'S CAR.
IT'S TOTALED NOW!
NOT THAT HE DOESN'T DESERVE IT, BUT ANYONE SEE IT HAPPEN?
OR, FOR THAT MATTER, WHERE WE CAN FIND BRAD OR--
H-HELP...
JUSTIN?!
C-CAN'T MOVE...
OHMIGOD. THEY'RE IN THE *TRUNK!*
DON'T WORRY, WE'LL GET YOU OUTTA THERE!
911!
THIS IS AN EMERGENCY, PLEASE HURRY.
DEAR LORD, WHO WOULD *DO* SUCH A THING?!

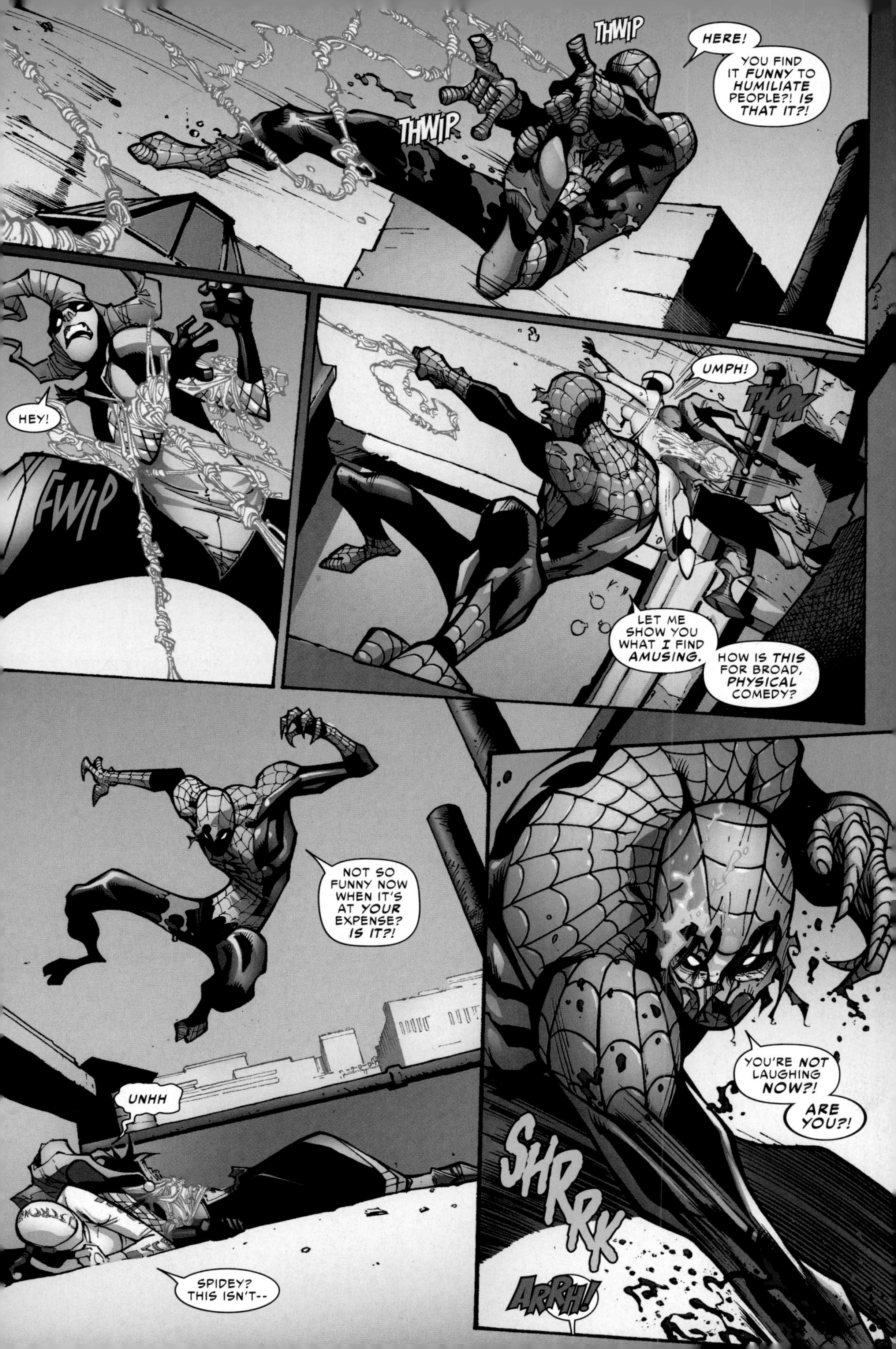
THWIP
THWIP
HERE!
YOU FIND IT FUNNY TO HUMILIATE PEOPLE?! IS THAT IT?!
HEY!
FWIP
UMPH!
THOK
LET ME SHOW YOU WHAT I FIND AMUSING.
HOW IS THIS FOR BROAD, PHYSICAL COMEDY?
NOT SO FUNNY NOW WHEN IT'S AT YOUR EXPENSE? IS IT?!
UNHH
SPIDEY? THIS ISN'T--
YOU'RE NOT LAUGHING NOW?!
ARE YOU?!
SHRRK
ARRH!

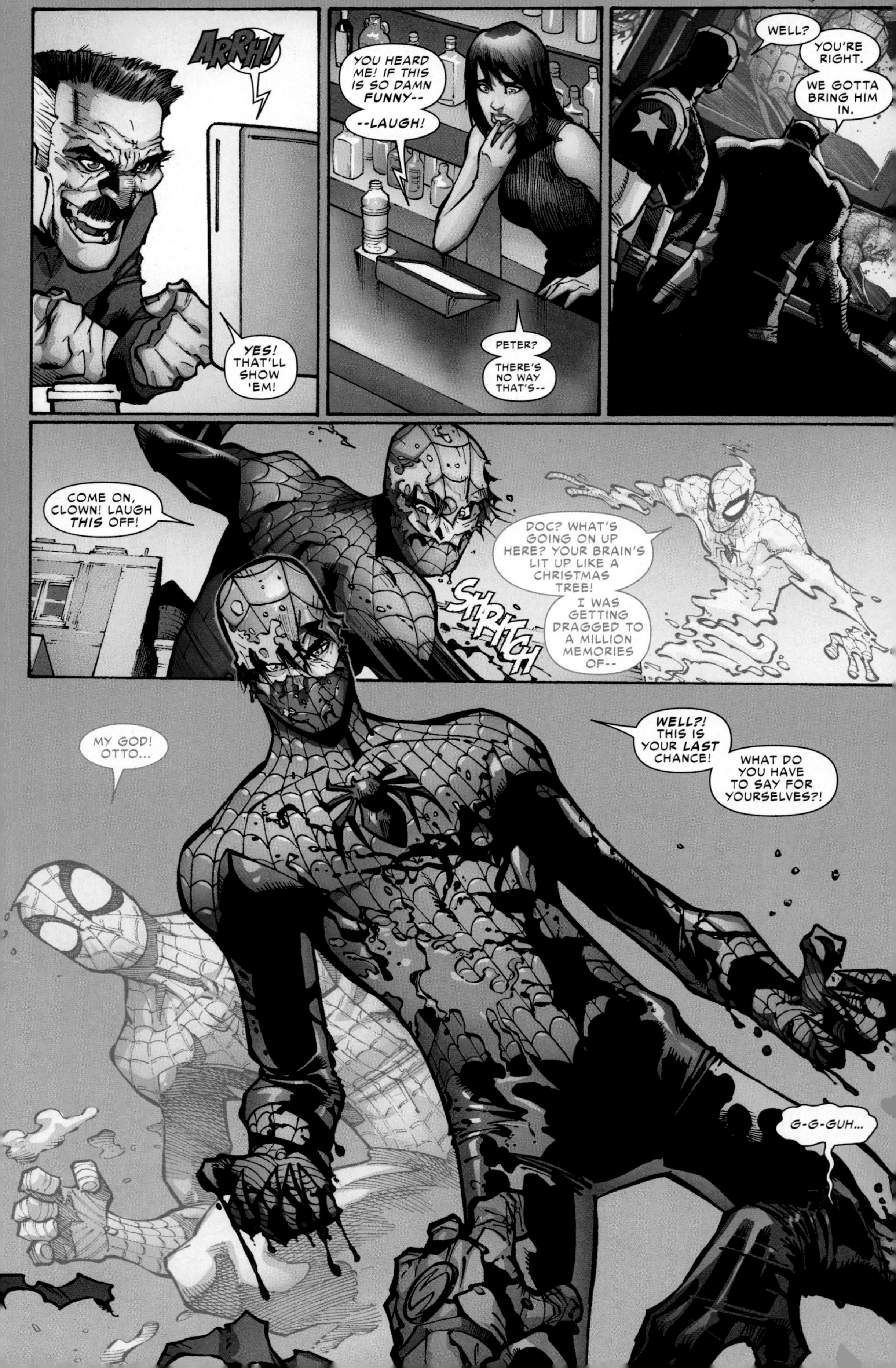
ARRH!
YES! THAT'LL SHOW 'EM!
YOU HEARD ME! IF THIS IS SO DAMN FUNNY--
--LAUGH!
PETER?
THERE'S NO WAY THAT'S--
WELL?
YOU'RE RIGHT.
WE GOTTA BRING HIM IN.
COME ON, CLOWN! LAUGH THIS OFF!
SHRITCH
DOC? WHAT'S GOING ON UP HERE? YOUR BRAIN'S LIT UP LIKE A CHRISTMAS TREE!
I WAS GETTING DRAGGED TO A MILLION MEMORIES OF--
MY GOD! OTTO...
WELL?! THIS IS YOUR LAST CHANCE!
WHAT DO YOU HAVE TO SAY FOR YOURSELVES?!
G-G-GUH...

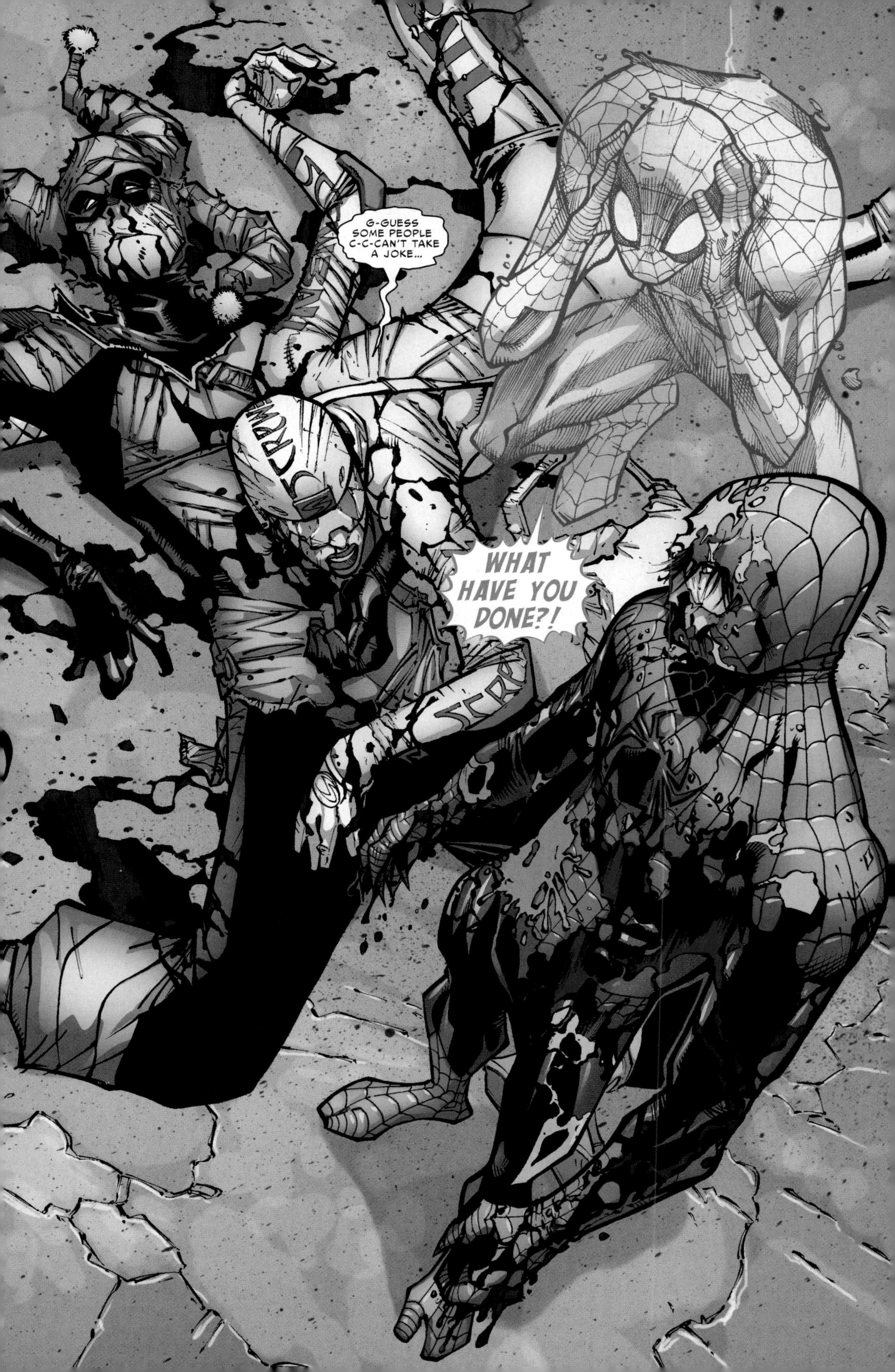
G-GUESS SOME PEOPLE C-C-CAN'T TAKE A JOKE...
WHAT HAVE YOU DONE?!

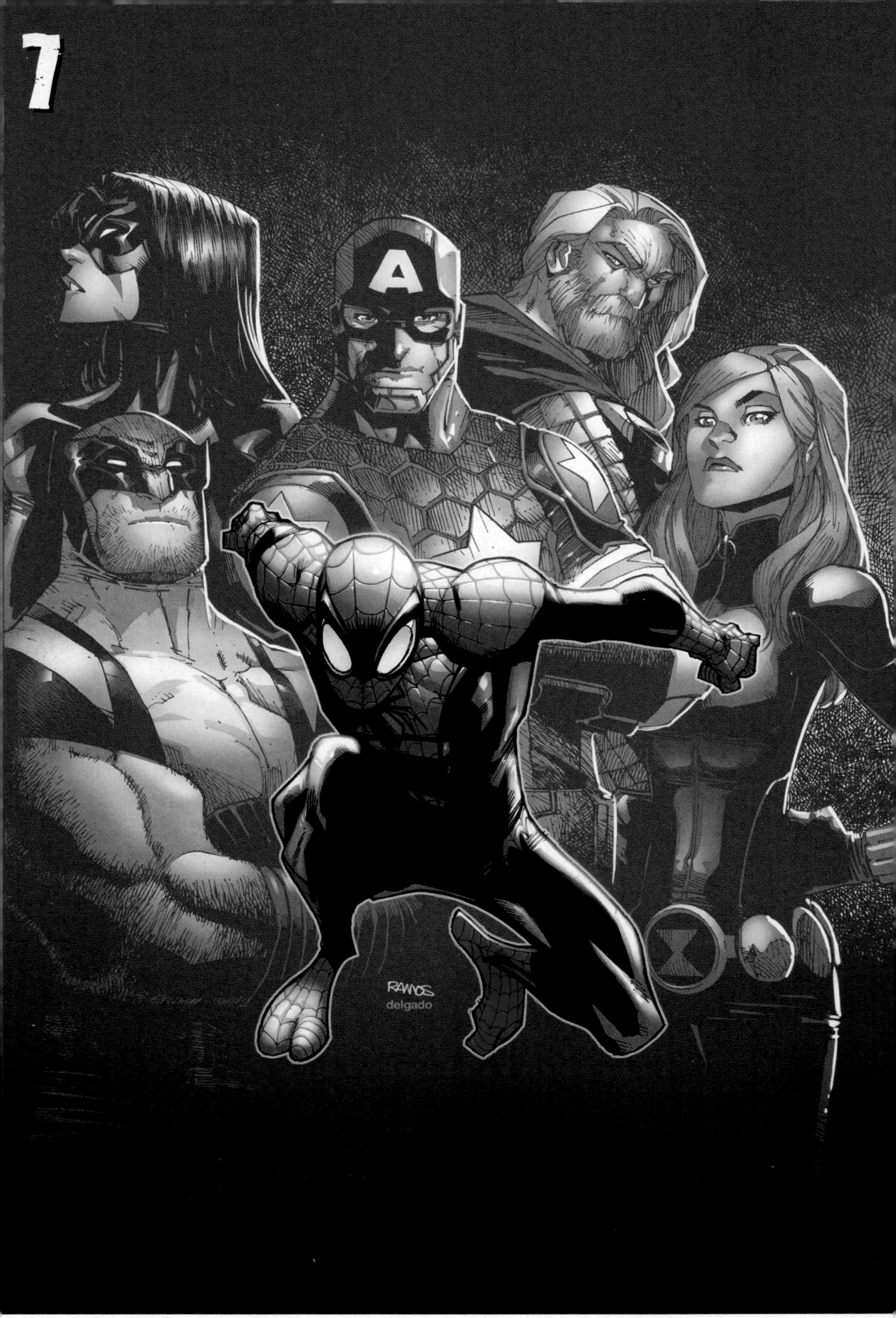
7
RAMOS
delgado

TROUBLED MIND PART ONE: RIGHT-HAND MAN

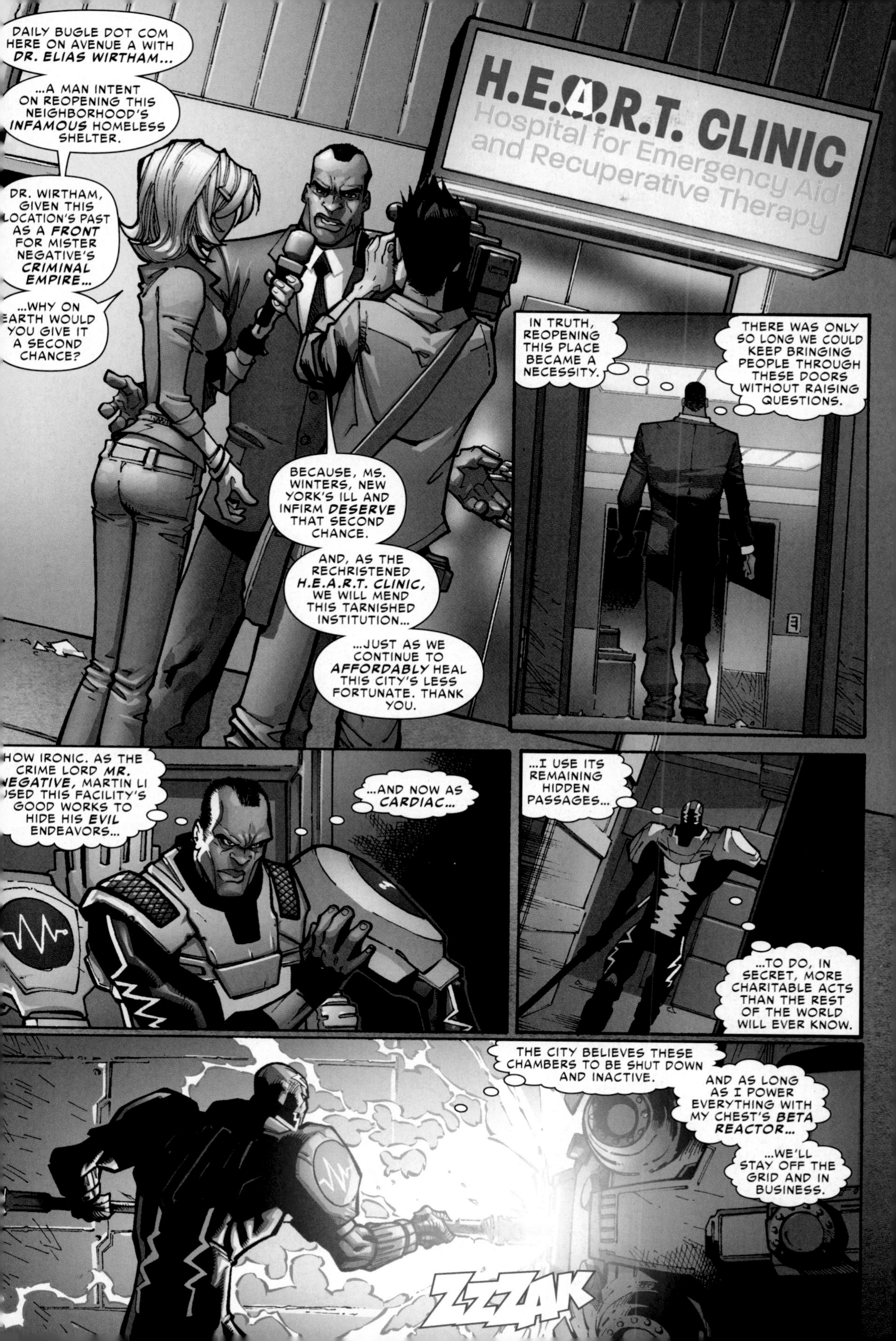
DAILY BUGLE DOT COM HERE ON AVENUE A WITH DR. ELIAS WIRTHAM...
...A MAN INTENT ON REOPENING THIS NEIGHBORHOOD'S INFAMOUS HOMELESS SHELTER.
H.E.A.R.T. CLINIC
Hospital for Emergency Aid and Recuperative Therapy
DR. WIRTHAM, GIVEN THIS LOCATION'S PAST AS A FRONT FOR MISTER NEGATIVE'S CRIMINAL EMPIRE...
...WHY ON EARTH WOULD YOU GIVE IT A SECOND CHANCE?
BECAUSE, MS. WINTERS, NEW YORK'S ILL AND INFIRM DESERVE THAT SECOND CHANCE.
AND, AS THE RECHRISTENED H.E.A.R.T. CLINIC, WE WILL MEND THIS TARNISHED INSTITUTION...
...JUST AS WE CONTINUE TO AFFORDABLY HEAL THIS CITY'S LESS FORTUNATE. THANK YOU.
IN TRUTH, REOPENING THIS PLACE BECAME A NECESSITY.
THERE WAS ONLY SO LONG WE COULD KEEP BRINGING PEOPLE THROUGH THESE DOORS WITHOUT RAISING QUESTIONS.
HOW IRONIC. AS THE CRIME LORD MR. NEGATIVE, MARTIN LI USED THIS FACILITY'S GOOD WORKS TO HIDE HIS EVIL ENDEAVORS...
...AND NOW AS CARDIAC...
...I USE ITS REMAINING HIDDEN PASSAGES...
...TO DO, IN SECRET, MORE CHARITABLE ACTS THAN THE REST OF THE WORLD WILL EVER KNOW.
THE CITY BELIEVES THESE CHAMBERS TO BE SHUT DOWN AND INACTIVE.
AND AS LONG AS I POWER EVERYTHING WITH MY CHEST'S BETA REACTOR...
...WE'LL STAY OFF THE GRID AND IN BUSINESS.
ZZZAK

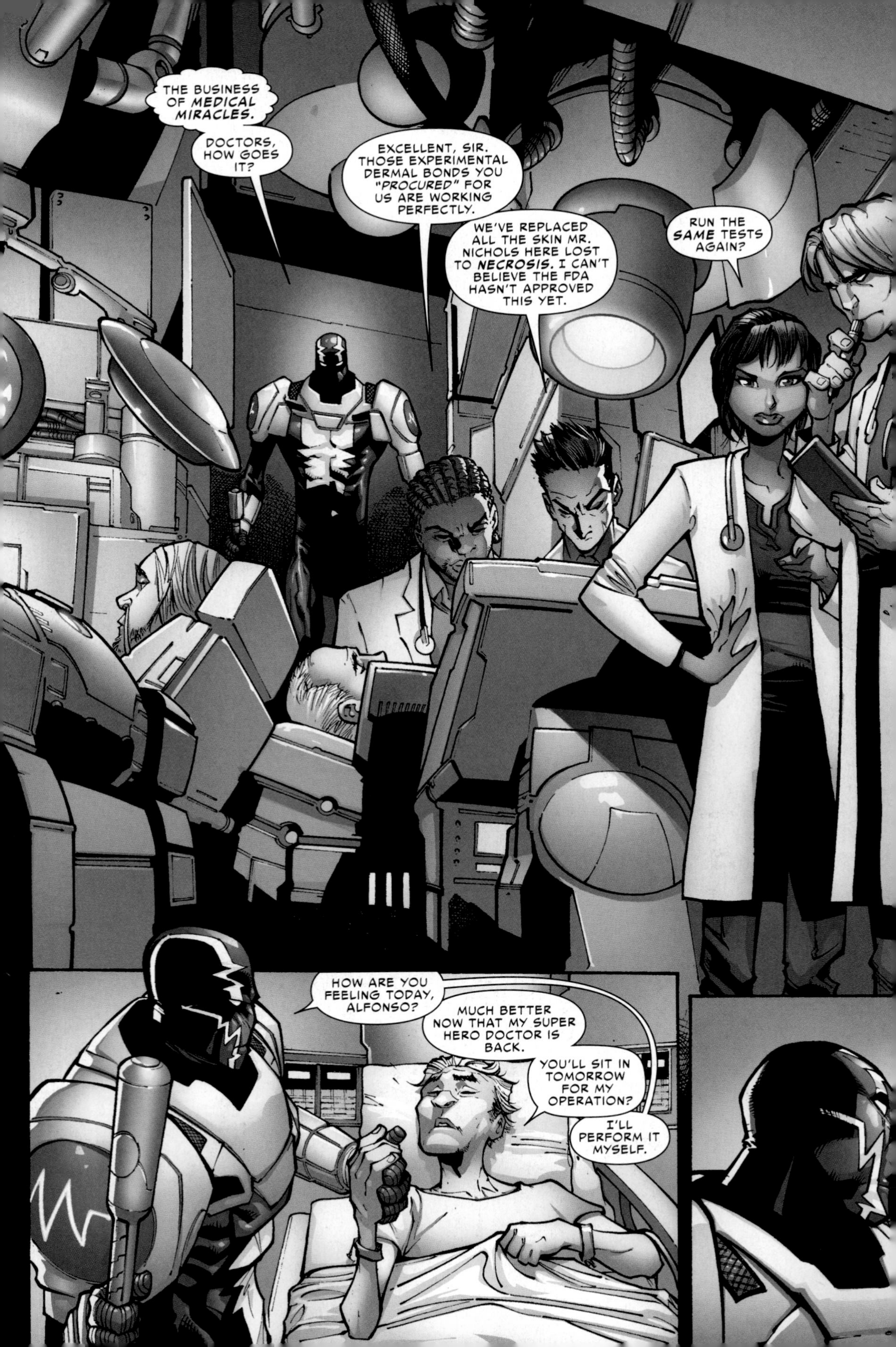

THE BUSINESS OF MEDICAL MIRACLES.
DOCTORS, HOW GOES IT?
EXCELLENT, SIR. THOSE EXPERIMENTAL DERMAL BONDS YOU "PROCURED" FOR US ARE WORKING PERFECTLY.
WE'VE REPLACED ALL THE SKIN MR. NICHOLS HERE LOST TO NECROSIS. I CAN'T BELIEVE THE FDA HASN'T APPROVED THIS YET.
RUN THE SAME TESTS AGAIN?
HOW ARE YOU FEELING TODAY, ALFONSO?
MUCH BETTER NOW THAT MY SUPER HERO DOCTOR IS BACK.
YOU'LL SIT IN TOMORROW FOR MY OPERATION?
I'LL PERFORM IT MYSELF.

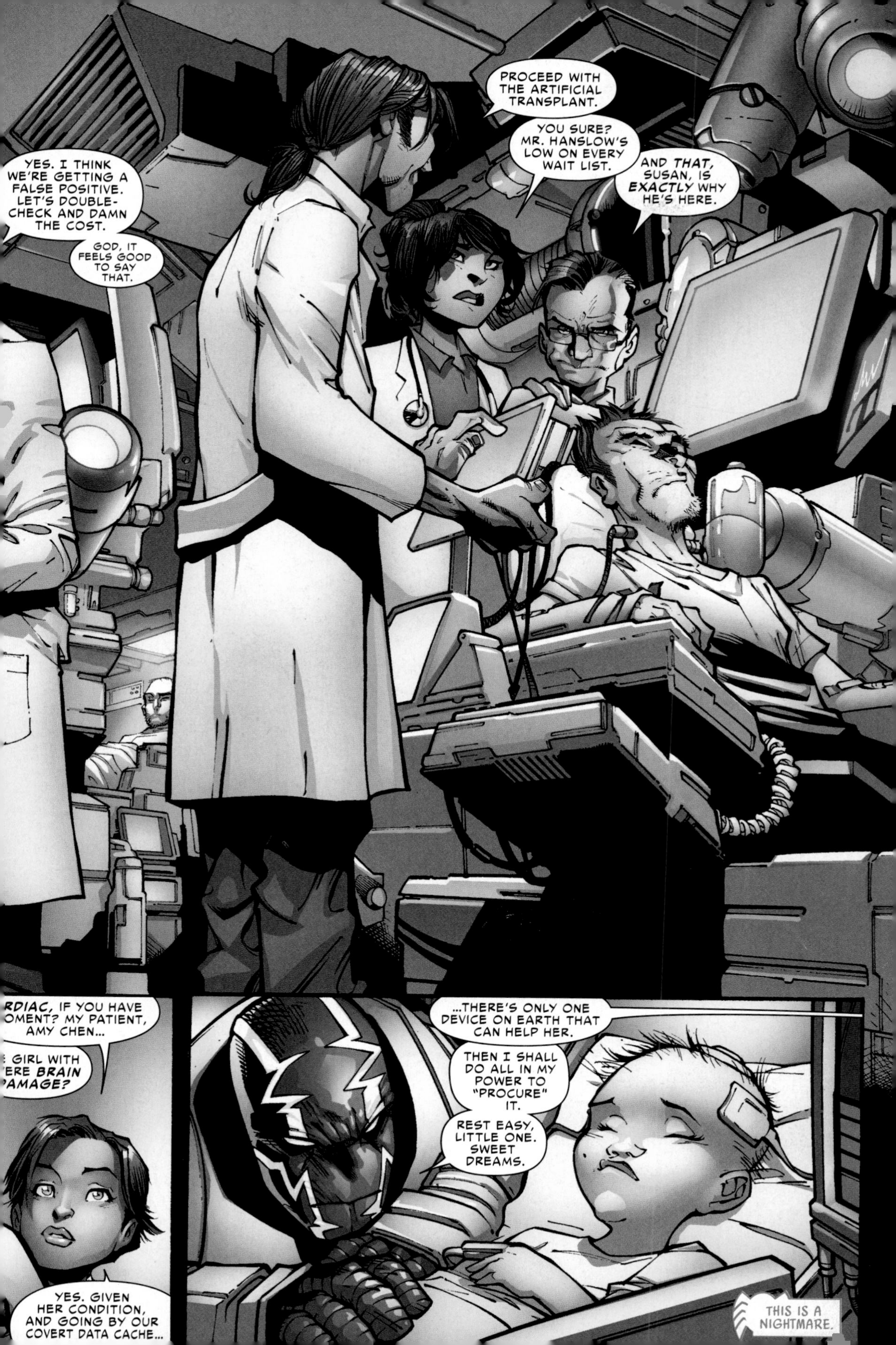

YES. I THINK WE'RE GETTING A FALSE POSITIVE. LET'S DOUBLE-CHECK AND DAMN THE COST.
GOD, IT FEELS GOOD TO SAY THAT.
PROCEED WITH THE ARTIFICIAL TRANSPLANT.
YOU SURE? MR. HANSLOW'S LOW ON EVERY WAIT LIST.
AND *THAT*, SUSAN, IS *EXACTLY* WHY HE'S HERE.
RDIAC, IF YOU HAVE OMENT? MY PATIENT, AMY CHEN...
E GIRL WITH ERE *BRAIN* AMAGE?
YES. GIVEN HER CONDITION, AND GOING BY OUR COVERT DATA CACHE...
...THERE'S ONLY ONE DEVICE ON EARTH THAT CAN HELP HER.
THEN I SHALL DO ALL IN MY POWER TO "PROCURE" IT.
REST EASY, LITTLE ONE. SWEET DREAMS.
THIS IS A NIGHTMARE.

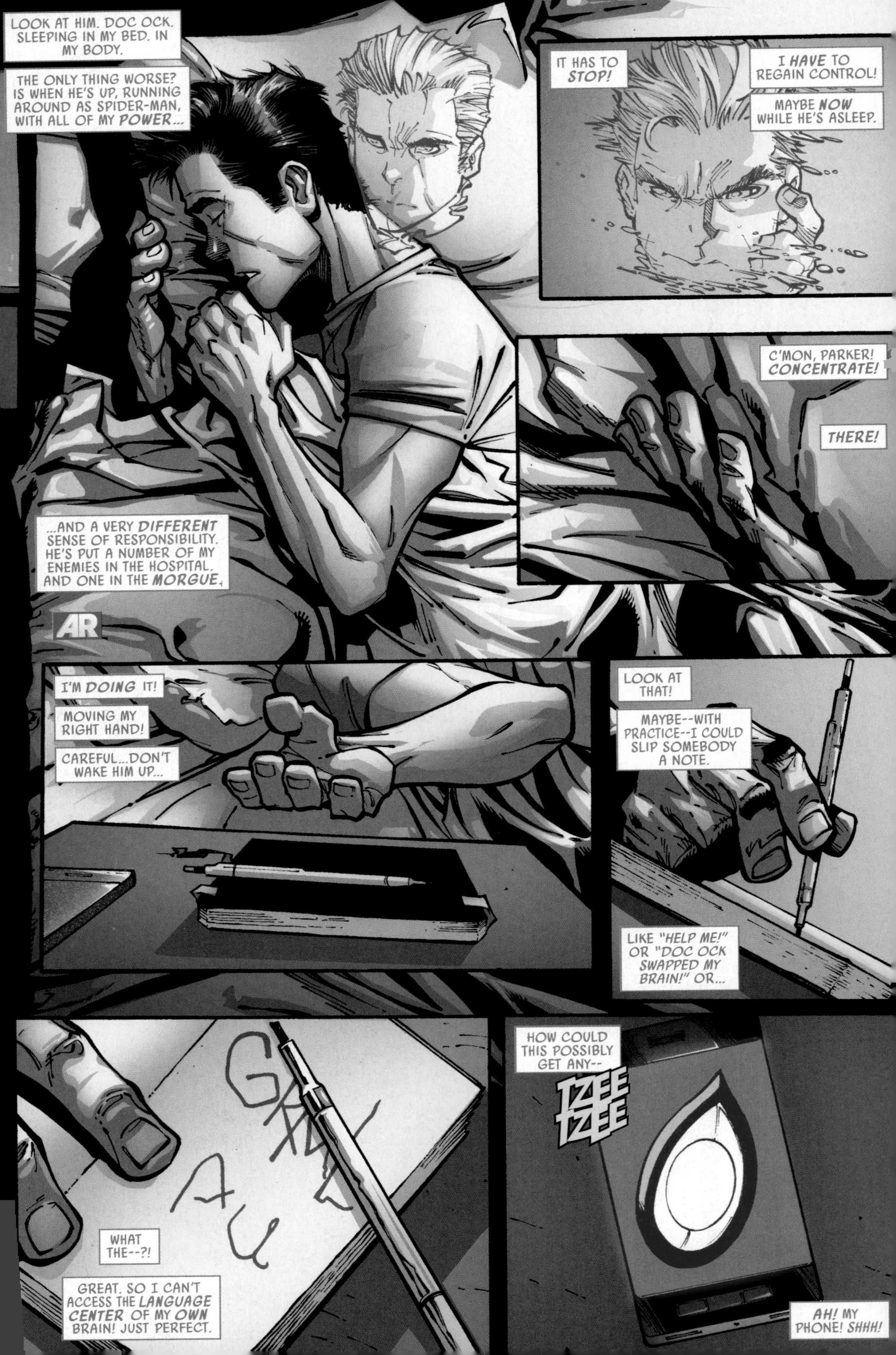
LOOK AT HIM. DOC OCK. SLEEPING IN MY BED. IN MY BODY.
THE ONLY THING WORSE? IS WHEN HE'S UP, RUNNING AROUND AS SPIDER-MAN, WITH ALL OF MY POWER...
...AND A VERY DIFFERENT SENSE OF RESPONSIBILITY. HE'S PUT A NUMBER OF MY ENEMIES IN THE HOSPITAL. AND ONE IN THE MORGUE.
IT HAS TO STOP!
I HAVE TO REGAIN CONTROL!
MAYBE NOW WHILE HE'S ASLEEP.
C'MON, PARKER! CONCENTRATE!
THERE!
I'M DOING IT!
MOVING MY RIGHT HAND!
CAREFUL...DON'T WAKE HIM UP...
LOOK AT THAT!
MAYBE--WITH PRACTICE--I COULD SLIP SOMEBODY A NOTE.
LIKE "HELP ME!" OR "DOC OCK SWAPPED MY BRAIN!" OR...
WHAT THE--?!
GREAT. SO I CAN'T ACCESS THE LANGUAGE CENTER OF MY OWN BRAIN! JUST PERFECT.
HOW COULD THIS POSSIBLY GET ANY--
TZEE TZEE
AH! MY PHONE! SHHH!

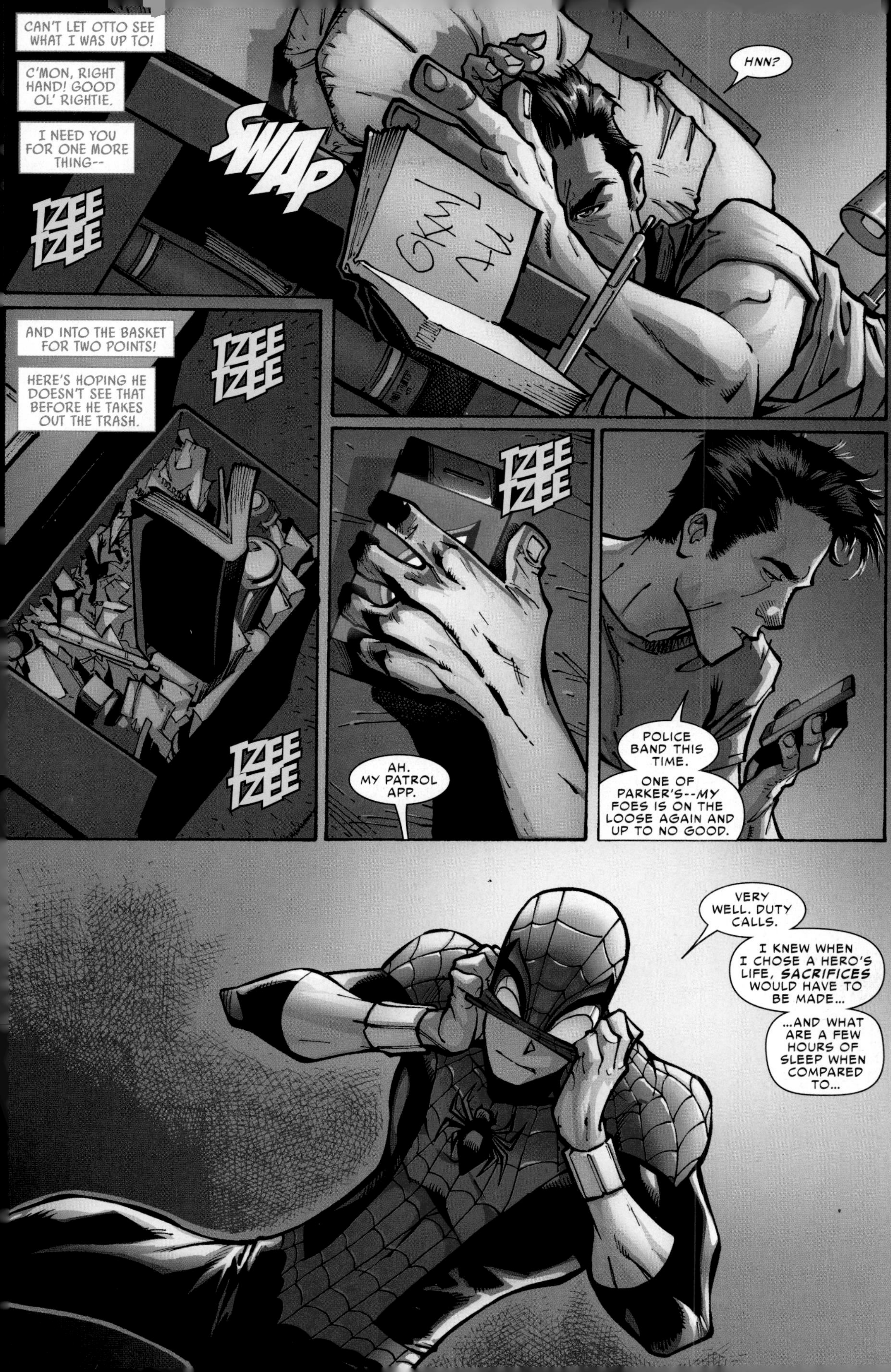
CAN'T LET OTTO SEE WHAT I WAS UP TO!
C'MON, RIGHT HAND! GOOD OL' RIGHTIE.
I NEED YOU FOR ONE MORE THING--
TZEE TZEE
SWAP
HNN?
AND INTO THE BASKET FOR TWO POINTS!
HERE'S HOPING HE DOESN'T SEE THAT BEFORE HE TAKES OUT THE TRASH.
TZEE TZEE
TZEE TZEE
TZEE TZEE
AH. MY PATROL APP.
POLICE BAND THIS TIME.
ONE OF PARKER'S--MY FOES IS ON THE LOOSE AGAIN AND UP TO NO GOOD.
VERY WELL. DUTY CALLS.
I KNEW WHEN I CHOSE A HERO'S LIFE, SACRIFICES WOULD HAVE TO BE MADE...
...AND WHAT ARE A FEW HOURS OF SLEEP WHEN COMPARED TO...

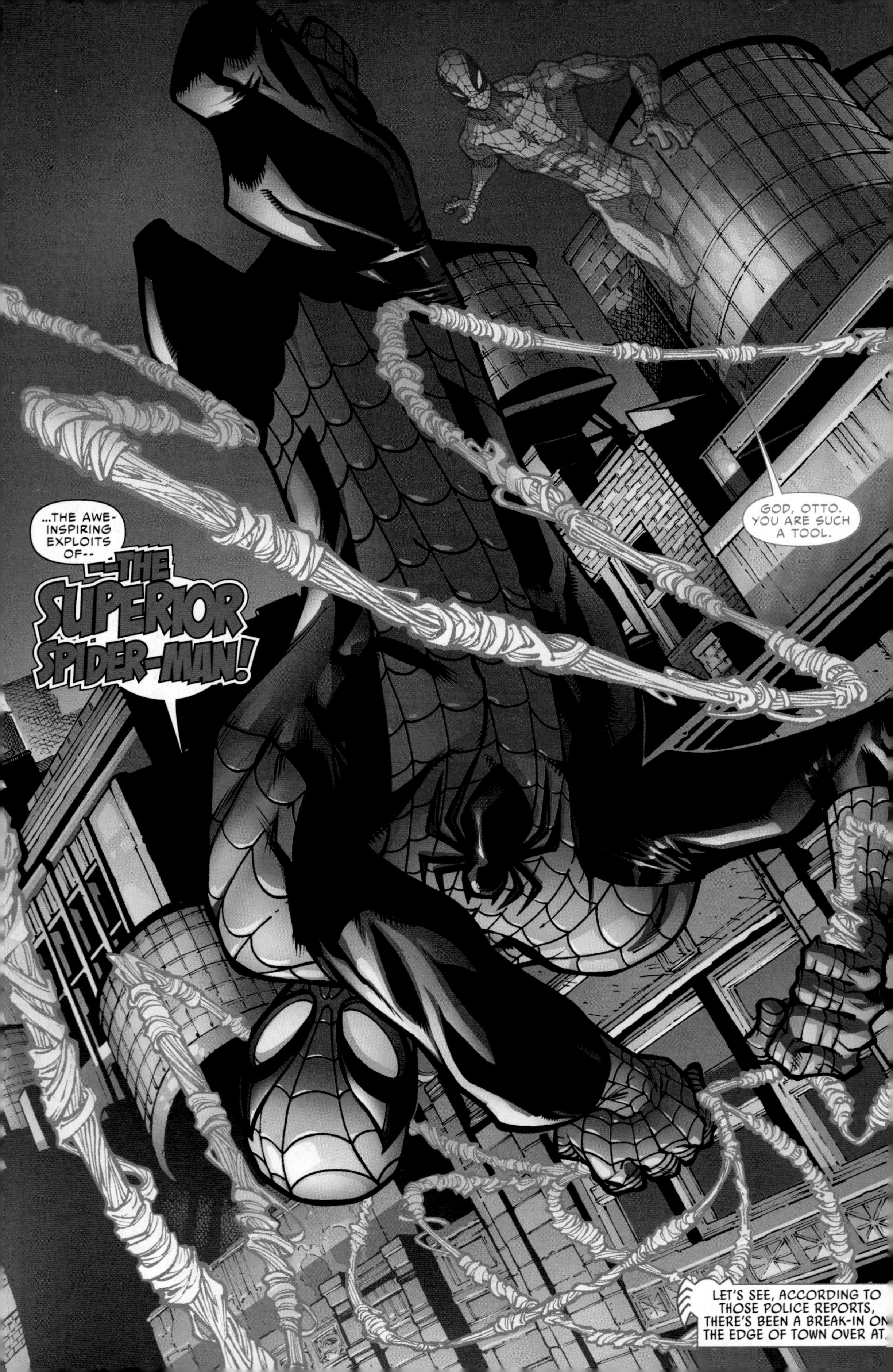
...THE AWE-INSPIRING EXPLOITS OF--
--THE SUPERIOR SPIDER-MAN!
GOD, OTTO. YOU ARE SUCH A TOOL.
LET'S SEE, ACCORDING TO THOSE POLICE REPORTS, THERE'S BEEN A BREAK-IN ON THE EDGE OF TOWN OVER AT...

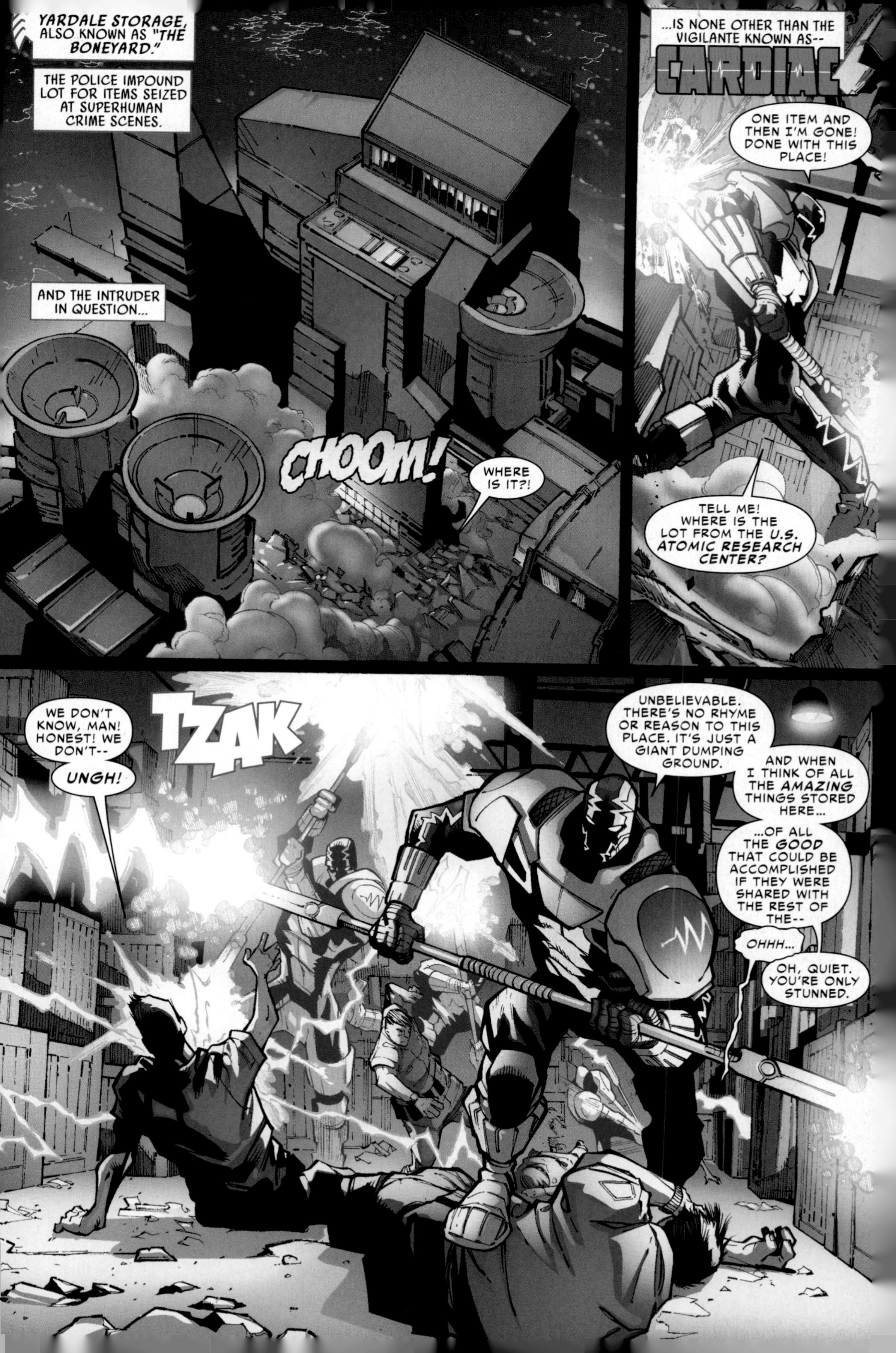
YARDALE STORAGE, ALSO KNOWN AS "THE BONEYARD."
THE POLICE IMPOUND LOT FOR ITEMS SEIZED AT SUPERHUMAN CRIME SCENES.
AND THE INTRUDER IN QUESTION...
CHOOM!
WHERE IS IT?!
...IS NONE OTHER THAN THE VIGILANTE KNOWN AS--
CARDIAC
ONE ITEM AND THEN I'M GONE! DONE WITH THIS PLACE!
TELL ME! WHERE IS THE LOT FROM THE U.S. ATOMIC RESEARCH CENTER?
WE DON'T KNOW, MAN! HONEST! WE DON'T--
UNGH!
TZAK
UNBELIEVABLE. THERE'S NO RHYME OR REASON TO THIS PLACE. IT'S JUST A GIANT DUMPING GROUND.
AND WHEN I THINK OF ALL THE AMAZING THINGS STORED HERE...
...OF ALL THE GOOD THAT COULD BE ACCOMPLISHED IF THEY WERE SHARED WITH THE REST OF THE--
OHHH...
OH, QUIET. YOU'RE ONLY STUNNED.

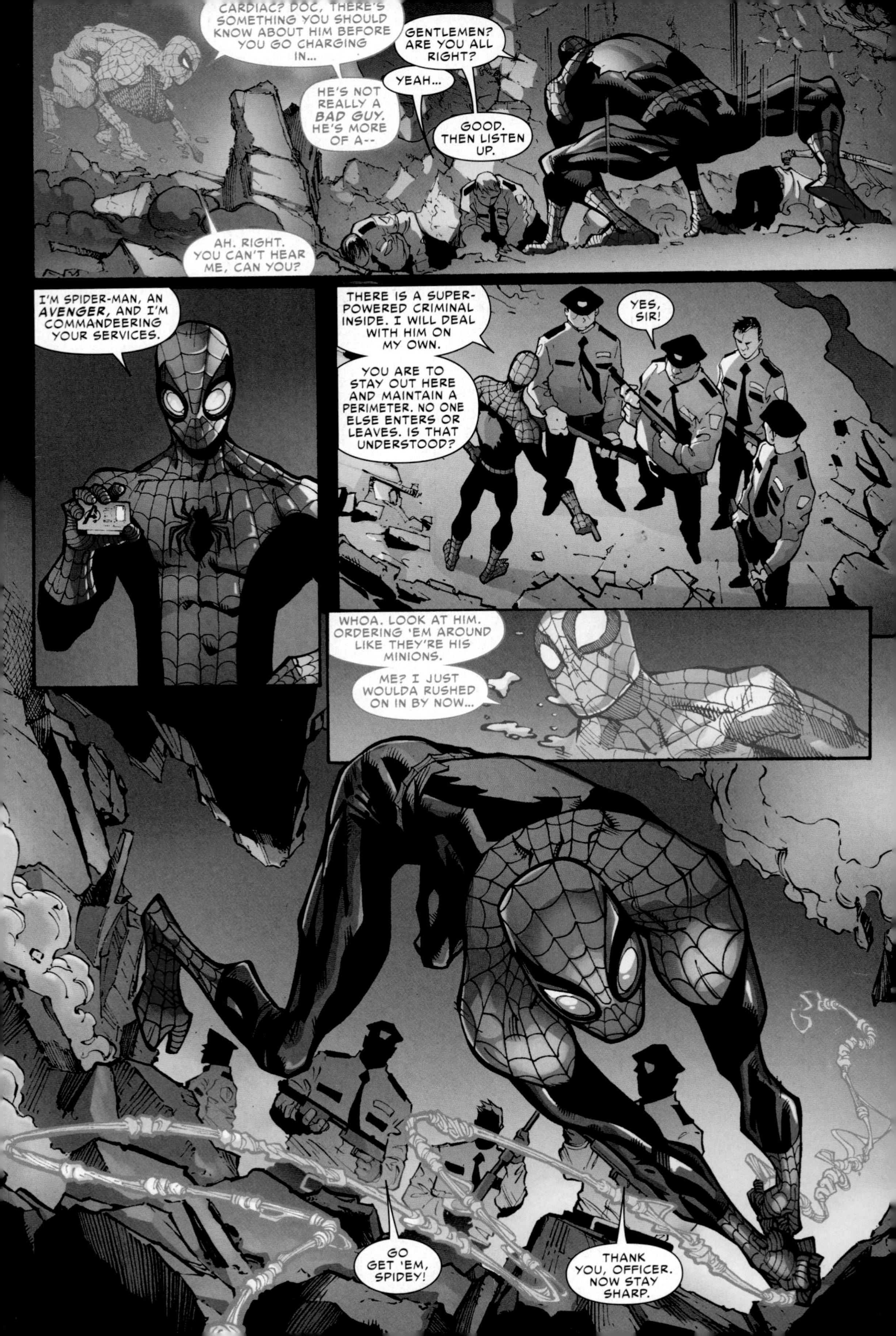

CARDIAC? DOC, THERE'S SOMETHING YOU SHOULD KNOW ABOUT HIM BEFORE YOU GO CHARGING IN...
GENTLEMEN? ARE YOU ALL RIGHT?
YEAH...
HE'S NOT REALLY A *BAD GUY*. HE'S MORE OF A--
GOOD. THEN LISTEN UP.
AH. RIGHT. YOU CAN'T HEAR ME, CAN YOU?
I'M SPIDER-MAN, AN *AVENGER*, AND I'M COMMANDEERING YOUR SERVICES.
THERE IS A SUPER-POWERED CRIMINAL INSIDE. I WILL DEAL WITH HIM ON MY OWN.
YOU ARE TO STAY OUT HERE AND MAINTAIN A PERIMETER. NO ONE ELSE ENTERS OR LEAVES. IS THAT UNDERSTOOD?
YES, SIR!
WHOA. LOOK AT HIM. ORDERING 'EM AROUND LIKE THEY'RE HIS MINIONS.
ME? I JUST WOULDA RUSHED ON IN BY NOW...
GO GET 'EM, SPIDEY!
THANK YOU, OFFICER. NOW STAY SHARP.

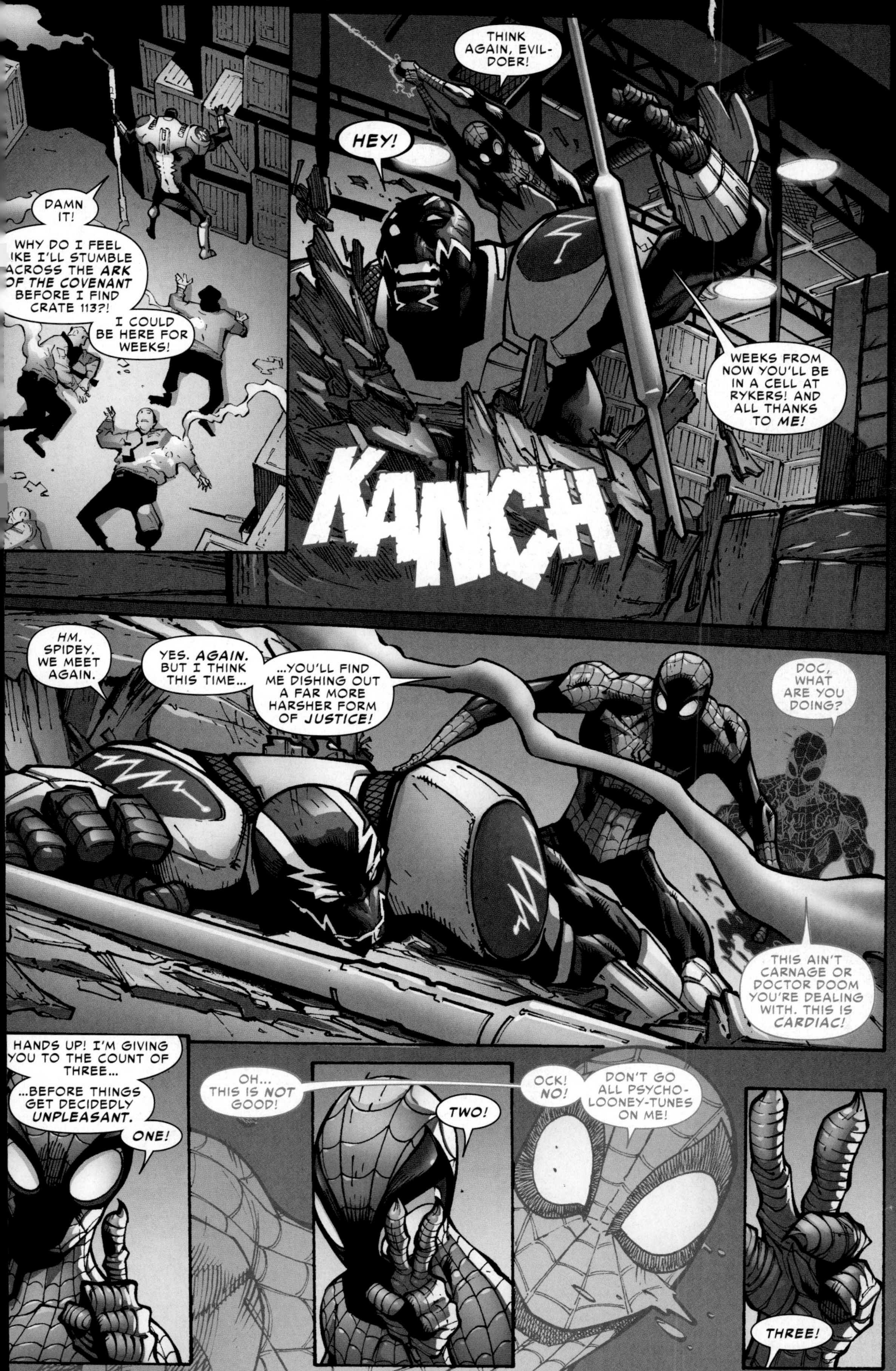

DAMN IT!
WHY DO I FEEL LIKE I'LL STUMBLE ACROSS THE ARK OF THE COVENANT BEFORE I FIND CRATE 113?!
I COULD BE HERE FOR WEEKS!
THINK AGAIN, EVIL-DOER!
HEY!
WEEKS FROM NOW YOU'LL BE IN A CELL AT RYKERS! AND ALL THANKS TO ME!
KANCH
HM. SPIDEY. WE MEET AGAIN.
YES. AGAIN. BUT I THINK THIS TIME...
...YOU'LL FIND ME DISHING OUT A FAR MORE HARSHER FORM OF JUSTICE!
DOC, WHAT ARE YOU DOING?
THIS AIN'T CARNAGE OR DOCTOR DOOM YOU'RE DEALING WITH. THIS IS CARDIAC!
HANDS UP! I'M GIVING YOU TO THE COUNT OF THREE...
...BEFORE THINGS GET DECIDEDLY UNPLEASANT.
ONE!
OH... THIS IS NOT GOOD!
TWO!
OCK! NO!
DON'T GO ALL PSYCHO-LOONEY-TUNES ON ME!
THREE!

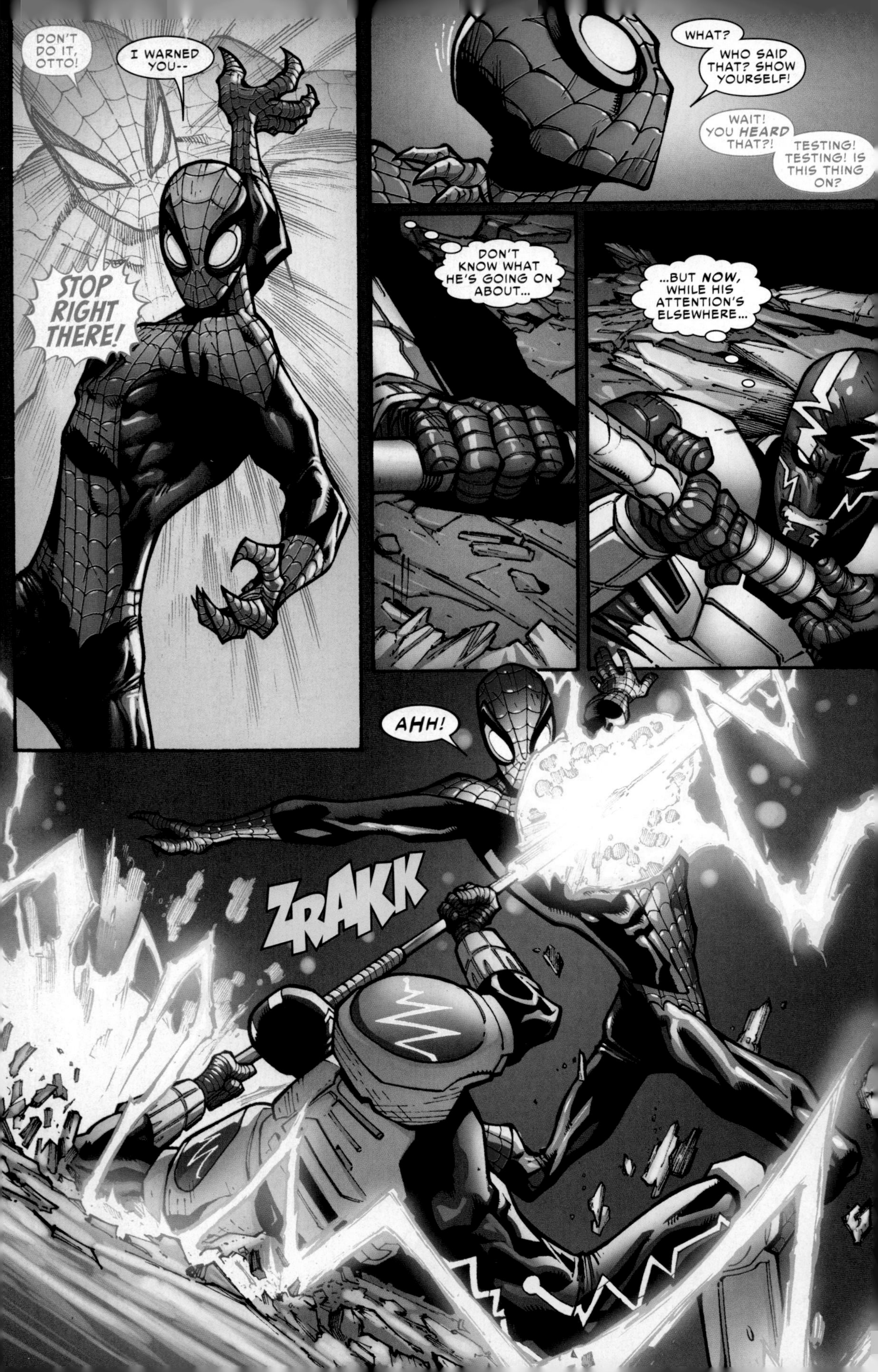
DON'T DO IT, OTTO!
I WARNED YOU--
STOP RIGHT THERE!
WHAT?
WHO SAID THAT? SHOW YOURSELF!
WAIT! YOU HEARD THAT?!
TESTING! TESTING! IS THIS THING ON?
DON'T KNOW WHAT HE'S GOING ON ABOUT...
...BUT NOW, WHILE HIS ATTENTION'S ELSEWHERE...
AHH!
ZRAKK

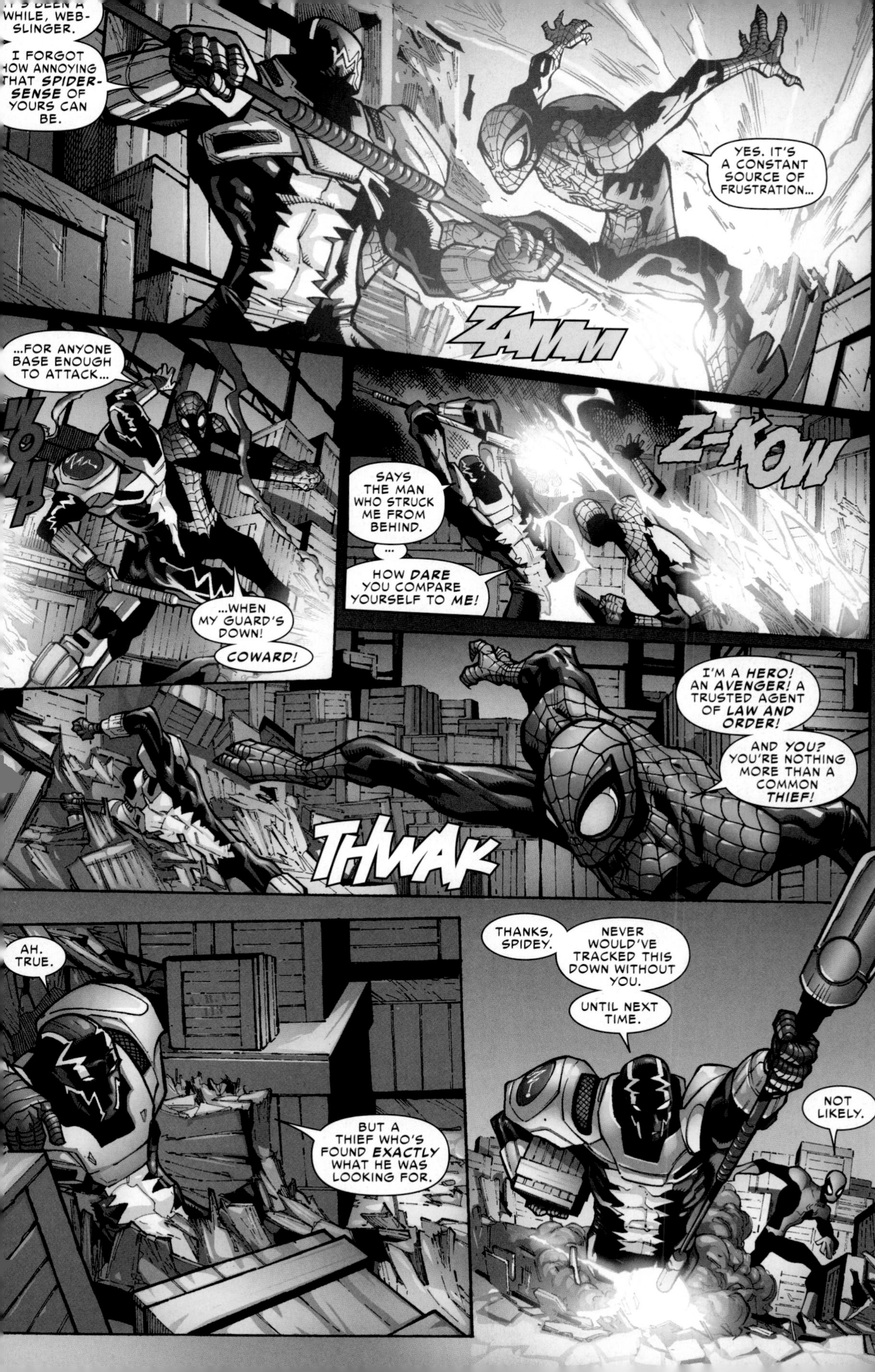
WHILE, WEB-SLINGER.
I FORGOT HOW ANNOYING THAT SPIDER-SENSE OF YOURS CAN BE.
YES. IT'S A CONSTANT SOURCE OF FRUSTRATION...
ZAMM
...FOR ANYONE BASE ENOUGH TO ATTACK...
WOMP
...WHEN MY GUARD'S DOWN!
COWARD!
SAYS THE MAN WHO STRUCK ME FROM BEHIND.
...
HOW DARE YOU COMPARE YOURSELF TO ME!
Z-KOW
I'M A HERO! AN AVENGER! A TRUSTED AGENT OF LAW AND ORDER!
AND YOU? YOU'RE NOTHING MORE THAN A COMMON THIEF!
THWAK
AH. TRUE.
BUT A THIEF WHO'S FOUND EXACTLY WHAT HE WAS LOOKING FOR.
THANKS, SPIDEY.
NEVER WOULD'VE TRACKED THIS DOWN WITHOUT YOU.
UNTIL NEXT TIME.
NOT LIKELY.

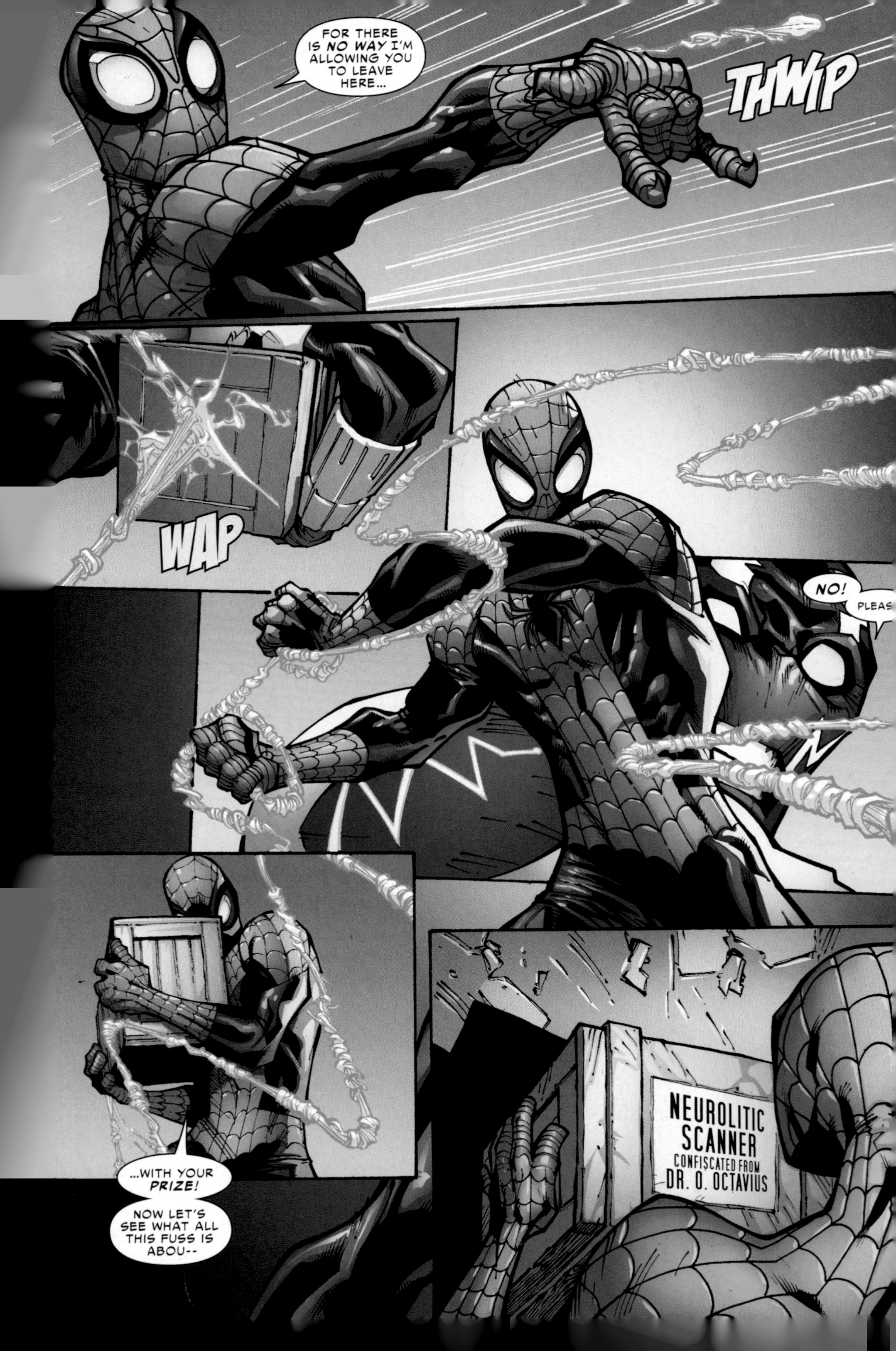
FOR THERE IS NO WAY I'M ALLOWING YOU TO LEAVE HERE...
THWIP
WAP
NO!
PLEAS
...WITH YOUR PRIZE!
NOW LET'S SEE WHAT ALL THIS FUSS IS ABOU--
NEUROLITIC SCANNER CONFISCATED FROM DR. O. OCTAVIUS

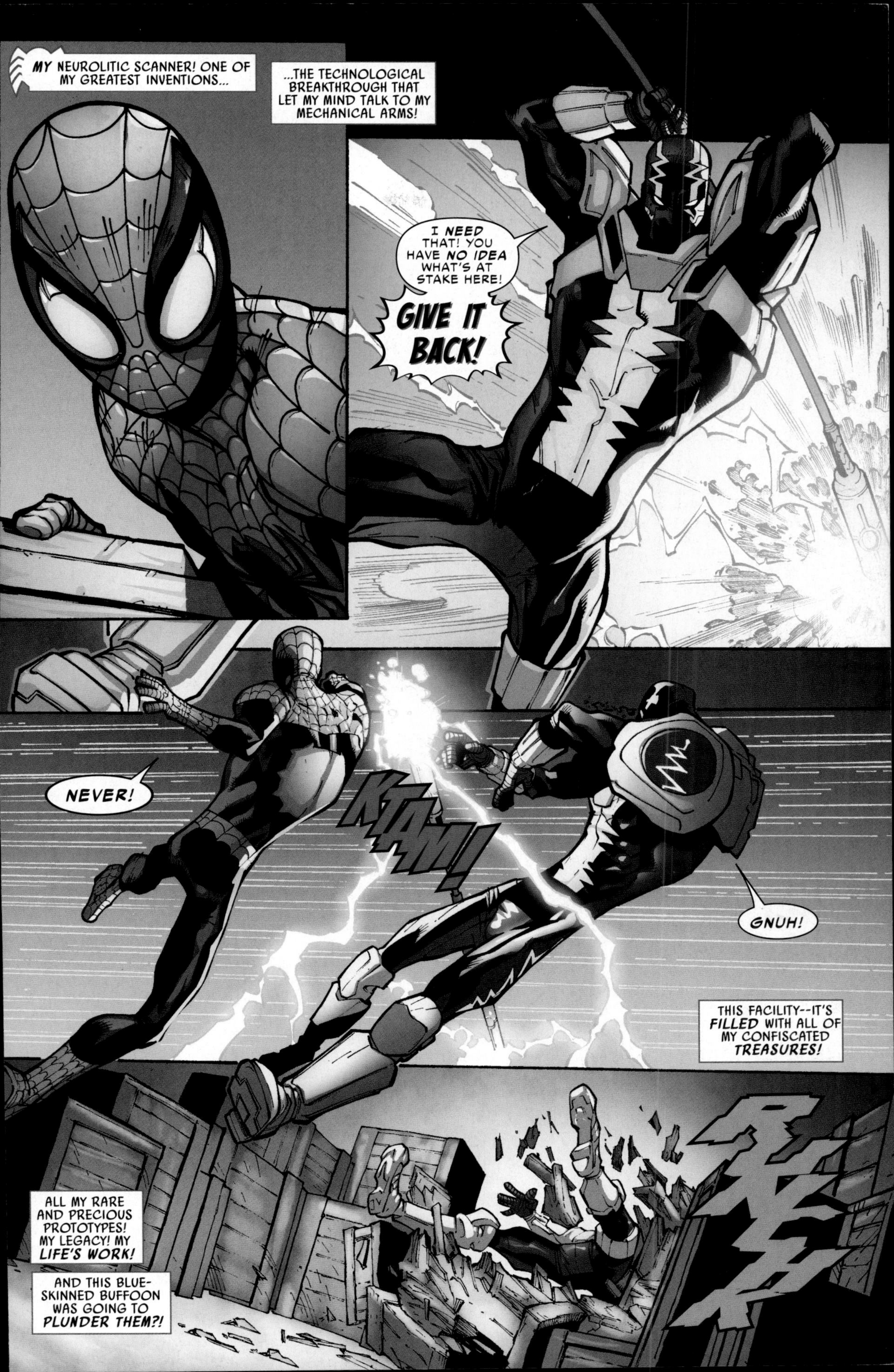
MY NEUROLITIC SCANNER! ONE OF MY GREATEST INVENTIONS...
...THE TECHNOLOGICAL BREAKTHROUGH THAT LET MY MIND TALK TO MY MECHANICAL ARMS!
I NEED THAT! YOU HAVE NO IDEA WHAT'S AT STAKE HERE!
GIVE IT BACK!
NEVER!
KTAM!
GNUH!
THIS FACILITY--IT'S FILLED WITH ALL OF MY CONFISCATED TREASURES!
ALL MY RARE AND PRECIOUS PROTOTYPES! MY LEGACY! MY LIFE'S WORK!
AND THIS BLUE-SKINNED BUFFOON WAS GOING TO PLUNDER THEM?!

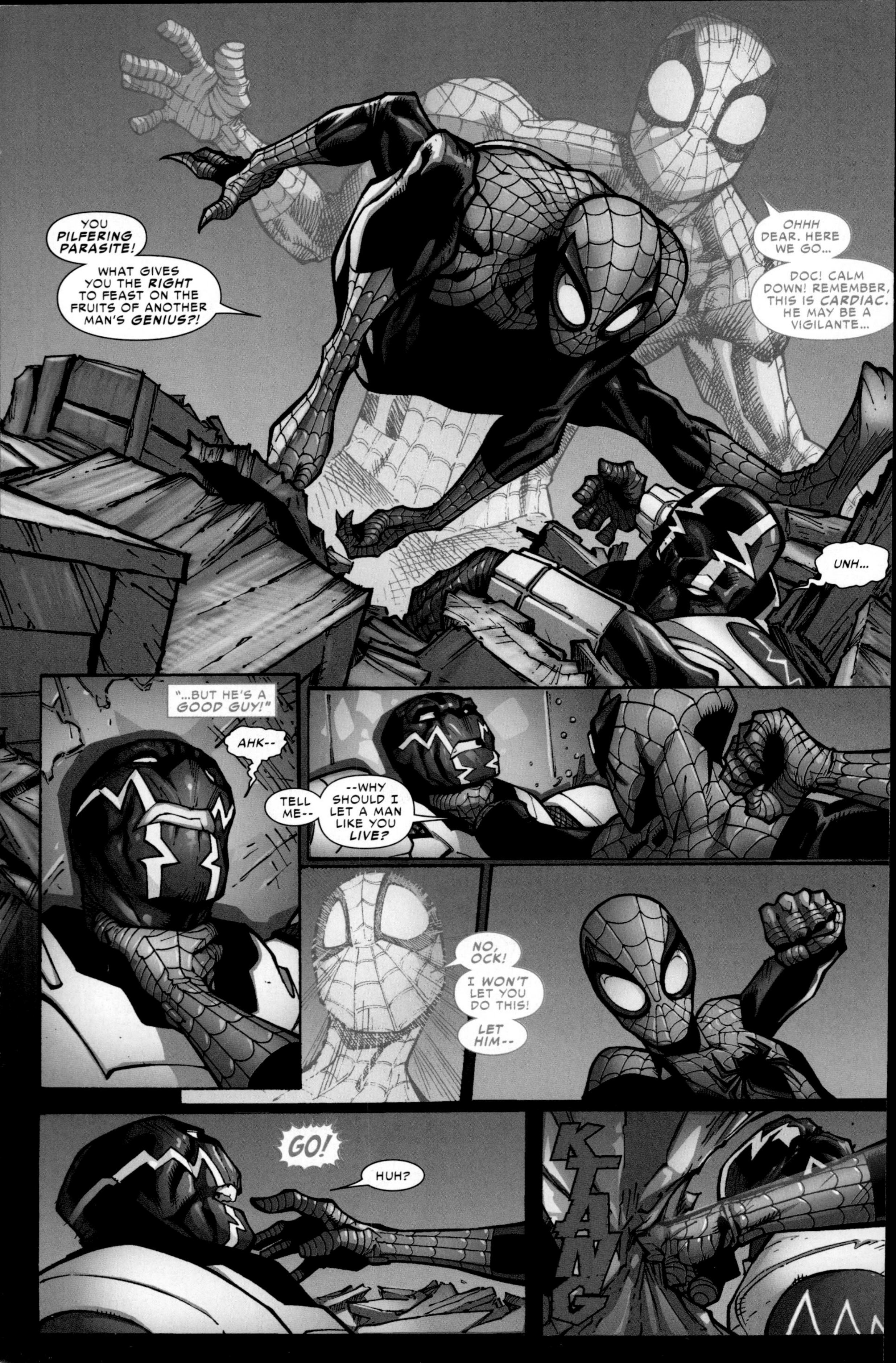
YOU PILFERING PARASITE!
WHAT GIVES YOU THE RIGHT TO FEAST ON THE FRUITS OF ANOTHER MAN'S GENIUS?!
OHHH DEAR. HERE WE GO...
DOC! CALM DOWN! REMEMBER, THIS IS CARDIAC. HE MAY BE A VIGILANTE...
UNH...
"...BUT HE'S A GOOD GUY!"
AHK--
TELL ME--
--WHY SHOULD I LET A MAN LIKE YOU LIVE?
NO, OCK!
I WON'T LET YOU DO THIS!
LET HIM--
GO!
HUH?
KLANG

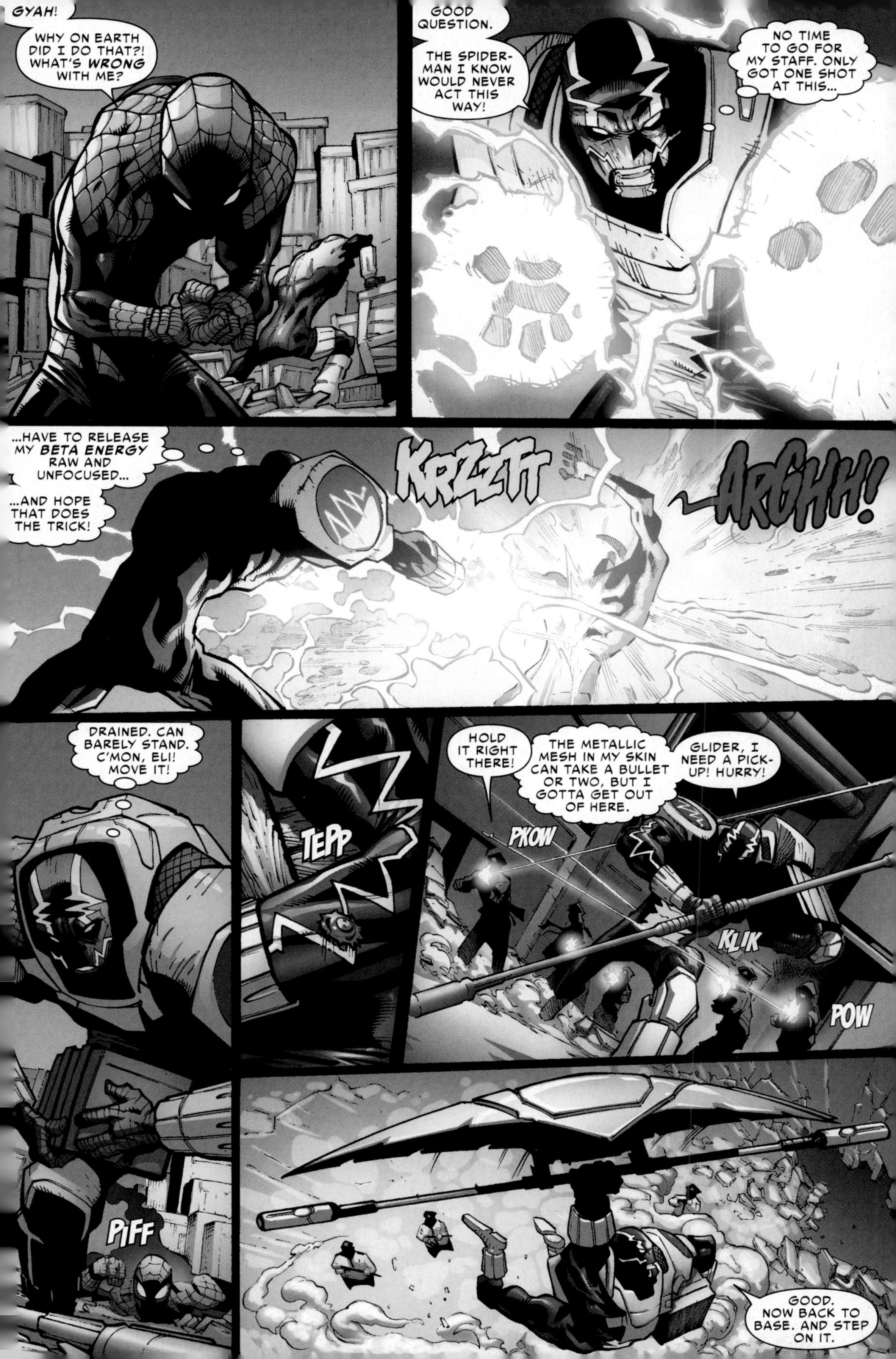

GYAH!
WHY ON EARTH DID I DO THAT?! WHAT'S WRONG WITH ME?
GOOD QUESTION.
THE SPIDER-MAN I KNOW WOULD NEVER ACT THIS WAY!
NO TIME TO GO FOR MY STAFF. ONLY GOT ONE SHOT AT THIS...
...HAVE TO RELEASE MY BETA ENERGY RAW AND UNFOCUSED...
...AND HOPE THAT DOES THE TRICK!
KRZZTT
ARGHH!
DRAINED. CAN BARELY STAND. C'MON, ELI! MOVE IT!
TEPP
HOLD IT RIGHT THERE!
THE METALLIC MESH IN MY SKIN CAN TAKE A BULLET OR TWO, BUT I GOTTA GET OUT OF HERE.
GLIDER, I NEED A PICK-UP! HURRY!
PKOW
KLIK
POW
PIFF
GOOD. NOW BACK TO BASE. AND STEP ON IT.

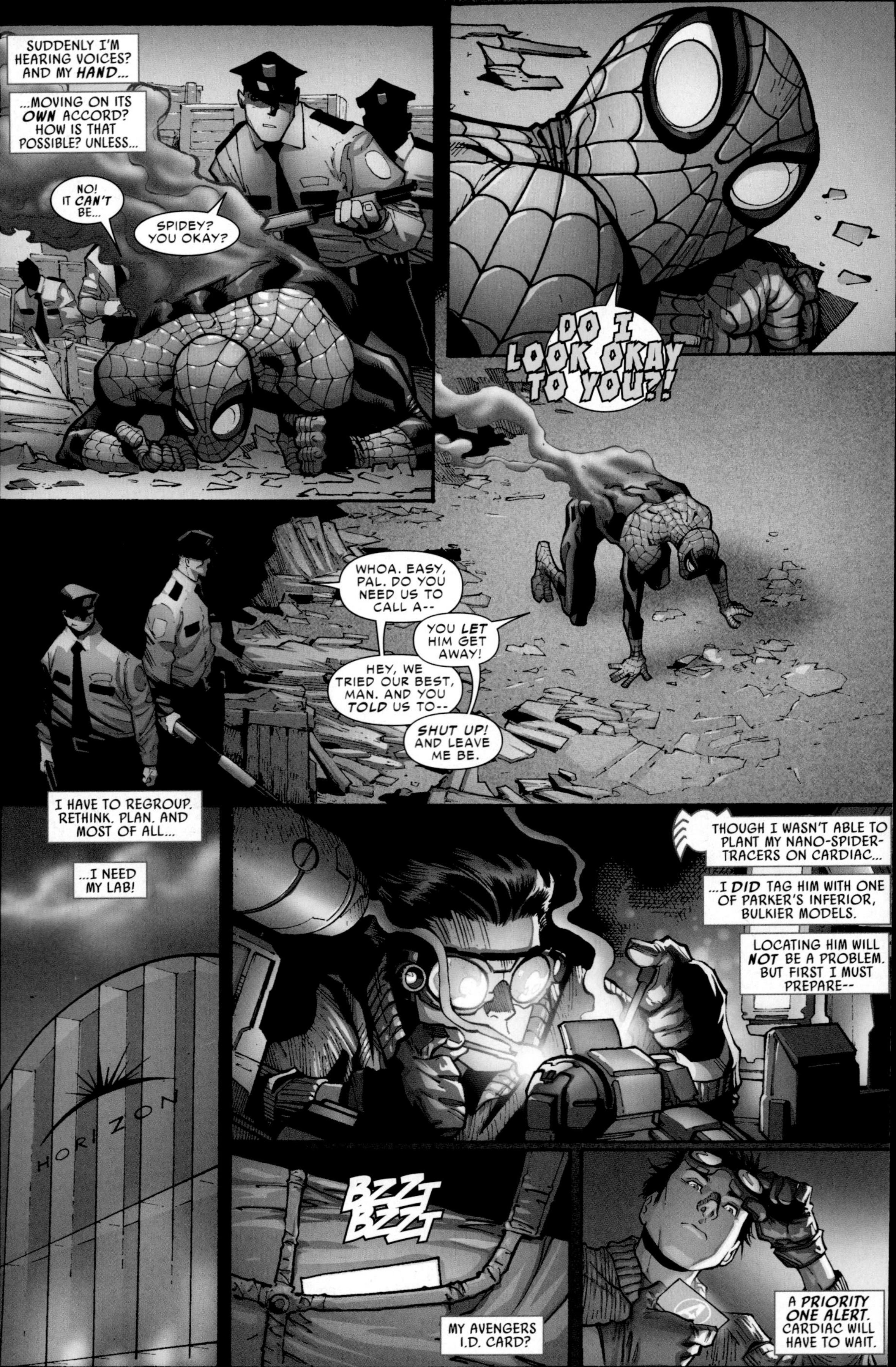
SUDDENLY I'M HEARING VOICES? AND MY HAND...
...MOVING ON ITS OWN ACCORD? HOW IS THAT POSSIBLE? UNLESS...
NO! IT CAN'T BE...
SPIDEY? YOU OKAY?
DO I LOOK OKAY TO YOU?!
WHOA. EASY, PAL. DO YOU NEED US TO CALL A--
YOU LET HIM GET AWAY!
HEY, WE TRIED OUR BEST, MAN. AND YOU TOLD US TO--
SHUT UP! AND LEAVE ME BE.
I HAVE TO REGROUP. RETHINK. PLAN. AND MOST OF ALL...
...I NEED MY LAB!
HORIZON
THOUGH I WASN'T ABLE TO PLANT MY NANO-SPIDER-TRACERS ON CARDIAC...
...I DID TAG HIM WITH ONE OF PARKER'S INFERIOR, BULKIER MODELS.
LOCATING HIM WILL NOT BE A PROBLEM. BUT FIRST I MUST PREPARE--
BZZT BZZT
MY AVENGERS I.D. CARD?
A PRIORITY ONE ALERT. CARDIAC WILL HAVE TO WAIT.

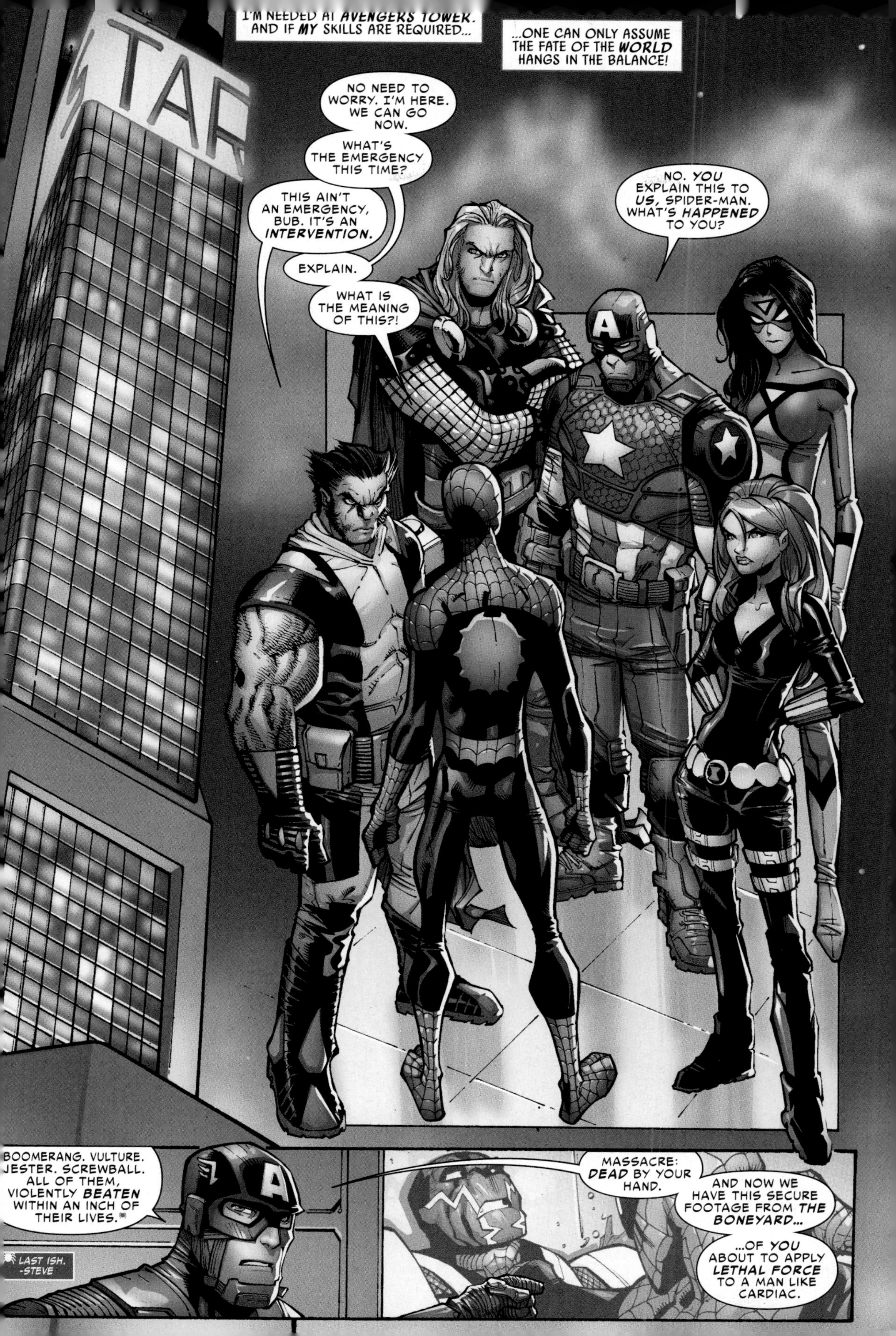
I'M NEEDED AT AVENGERS TOWER. AND IF MY SKILLS ARE REQUIRED...
...ONE CAN ONLY ASSUME THE FATE OF THE WORLD HANGS IN THE BALANCE!
NO NEED TO WORRY. I'M HERE. WE CAN GO NOW.
WHAT'S THE EMERGENCY THIS TIME?
THIS AIN'T AN EMERGENCY, BUB. IT'S AN INTERVENTION.
EXPLAIN.
WHAT IS THE MEANING OF THIS?!
NO. YOU EXPLAIN THIS TO US, SPIDER-MAN. WHAT'S HAPPENED TO YOU?
BOOMERANG. VULTURE. JESTER. SCREWBALL. ALL OF THEM, VIOLENTLY BEATEN WITHIN AN INCH OF THEIR LIVES.
LAST ISH. -STEVE
MASSACRE: DEAD BY YOUR HAND.
AND NOW WE HAVE THIS SECURE FOOTAGE FROM THE BONEYARD...
...OF YOU ABOUT TO APPLY LETHAL FORCE TO A MAN LIKE CARDIAC.

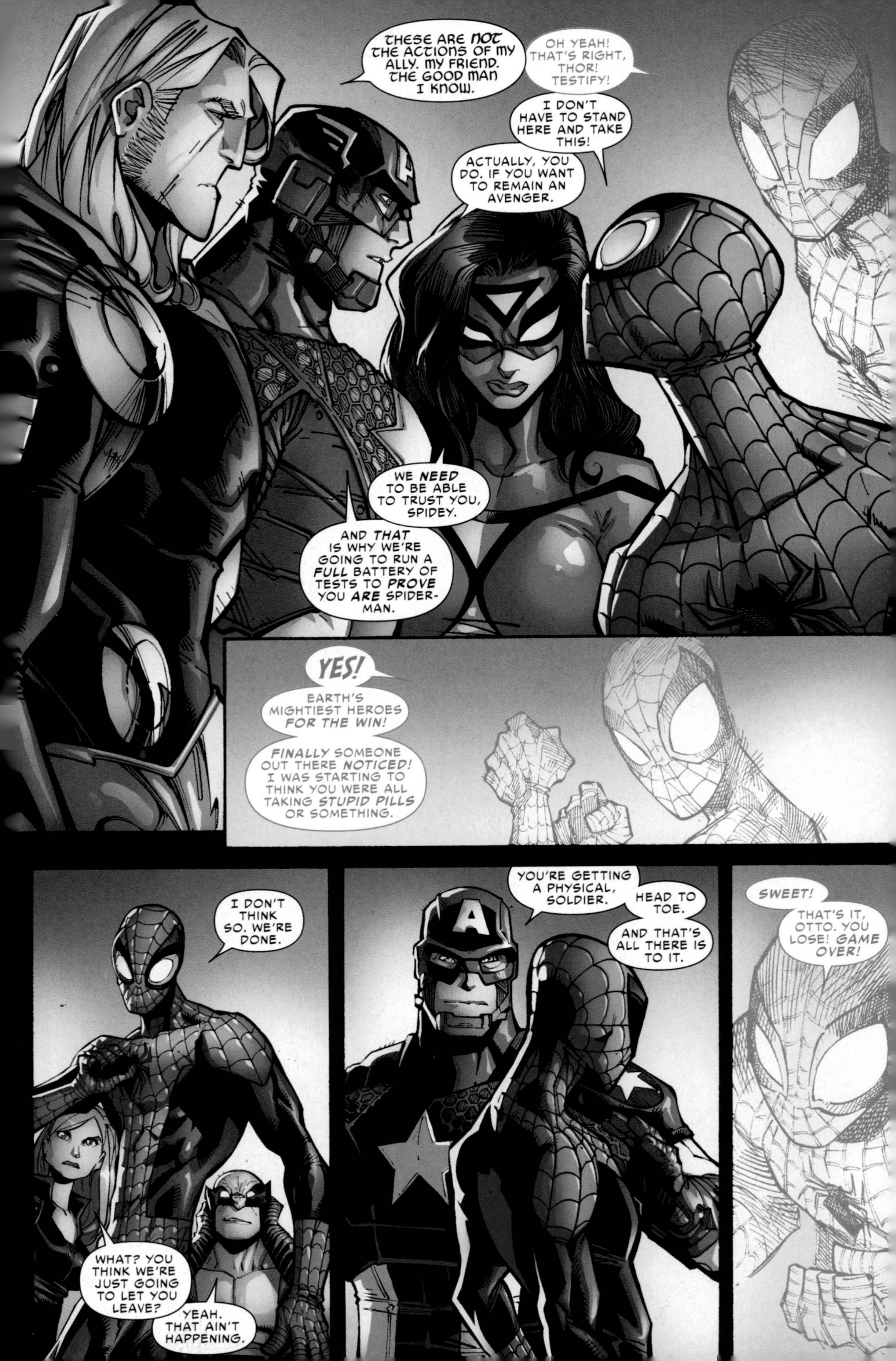
THESE ARE NOT THE ACTIONS OF MY ALLY. MY FRIEND. THE GOOD MAN I KNOW.
OH YEAH! THAT'S RIGHT, THOR! TESTIFY!
I DON'T HAVE TO STAND HERE AND TAKE THIS!
ACTUALLY, YOU DO. IF YOU WANT TO REMAIN AN AVENGER.
WE NEED TO BE ABLE TO TRUST YOU, SPIDEY.
AND THAT IS WHY WE'RE GOING TO RUN A FULL BATTERY OF TESTS TO PROVE YOU ARE SPIDER-MAN.
YES!
EARTH'S MIGHTIEST HEROES FOR THE WIN!
FINALLY SOMEONE OUT THERE NOTICED! I WAS STARTING TO THINK YOU WERE ALL TAKING STUPID PILLS OR SOMETHING.
I DON'T THINK SO. WE'RE DONE.
WHAT? YOU THINK WE'RE JUST GOING TO LET YOU LEAVE?
YEAH. THAT AIN'T HAPPENING.
YOU'RE GETTING A PHYSICAL, SOLDIER.
HEAD TO TOE.
AND THAT'S ALL THERE IS TO IT.
SWEET!
THAT'S IT, OTTO. YOU LOSE! GAME OVER!

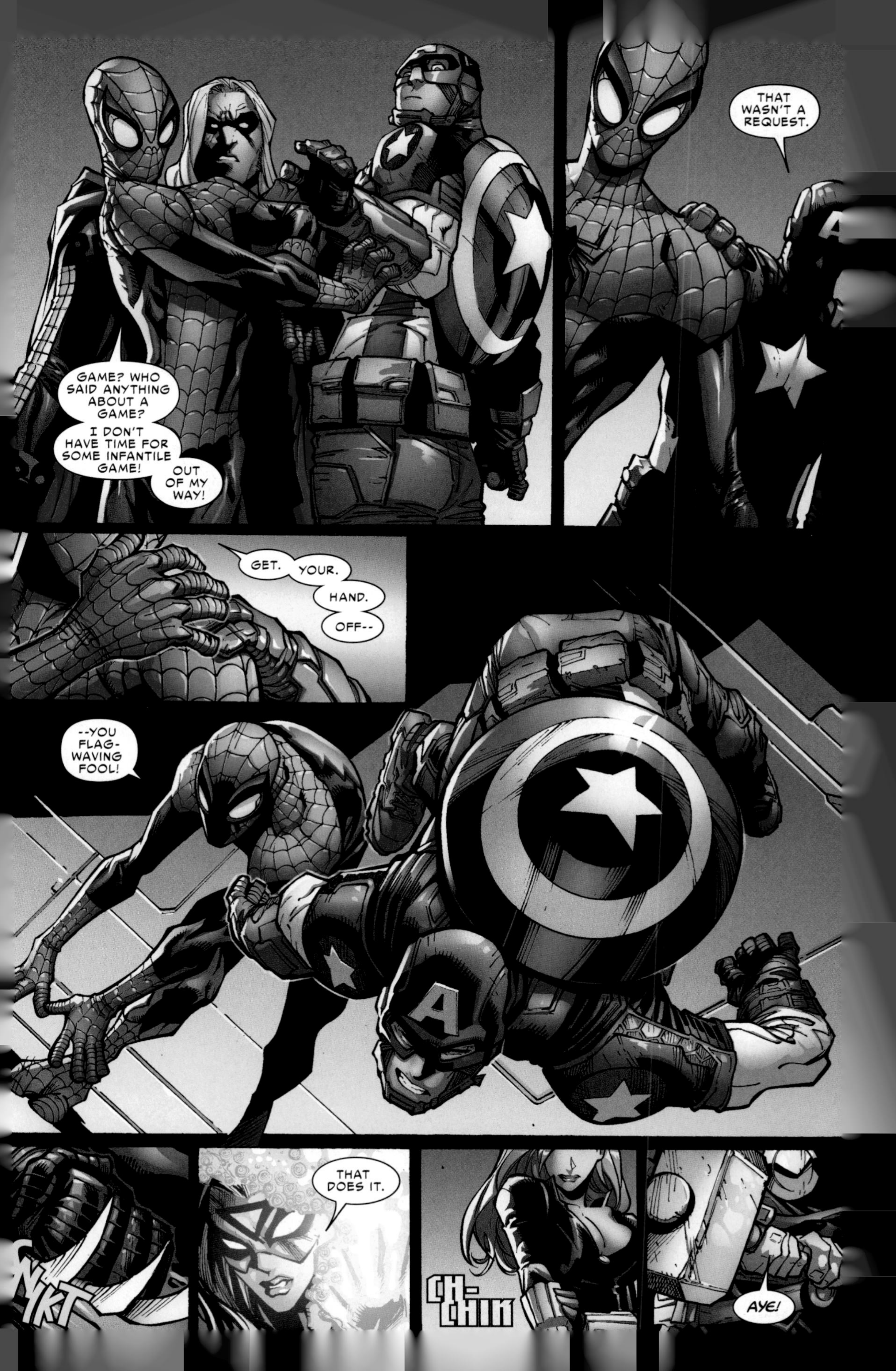

GAME? WHO SAID ANYTHING ABOUT A GAME?
I DON'T HAVE TIME FOR SOME INFANTILE GAME!
OUT OF MY WAY!
THAT WASN'T A REQUEST.
GET.
YOUR.
HAND.
OFF--
--YOU FLAG-WAVING FOOL!
NKT
THAT DOES IT.
CH-CHIN
AYE!

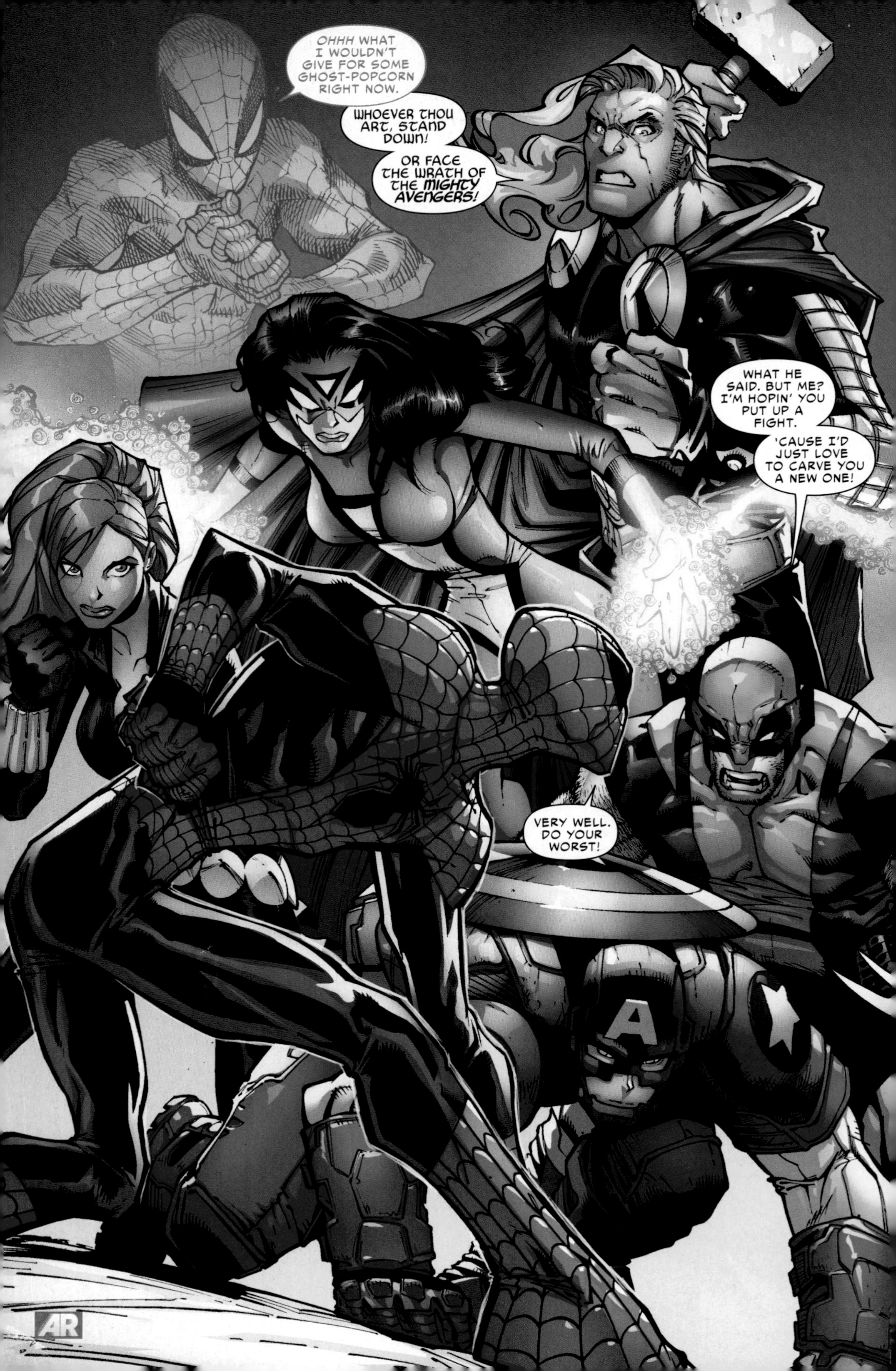

OHHH WHAT I WOULDN'T GIVE FOR SOME GHOST-POPCORN RIGHT NOW.
WHOEVER THOU ART, STAND DOWN!
OR FACE THE WRATH OF THE MIGHTY AVENGERS!
WHAT HE SAID. BUT ME? I'M HOPIN' YOU PUT UP A FIGHT.
'CAUSE I'D JUST LOVE TO CARVE YOU A NEW ONE!
VERY WELL. DO YOUR WORST!

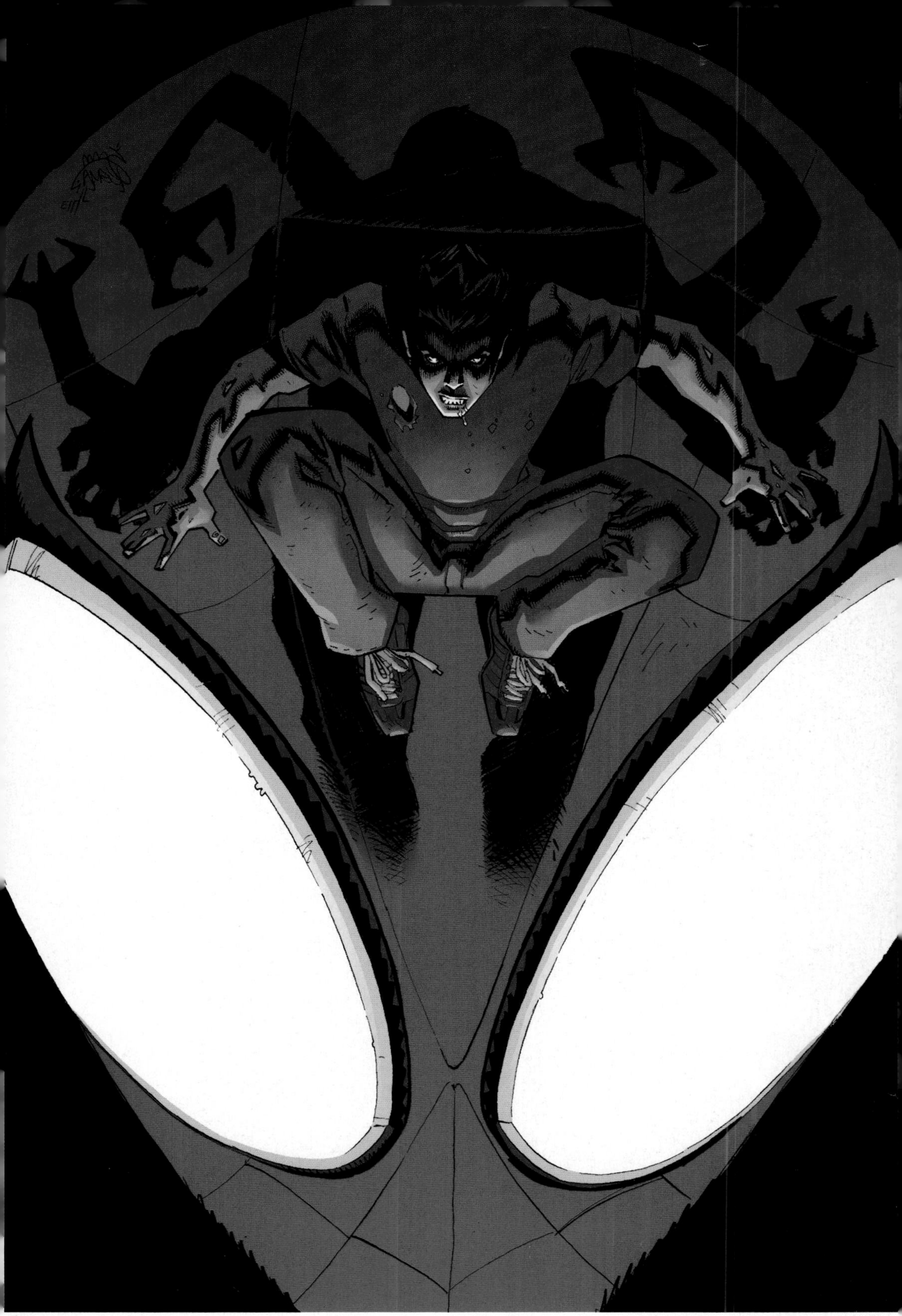

#9 VARIANT
BY RYAN STEGMAN & JASON HOWARD

8

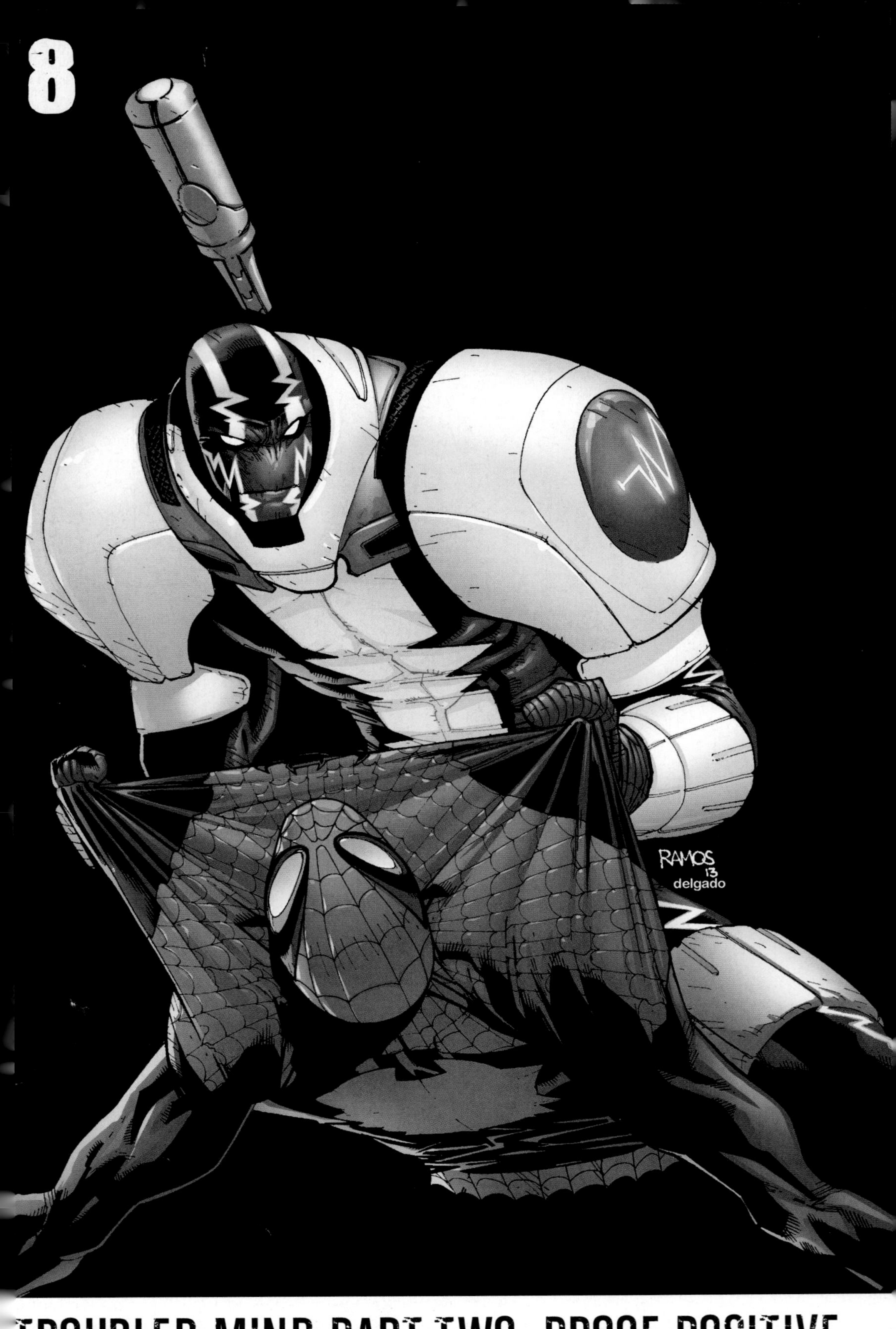
RAMOS
13
delgado

TROUBLED MIND PART TWO: PROOF POSITIVE

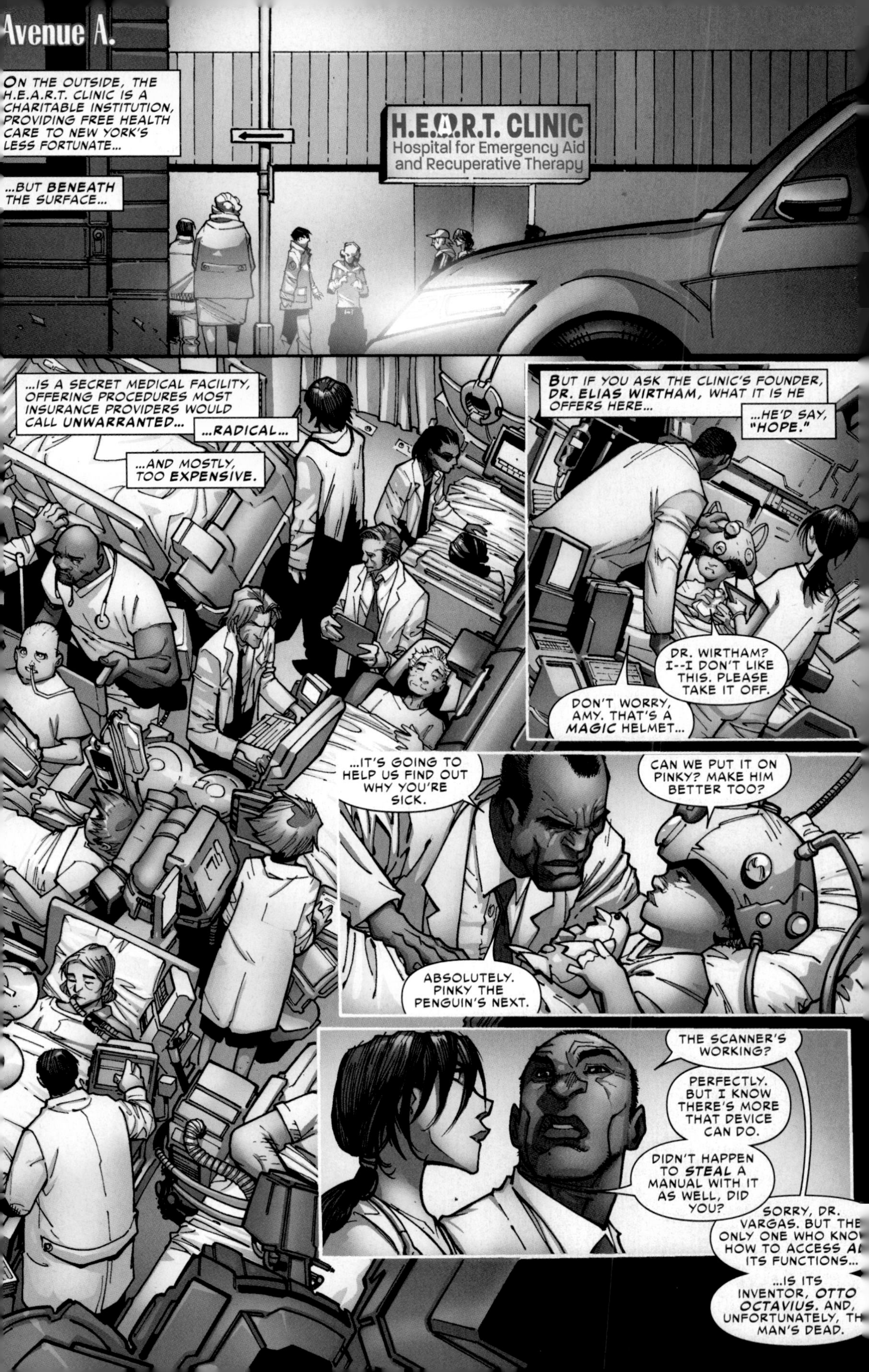
Avenue A.
ON THE OUTSIDE, THE H.E.A.R.T. CLINIC IS A CHARITABLE INSTITUTION, PROVIDING FREE HEALTH CARE TO NEW YORK'S LESS FORTUNATE...
H.E.A.R.T. CLINIC
Hospital for Emergency Aid and Recuperative Therapy
...BUT BENEATH THE SURFACE...
...IS A SECRET MEDICAL FACILITY, OFFERING PROCEDURES MOST INSURANCE PROVIDERS WOULD CALL UNWARRANTED...
...RADICAL...
...AND MOSTLY, TOO EXPENSIVE.
BUT IF YOU ASK THE CLINIC'S FOUNDER, DR. ELIAS WIRTHAM, WHAT IT IS HE OFFERS HERE...
...HE'D SAY, "HOPE."
DR. WIRTHAM? I--I DON'T LIKE THIS. PLEASE TAKE IT OFF.
DON'T WORRY, AMY. THAT'S A MAGIC HELMET...
...IT'S GOING TO HELP US FIND OUT WHY YOU'RE SICK.
CAN WE PUT IT ON PINKY? MAKE HIM BETTER TOO?
ABSOLUTELY. PINKY THE PENGUIN'S NEXT.
THE SCANNER'S WORKING?
PERFECTLY. BUT I KNOW THERE'S MORE THAT DEVICE CAN DO.
DIDN'T HAPPEN TO STEAL A MANUAL WITH IT AS WELL, DID YOU?
SORRY, DR. VARGAS. BUT THE ONLY ONE WHO KNOW HOW TO ACCESS A ITS FUNCTIONS...
...IS ITS INVENTOR, OTTO OCTAVIUS. AND, UNFORTUNATELY, TH MAN'S DEAD.

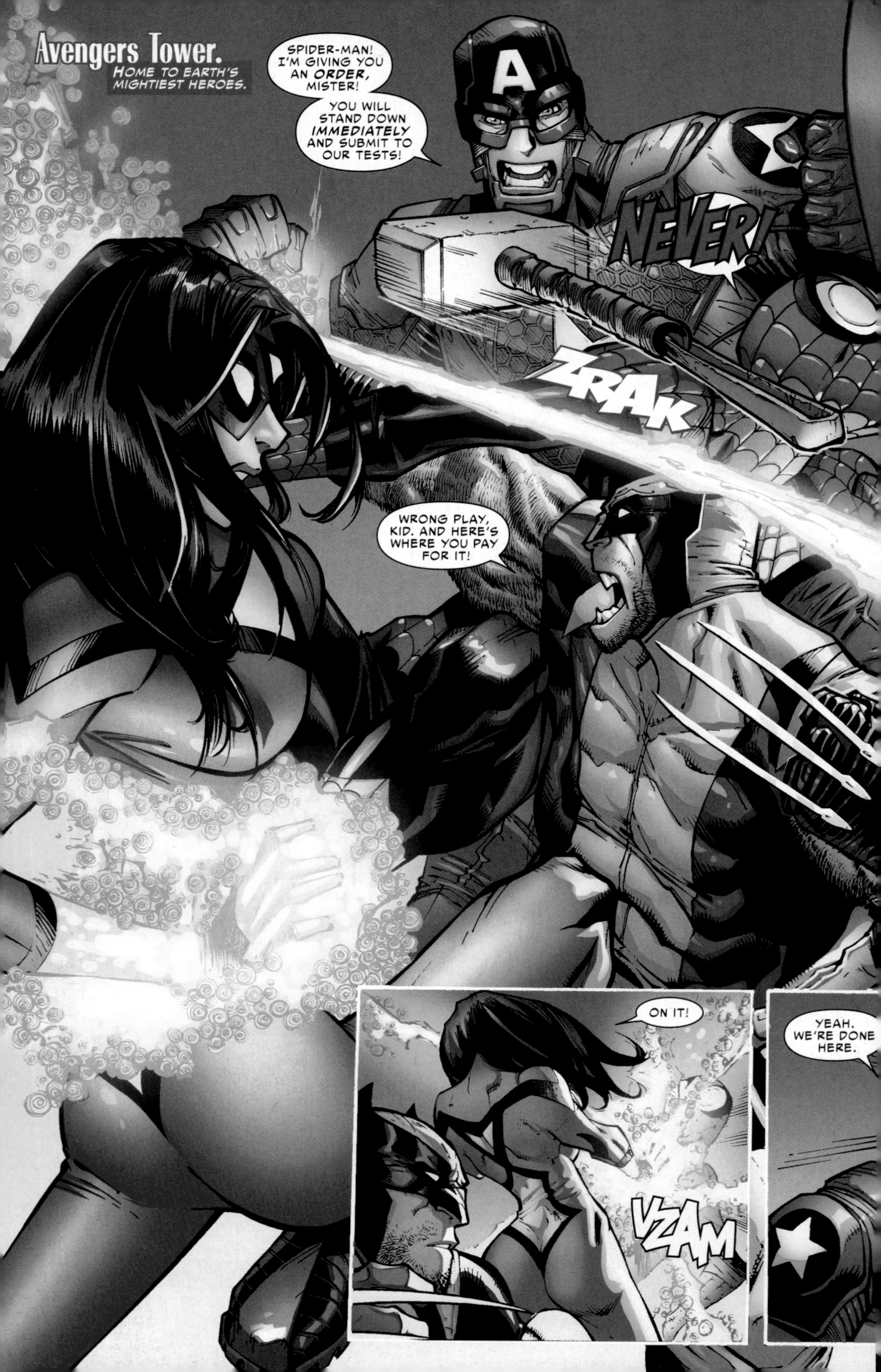
Avengers Tower.
HOME TO EARTH'S MIGHTIEST HEROES.
SPIDER-MAN! I'M GIVING YOU AN ORDER, MISTER!
YOU WILL STAND DOWN IMMEDIATELY AND SUBMIT TO OUR TESTS!
NEVER!
ZRAK
WRONG PLAY, KID. AND HERE'S WHERE YOU PAY FOR IT!
ON IT!
VZAM
YEAH. WE'RE DONE HERE.

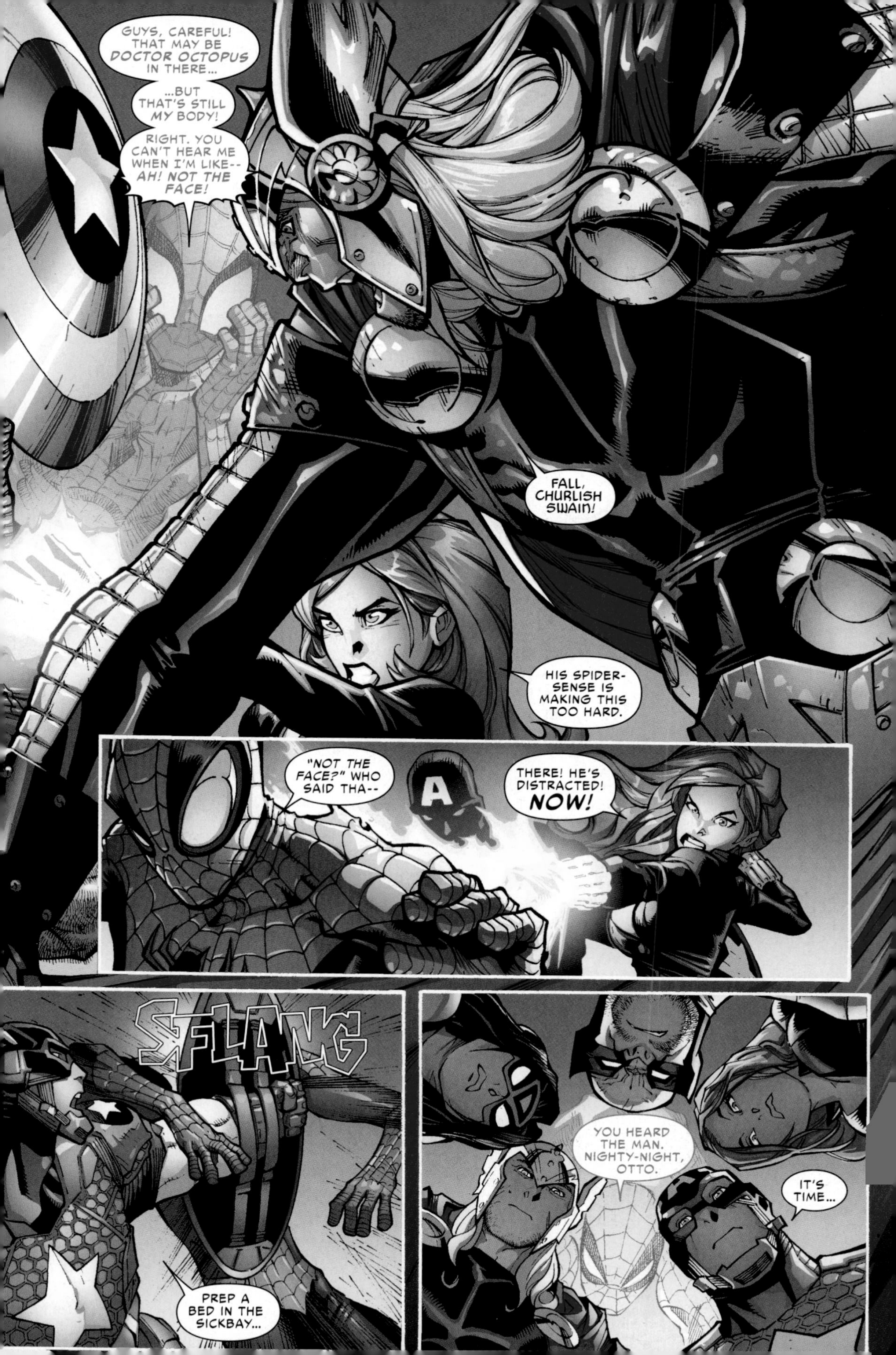
GUYS, CAREFUL! THAT MAY BE DOCTOR OCTOPUS IN THERE...
...BUT THAT'S STILL MY BODY!
RIGHT. YOU CAN'T HEAR ME WHEN I'M LIKE-- AH! NOT THE FACE!
FALL, CHURLISH SWAIN!
HIS SPIDER-SENSE IS MAKING THIS TOO HARD.
"NOT THE FACE?" WHO SAID THA--
THERE! HE'S DISTRACTED! NOW!
SFLANG
PREP A BED IN THE SICKBAY...
YOU HEARD THE MAN. NIGHTY-NIGHT, OTTO.
IT'S TIME...

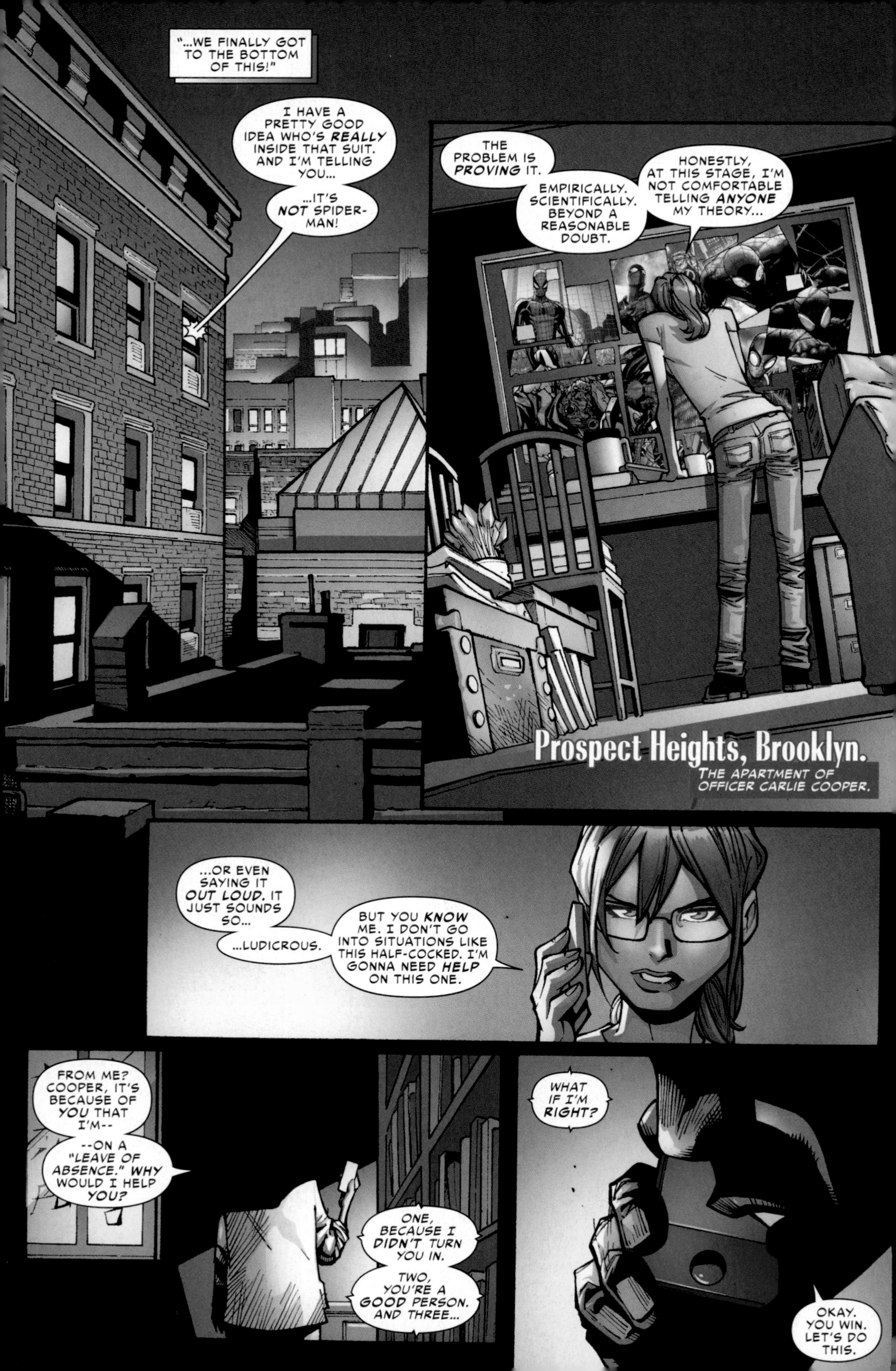
"...WE FINALLY GOT TO THE BOTTOM OF THIS!"
I HAVE A PRETTY GOOD IDEA WHO'S REALLY INSIDE THAT SUIT. AND I'M TELLING YOU...
...IT'S NOT SPIDER-MAN!
THE PROBLEM IS PROVING IT.
EMPIRICALLY. SCIENTIFICALLY. BEYOND A REASONABLE DOUBT.
HONESTLY, AT THIS STAGE, I'M NOT COMFORTABLE TELLING ANYONE MY THEORY...
Prospect Heights, Brooklyn.
THE APARTMENT OF OFFICER CARLIE COOPER.
...OR EVEN SAYING IT OUT LOUD. IT JUST SOUNDS SO...
...LUDICROUS.
BUT YOU KNOW ME. I DON'T GO INTO SITUATIONS LIKE THIS HALF-COCKED. I'M GONNA NEED HELP ON THIS ONE.
FROM ME? COOPER, IT'S BECAUSE OF YOU THAT I'M--
--ON A "LEAVE OF ABSENCE." WHY WOULD I HELP YOU?
ONE, BECAUSE I DIDN'T TURN YOU IN.
TWO, YOU'RE A GOOD PERSON. AND THREE...
WHAT IF I'M RIGHT?
OKAY. YOU WIN. LET'S DO THIS.

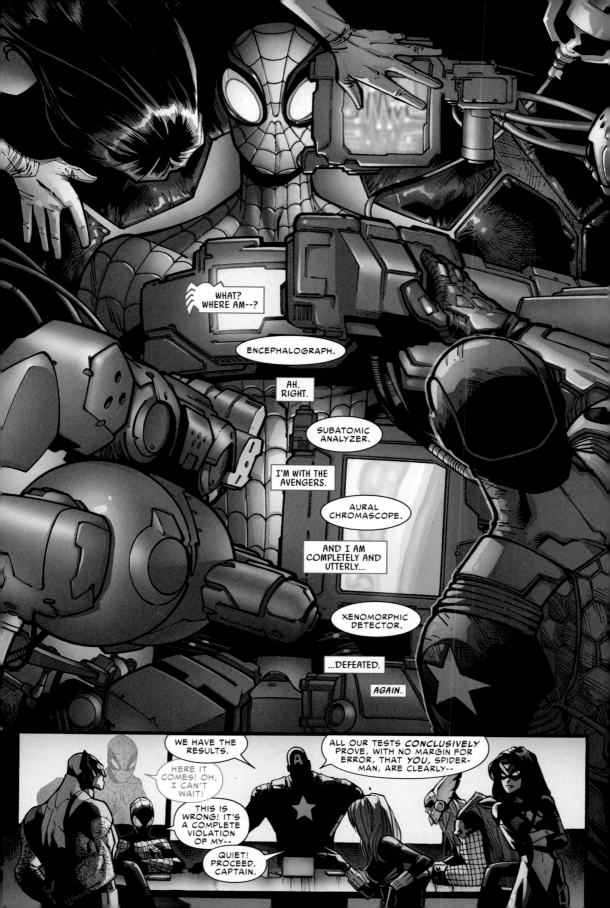

WHAT? WHERE AM--?

ENCEPHALOGRAPH.

AH. RIGHT.

SUBATOMIC ANALYZER.

I'M WITH THE AVENGERS.

AURAL CHROMASCOPE.

AND I AM COMPLETELY AND UTTERLY...

XENOMORPHIC DETECTOR.

...DEFEATED.

AGAIN.

WE HAVE THE RESULTS.

HERE IT COMES! OH, I CAN'T WAIT!

ALL OUR TESTS *CONCLUSIVELY* PROVE, WITH NO MARGIN FOR ERROR, THAT *YOU,* SPIDER-MAN, ARE CLEARLY--

THIS IS WRONG! IT'S A COMPLETE VIOLATION OF MY--

QUIET! PROCEED, CAPTAIN.

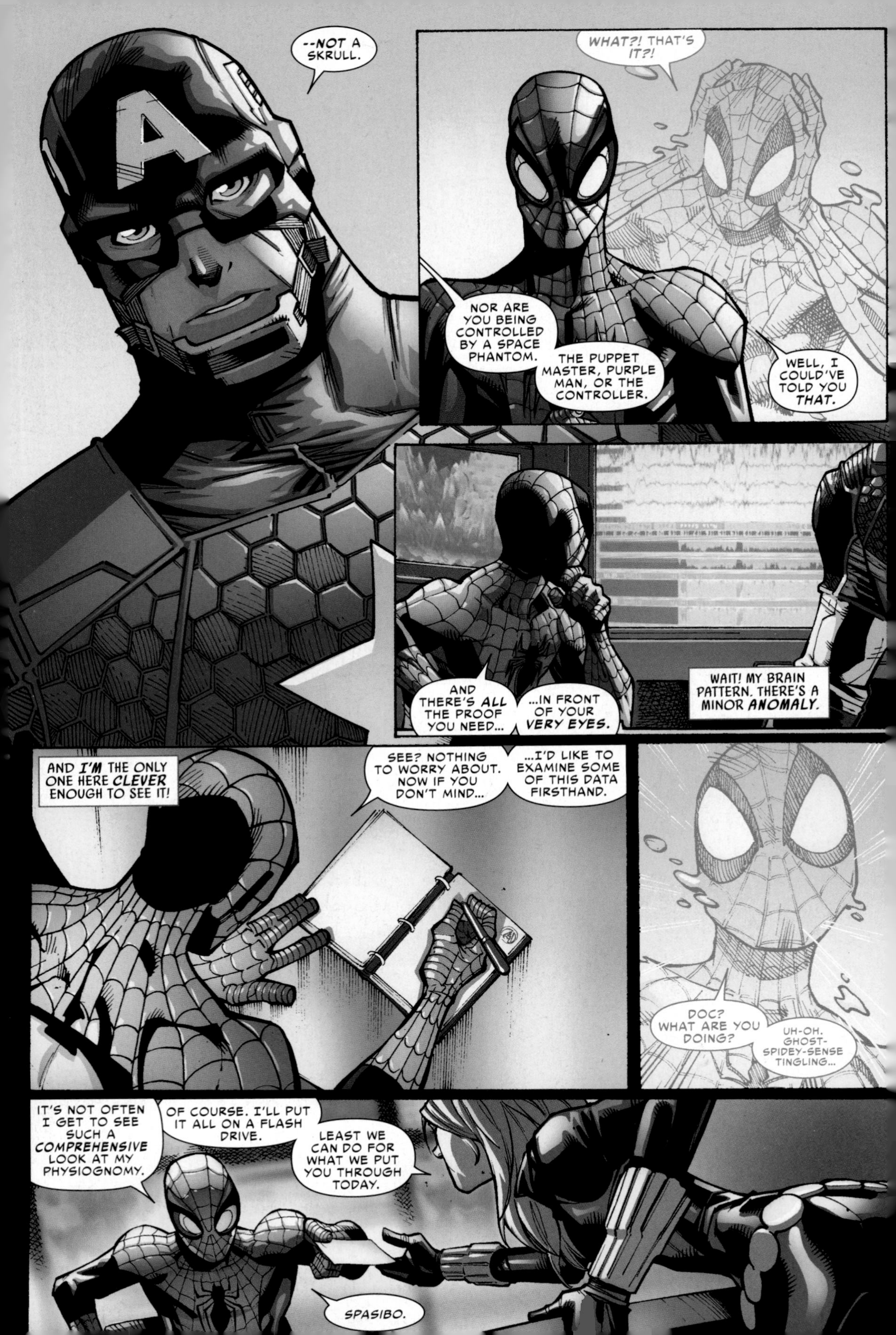
--NOT A SKRULL.
WHAT?! THAT'S IT?!
NOR ARE YOU BEING CONTROLLED BY A SPACE PHANTOM.
THE PUPPET MASTER, PURPLE MAN, OR THE CONTROLLER.
WELL, I COULD'VE TOLD YOU THAT.
AND THERE'S ALL THE PROOF YOU NEED...
...IN FRONT OF YOUR VERY EYES.
WAIT! MY BRAIN PATTERN. THERE'S A MINOR ANOMALY.
AND I'M THE ONLY ONE HERE CLEVER ENOUGH TO SEE IT!
SEE? NOTHING TO WORRY ABOUT. NOW IF YOU DON'T MIND...
...I'D LIKE TO EXAMINE SOME OF THIS DATA FIRSTHAND.
DOC? WHAT ARE YOU DOING?
UH-OH. GHOST-SPIDEY-SENSE TINGLING...
IT'S NOT OFTEN I GET TO SEE SUCH A COMPREHENSIVE LOOK AT MY PHYSIOGNOMY.
OF COURSE. I'LL PUT IT ALL ON A FLASH DRIVE.
LEAST WE CAN DO FOR WHAT WE PUT YOU THROUGH TODAY.
SPASIBO.

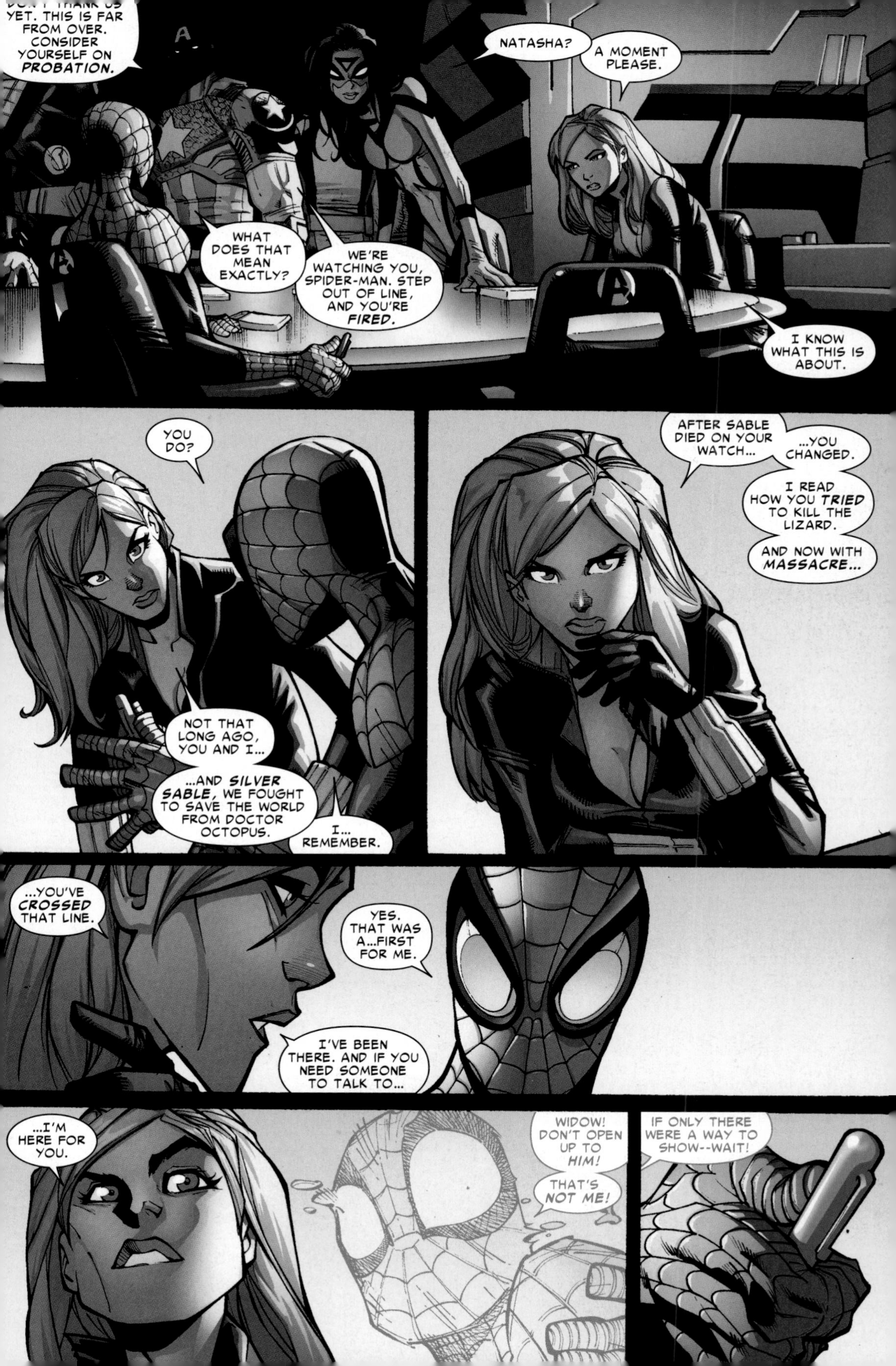

YET. THIS IS FAR FROM OVER. CONSIDER YOURSELF ON PROBATION.
NATASHA?
A MOMENT PLEASE.
WHAT DOES THAT MEAN EXACTLY?
WE'RE WATCHING YOU, SPIDER-MAN. STEP OUT OF LINE, AND YOU'RE FIRED.
I KNOW WHAT THIS IS ABOUT.
YOU DO?
NOT THAT LONG AGO, YOU AND I...
...AND SILVER SABLE, WE FOUGHT TO SAVE THE WORLD FROM DOCTOR OCTOPUS.
I... REMEMBER.
AFTER SABLE DIED ON YOUR WATCH...
...YOU CHANGED.
I READ HOW YOU TRIED TO KILL THE LIZARD.
AND NOW WITH MASSACRE...
...YOU'VE CROSSED THAT LINE.
YES. THAT WAS A...FIRST FOR ME.
I'VE BEEN THERE. AND IF YOU NEED SOMEONE TO TALK TO...
...I'M HERE FOR YOU.
WIDOW! DON'T OPEN UP TO HIM!
THAT'S NOT ME!
IF ONLY THERE WERE A WAY TO SHOW--WAIT!

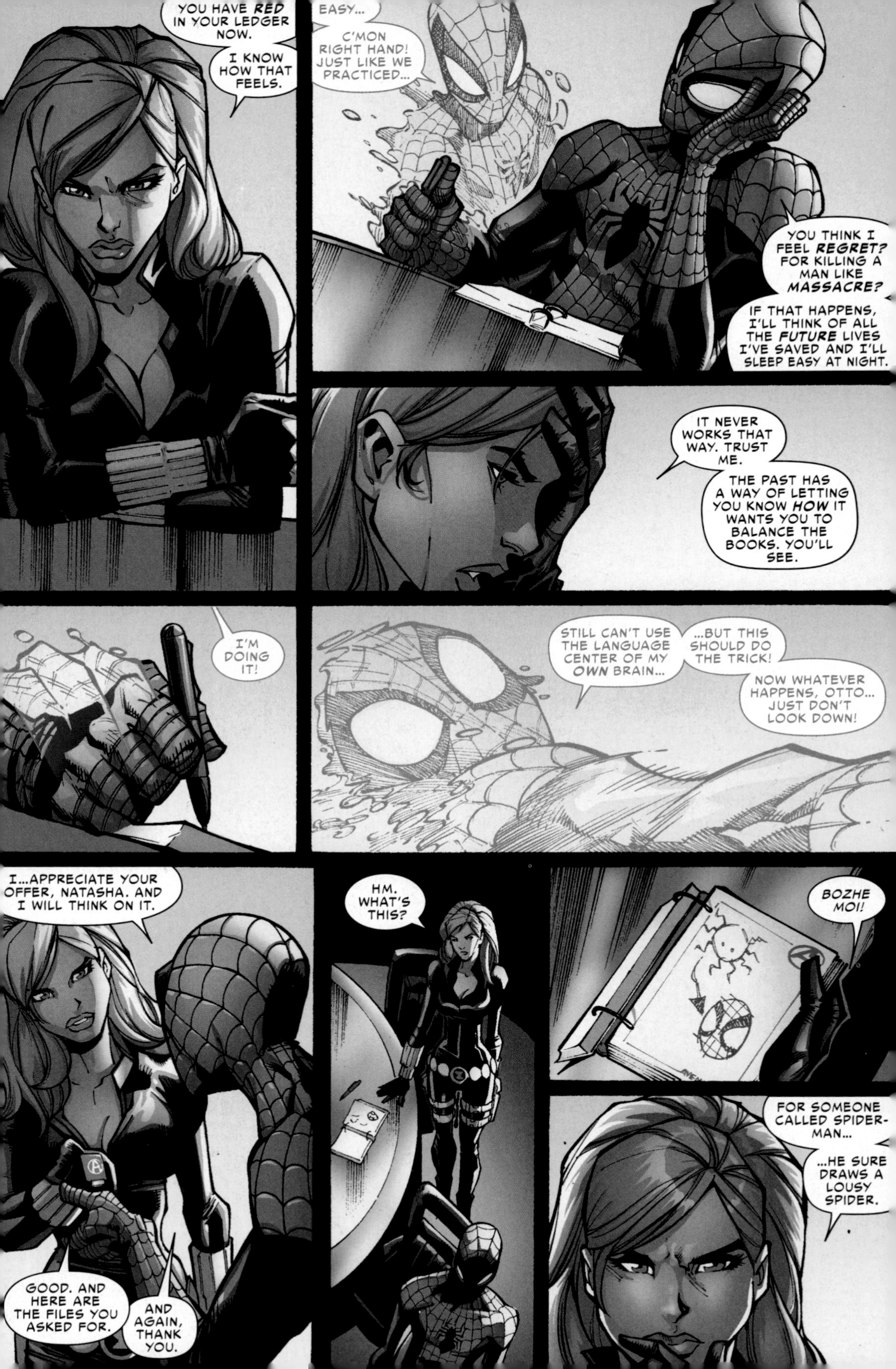
YOU HAVE RED IN YOUR LEDGER NOW.
I KNOW HOW THAT FEELS.
EASY...
C'MON RIGHT HAND! JUST LIKE WE PRACTICED...
YOU THINK I FEEL REGRET? FOR KILLING A MAN LIKE MASSACRE?
IF THAT HAPPENS, I'LL THINK OF ALL THE FUTURE LIVES I'VE SAVED AND I'LL SLEEP EASY AT NIGHT.
IT NEVER WORKS THAT WAY. TRUST ME.
THE PAST HAS A WAY OF LETTING YOU KNOW HOW IT WANTS YOU TO BALANCE THE BOOKS. YOU'LL SEE.
I'M DOING IT!
STILL CAN'T USE THE LANGUAGE CENTER OF MY OWN BRAIN...
...BUT THIS SHOULD DO THE TRICK!
NOW WHATEVER HAPPENS, OTTO... JUST DON'T LOOK DOWN!
I...APPRECIATE YOUR OFFER, NATASHA. AND I WILL THINK ON IT.
GOOD. AND HERE ARE THE FILES YOU ASKED FOR.
AND AGAIN, THANK YOU.
HM. WHAT'S THIS?
BOZHE MOI!
FOR SOMEONE CALLED SPIDER-MAN...
...HE SURE DRAWS A LOUSY SPIDER.

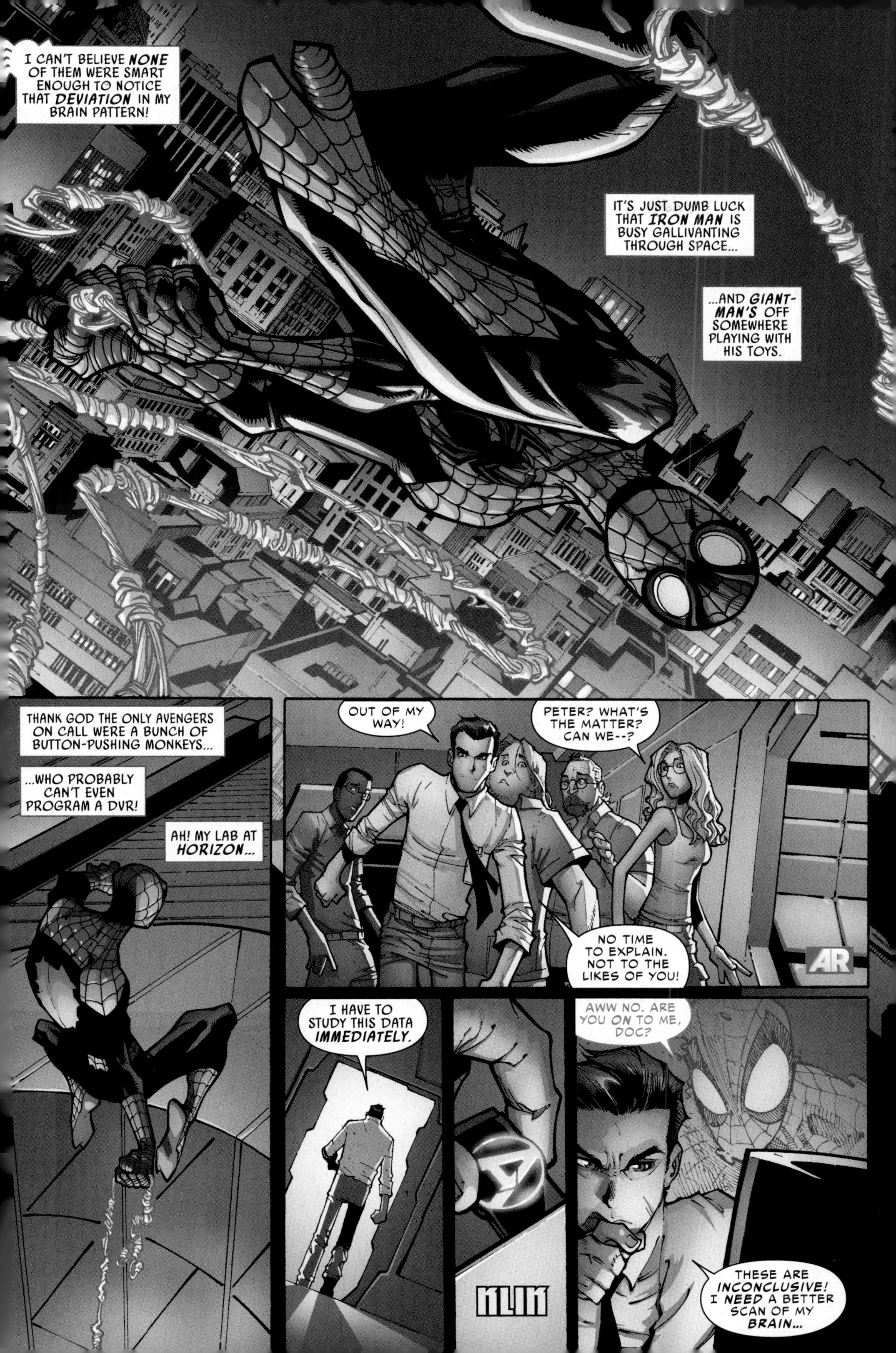

I CAN'T BELIEVE NONE OF THEM WERE SMART ENOUGH TO NOTICE THAT DEVIATION IN MY BRAIN PATTERN!
IT'S JUST DUMB LUCK THAT IRON MAN IS BUSY GALLIVANTING THROUGH SPACE...
...AND GIANT-MAN'S OFF SOMEWHERE PLAYING WITH HIS TOYS.
THANK GOD THE ONLY AVENGERS ON CALL WERE A BUNCH OF BUTTON-PUSHING MONKEYS...
...WHO PROBABLY CAN'T EVEN PROGRAM A DVR!
AH! MY LAB AT HORIZON...
OUT OF MY WAY!
PETER? WHAT'S THE MATTER? CAN WE--?
NO TIME TO EXPLAIN. NOT TO THE LIKES OF YOU!
AR
I HAVE TO STUDY THIS DATA IMMEDIATELY.
KLIK
AWW NO. ARE YOU ON TO ME, DOC?
THESE ARE INCONCLUSIVE! I NEED A BETTER SCAN OF MY BRAIN...

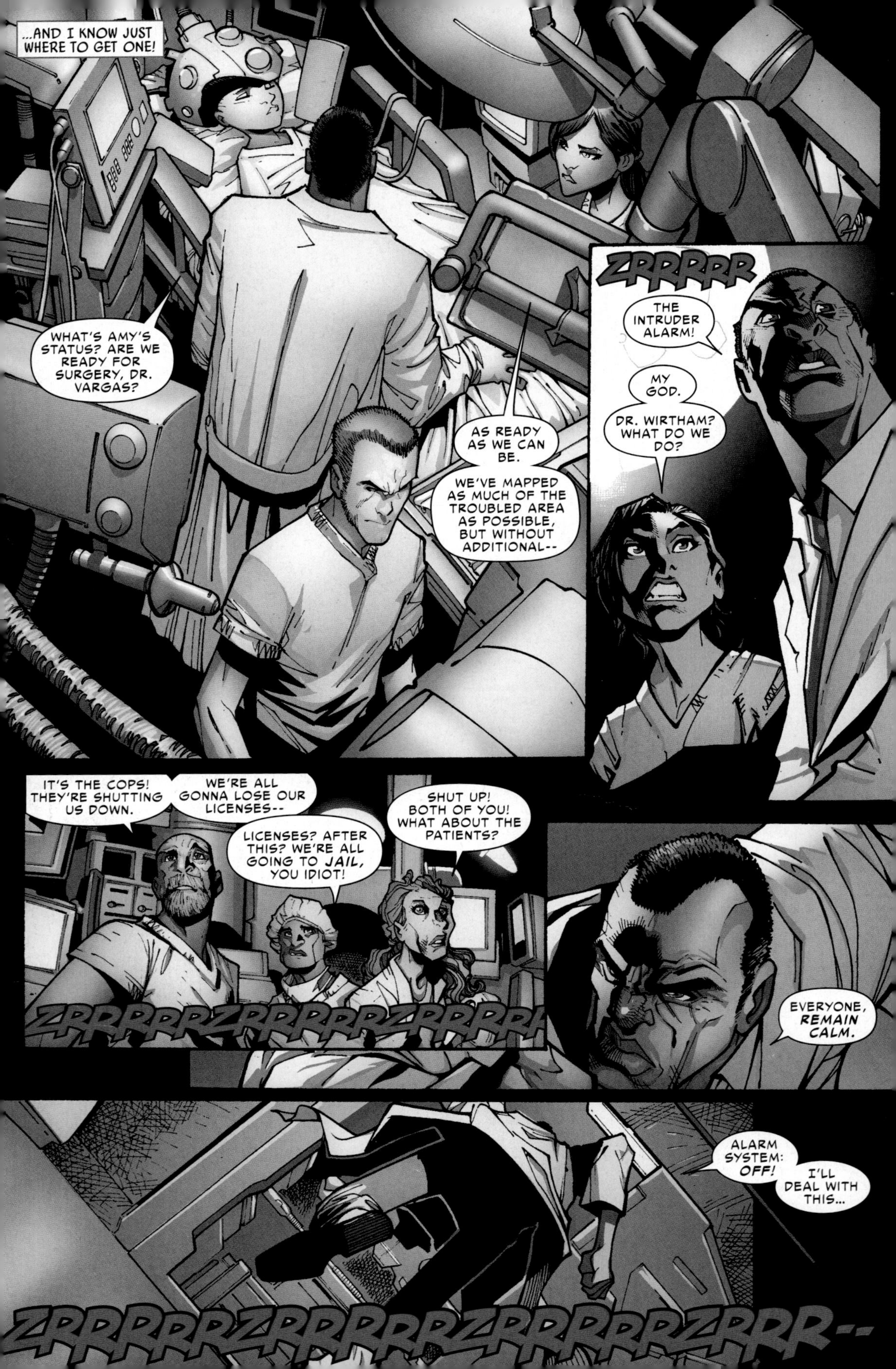
...AND I KNOW JUST WHERE TO GET ONE!
WHAT'S AMY'S STATUS? ARE WE READY FOR SURGERY, DR. VARGAS?
AS READY AS WE CAN BE.
WE'VE MAPPED AS MUCH OF THE TROUBLED AREA AS POSSIBLE, BUT WITHOUT ADDITIONAL--
ZRRRRR
THE INTRUDER ALARM!
MY GOD.
DR. WIRTHAM? WHAT DO WE DO?
IT'S THE COPS! THEY'RE SHUTTING US DOWN.
WE'RE ALL GONNA LOSE OUR LICENSES--
LICENSES? AFTER THIS? WE'RE ALL GOING TO JAIL, YOU IDIOT!
SHUT UP! BOTH OF YOU! WHAT ABOUT THE PATIENTS?
ZRRRRRZRRRRRZRRRRR
EVERYONE, REMAIN CALM.
ALARM SYSTEM: OFF!
I'LL DEAL WITH THIS...
ZRRRRRZRRRRRRZRRRRRRZRRRR--

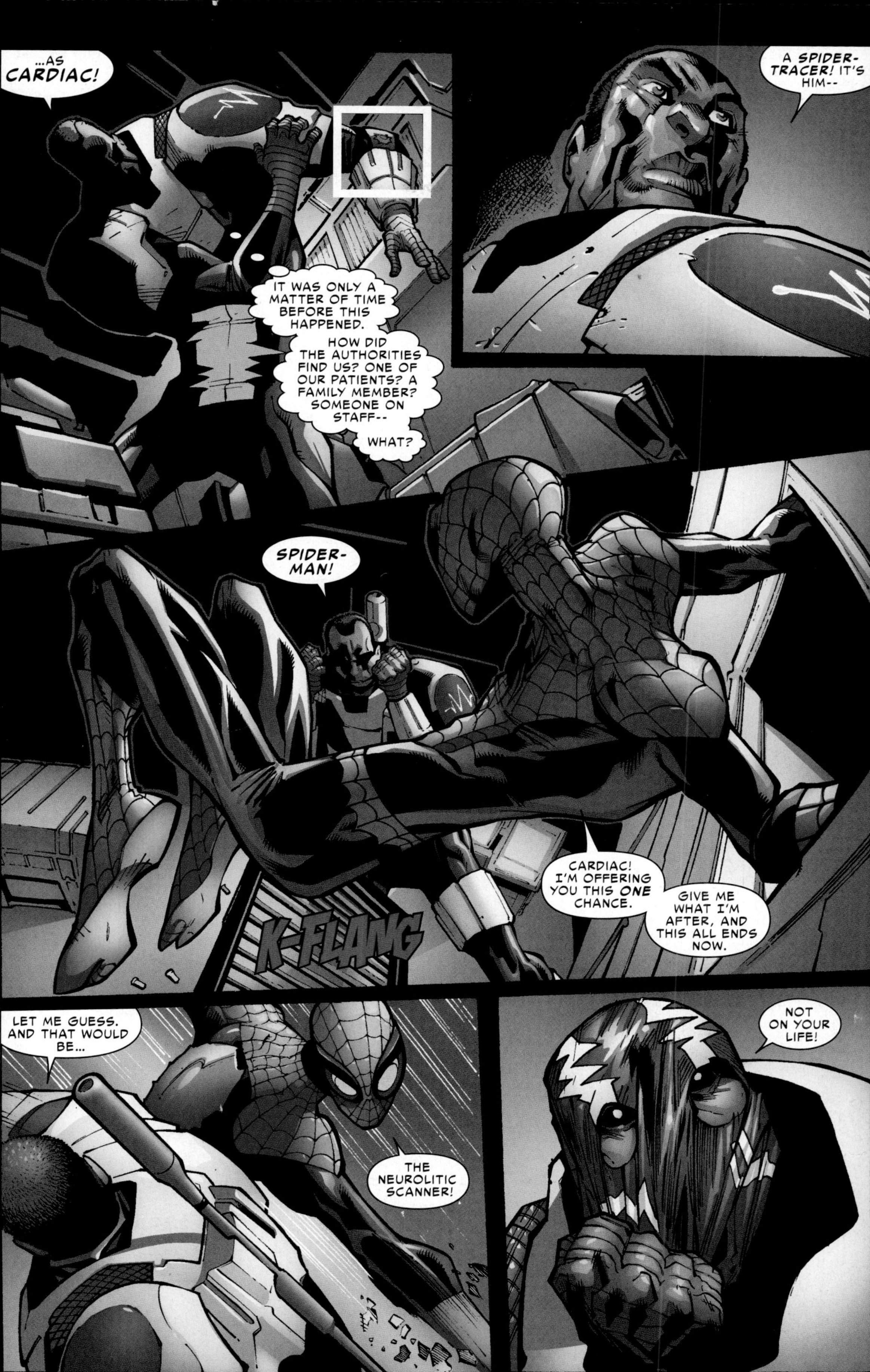

...AS CARDIAC!
A SPIDER-TRACER! IT'S HIM--
IT WAS ONLY A MATTER OF TIME BEFORE THIS HAPPENED.
HOW DID THE AUTHORITIES FIND US? ONE OF OUR PATIENTS? A FAMILY MEMBER? SOMEONE ON STAFF--
WHAT?
SPIDER-MAN!
CARDIAC! I'M OFFERING YOU THIS ONE CHANCE.
GIVE ME WHAT I'M AFTER, AND THIS ALL ENDS NOW.
K-FLANG
LET ME GUESS. AND THAT WOULD BE...
THE NEUROLITIC SCANNER!
NOT ON YOUR LIFE!

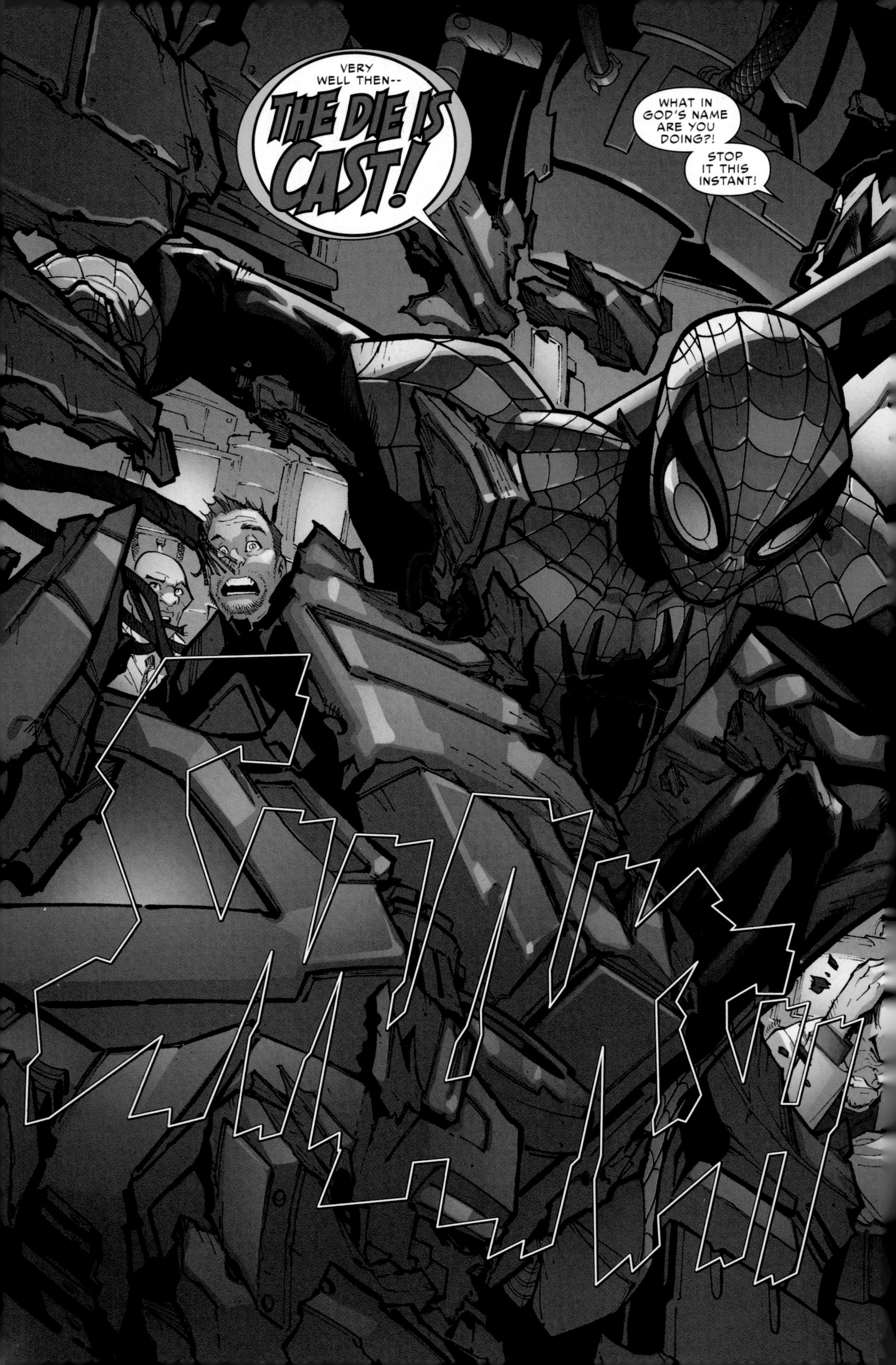
VERY WELL THEN--
THE DIE IS CAST!
WHAT IN GOD'S NAME ARE YOU DOING?!
STOP IT THIS INSTANT!

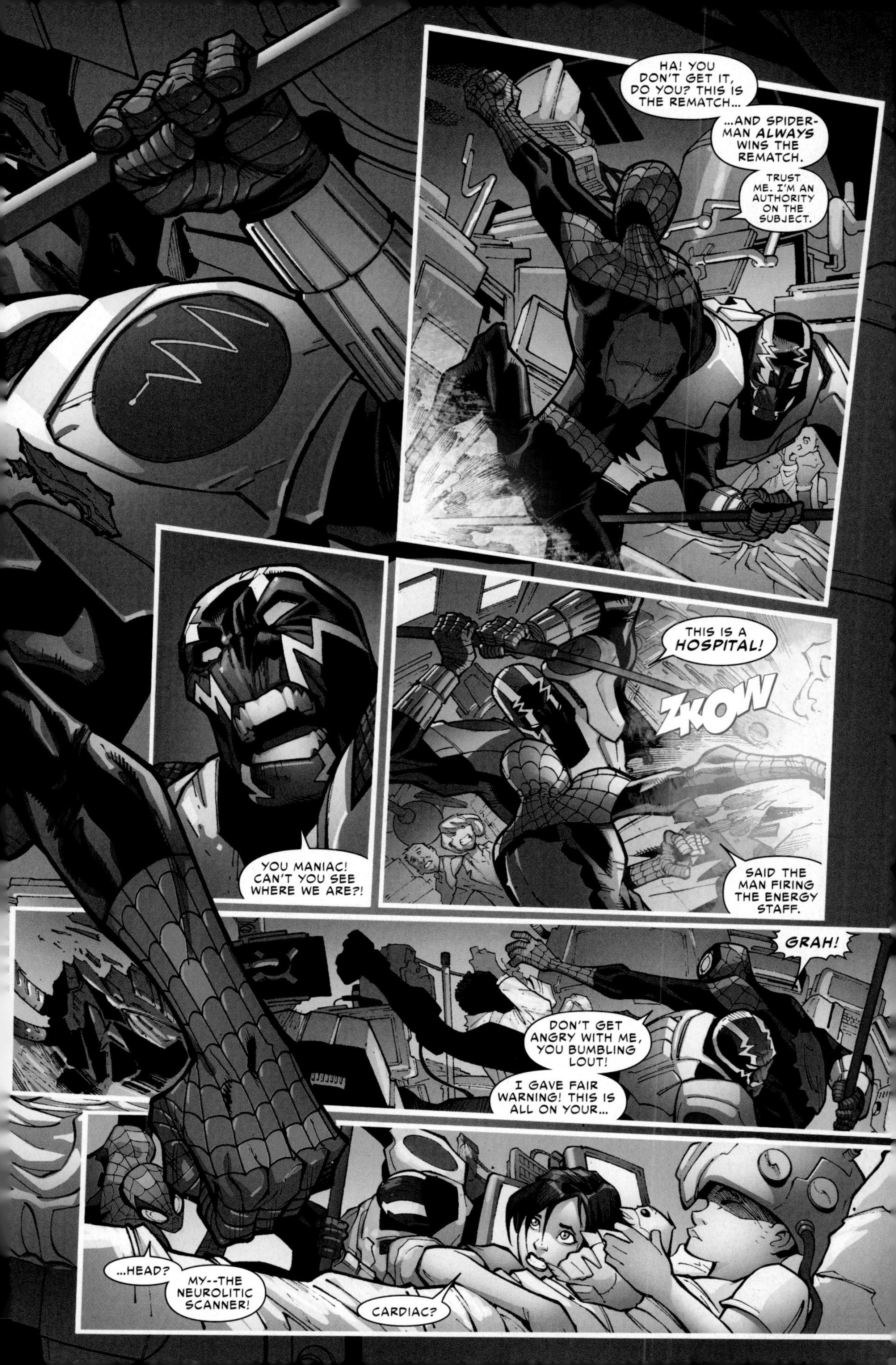
HA! YOU DON'T GET IT, DO YOU? THIS IS THE REMATCH...
...AND SPIDER-MAN ALWAYS WINS THE REMATCH.
TRUST ME. I'M AN AUTHORITY ON THE SUBJECT.
YOU MANIAC! CAN'T YOU SEE WHERE WE ARE?!
THIS IS A HOSPITAL!
ZKOW
SAID THE MAN FIRING THE ENERGY STAFF.
GRAH!
DON'T GET ANGRY WITH ME, YOU BUMBLING LOUT!
I GAVE FAIR WARNING! THIS IS ALL ON YOUR...
...HEAD?
MY--THE NEUROLITIC SCANNER!
CARDIAC?

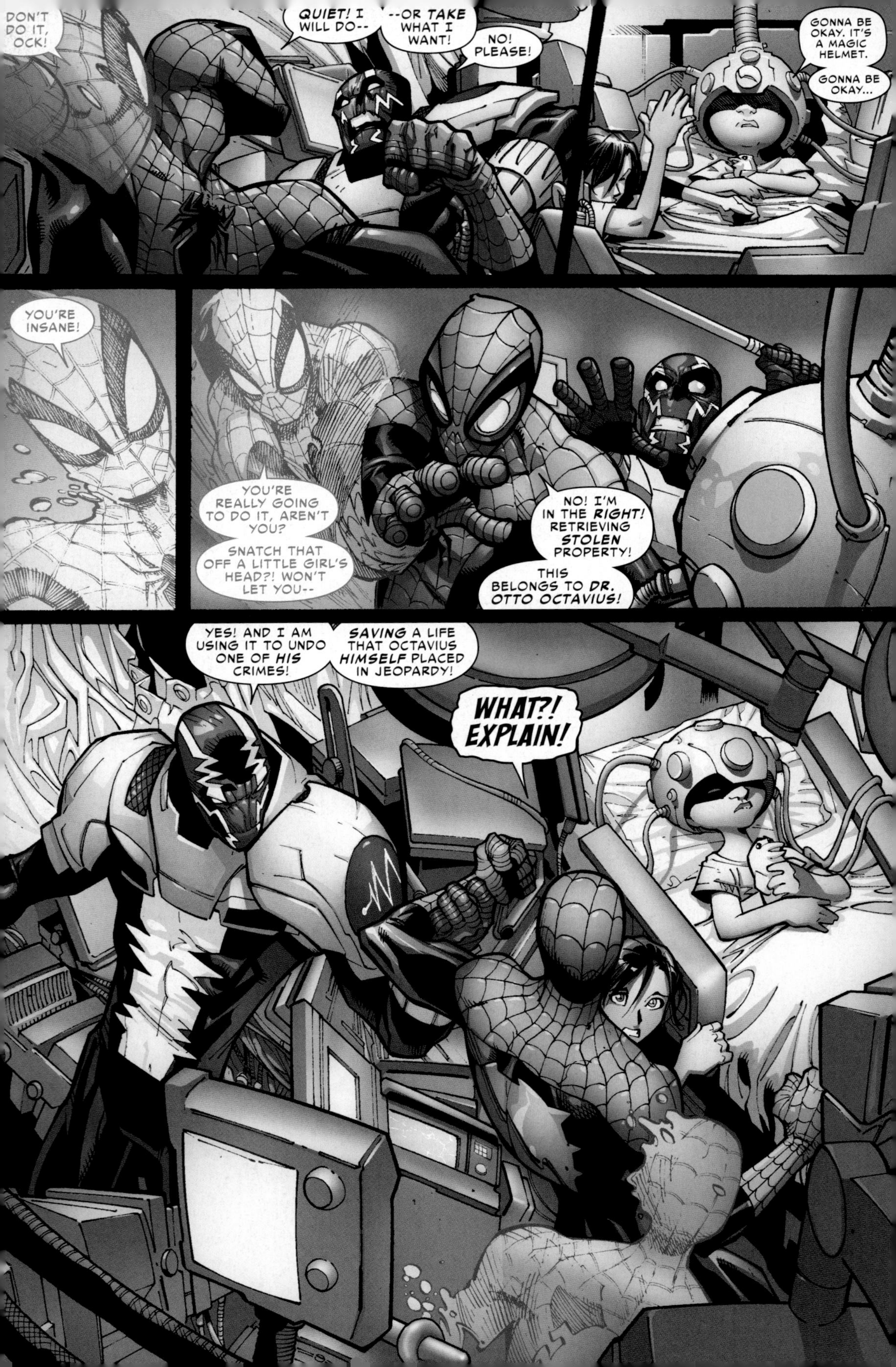
DON'T DO IT, OCK!
QUIET! I WILL DO--
--OR TAKE WHAT I WANT!
NO! PLEASE!
GONNA BE OKAY. IT'S A MAGIC HELMET.
GONNA BE OKAY...
YOU'RE INSANE!
YOU'RE REALLY GOING TO DO IT, AREN'T YOU?
SNATCH THAT OFF A LITTLE GIRL'S HEAD?! WON'T LET YOU--
NO! I'M IN THE RIGHT! RETRIEVING STOLEN PROPERTY!
THIS BELONGS TO DR. OTTO OCTAVIUS!
YES! AND I AM USING IT TO UNDO ONE OF HIS CRIMES!
SAVING A LIFE THAT OCTAVIUS HIMSELF PLACED IN JEOPARDY!
WHAT?! EXPLAIN!

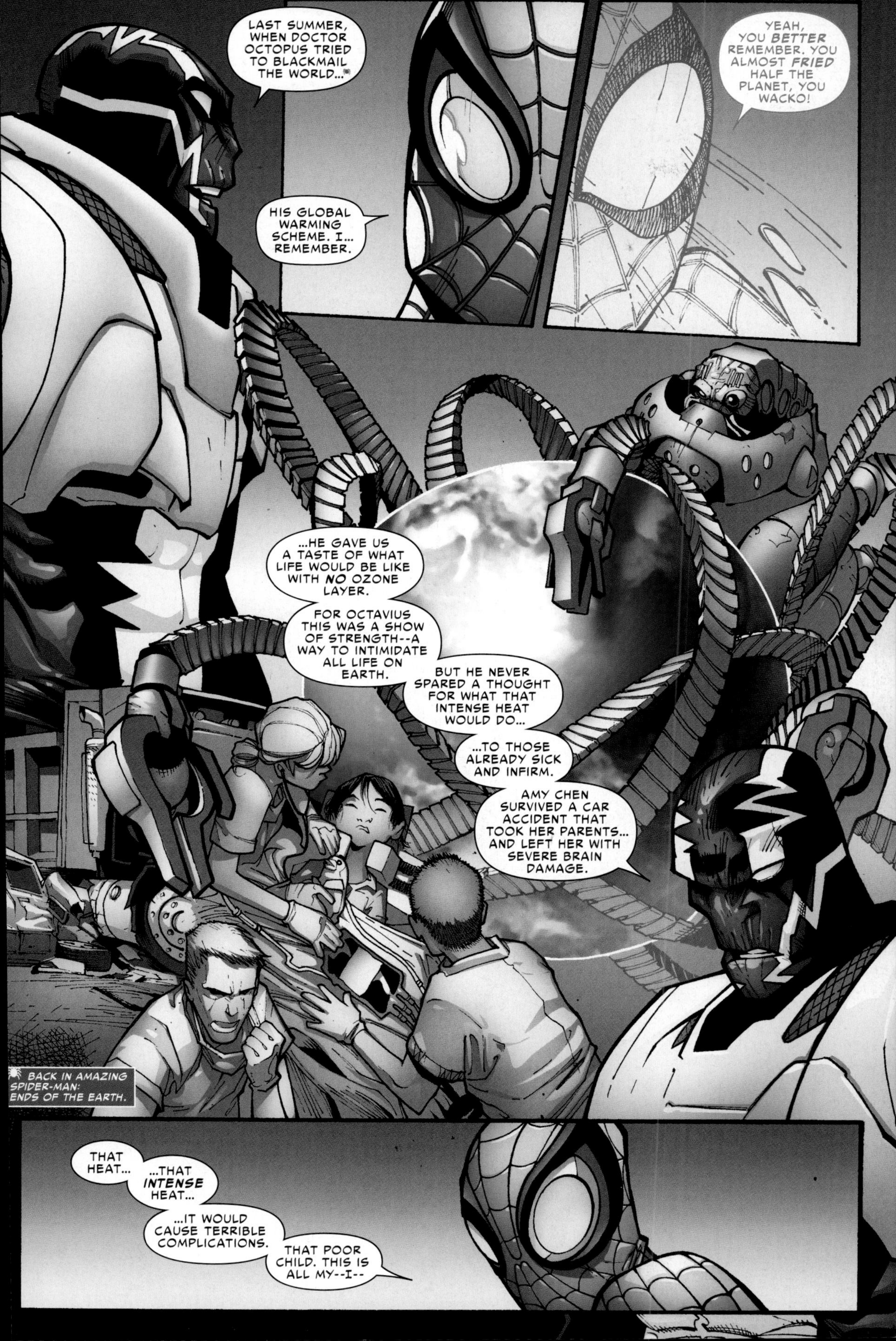
LAST SUMMER, WHEN DOCTOR OCTOPUS TRIED TO BLACKMAIL THE WORLD...*
YEAH, YOU BETTER REMEMBER. YOU ALMOST FRIED HALF THE PLANET, YOU WACKO!
HIS GLOBAL WARMING SCHEME. I... REMEMBER.
...HE GAVE US A TASTE OF WHAT LIFE WOULD BE LIKE WITH NO OZONE LAYER.
FOR OCTAVIUS THIS WAS A SHOW OF STRENGTH--A WAY TO INTIMIDATE ALL LIFE ON EARTH.
BUT HE NEVER SPARED A THOUGHT FOR WHAT THAT INTENSE HEAT WOULD DO...
...TO THOSE ALREADY SICK AND INFIRM.
AMY CHEN SURVIVED A CAR ACCIDENT THAT TOOK HER PARENTS... AND LEFT HER WITH SEVERE BRAIN DAMAGE.
* BACK IN AMAZING SPIDER-MAN: ENDS OF THE EARTH.
THAT HEAT...
...THAT INTENSE HEAT...
...IT WOULD CAUSE TERRIBLE COMPLICATIONS.
THAT POOR CHILD. THIS IS ALL MY--I--

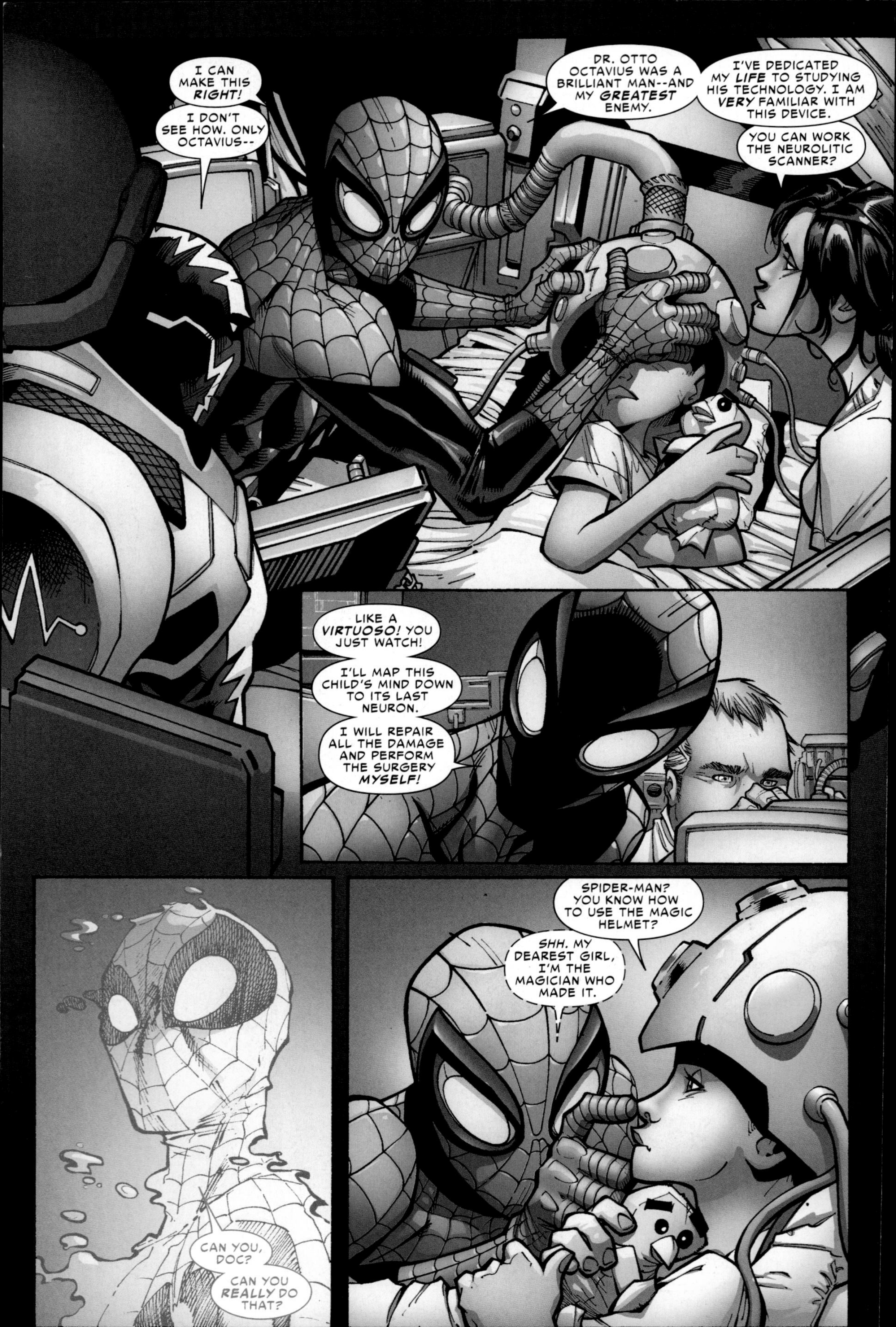
I CAN MAKE THIS RIGHT!
I DON'T SEE HOW. ONLY OCTAVIUS--
DR. OTTO OCTAVIUS WAS A BRILLIANT MAN--AND MY GREATEST ENEMY.
I'VE DEDICATED MY LIFE TO STUDYING HIS TECHNOLOGY. I AM VERY FAMILIAR WITH THIS DEVICE.
YOU CAN WORK THE NEUROLITIC SCANNER?
LIKE A VIRTUOSO! YOU JUST WATCH!
I'LL MAP THIS CHILD'S MIND DOWN TO ITS LAST NEURON.
I WILL REPAIR ALL THE DAMAGE AND PERFORM THE SURGERY MYSELF!
CAN YOU, DOC?
CAN YOU REALLY DO THAT?
SPIDER-MAN? YOU KNOW HOW TO USE THE MAGIC HELMET?
SHH. MY DEAREST GIRL, I'M THE MAGICIAN WHO MADE IT.

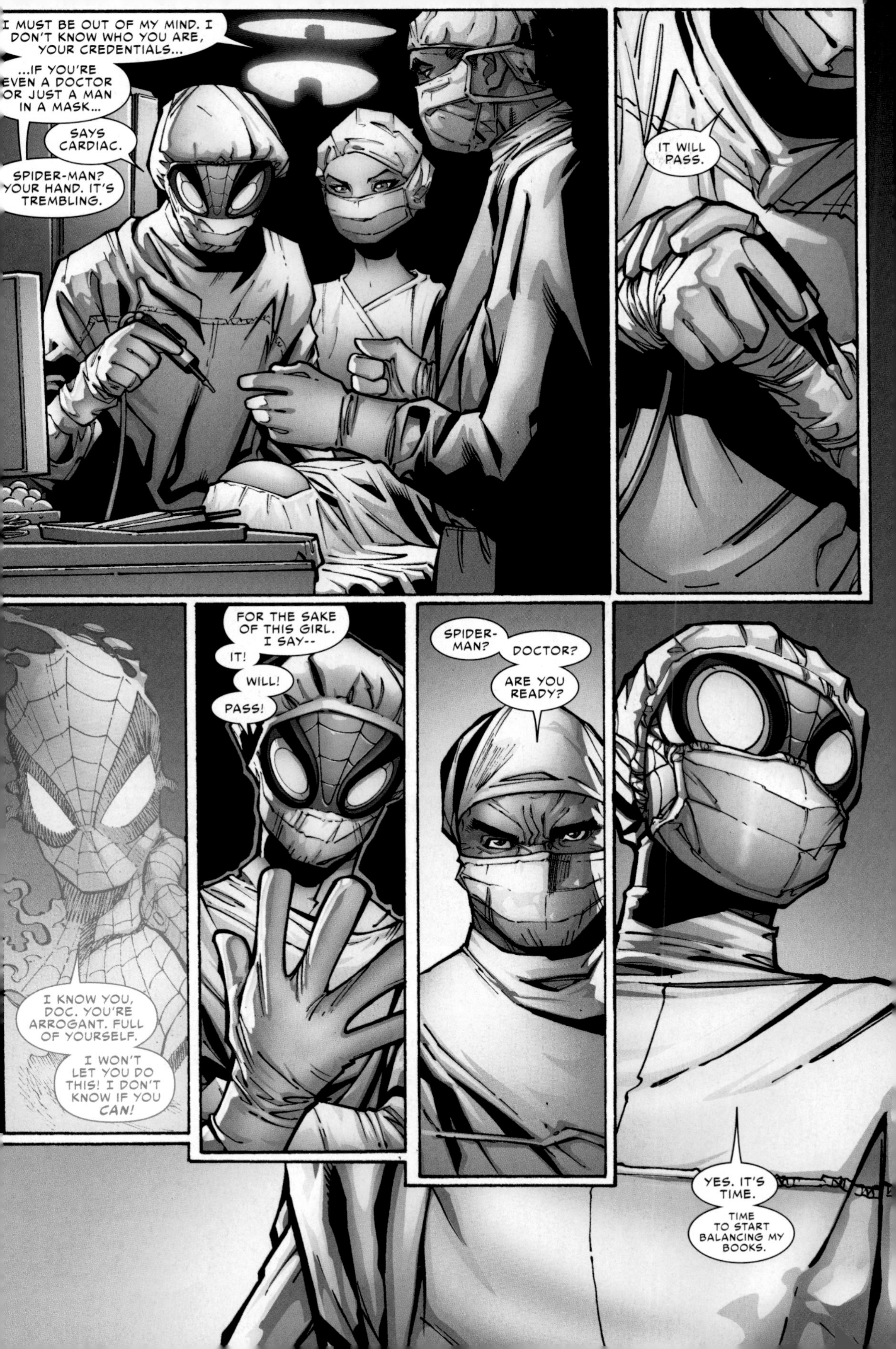

I MUST BE OUT OF MY MIND. I DON'T KNOW WHO YOU ARE, YOUR CREDENTIALS...
...IF YOU'RE EVEN A DOCTOR OR JUST A MAN IN A MASK...
SAYS CARDIAC.
SPIDER-MAN? YOUR HAND. IT'S TREMBLING.
IT WILL PASS.
I KNOW YOU, DOC. YOU'RE ARROGANT. FULL OF YOURSELF.
I WON'T LET YOU DO THIS! I DON'T KNOW IF YOU *CAN!*
FOR THE SAKE OF THIS GIRL. I SAY--
IT!
WILL!
PASS!
SPIDER-MAN?
DOCTOR?
ARE YOU READY?
YES. IT'S TIME.
TIME TO START BALANCING MY BOOKS.

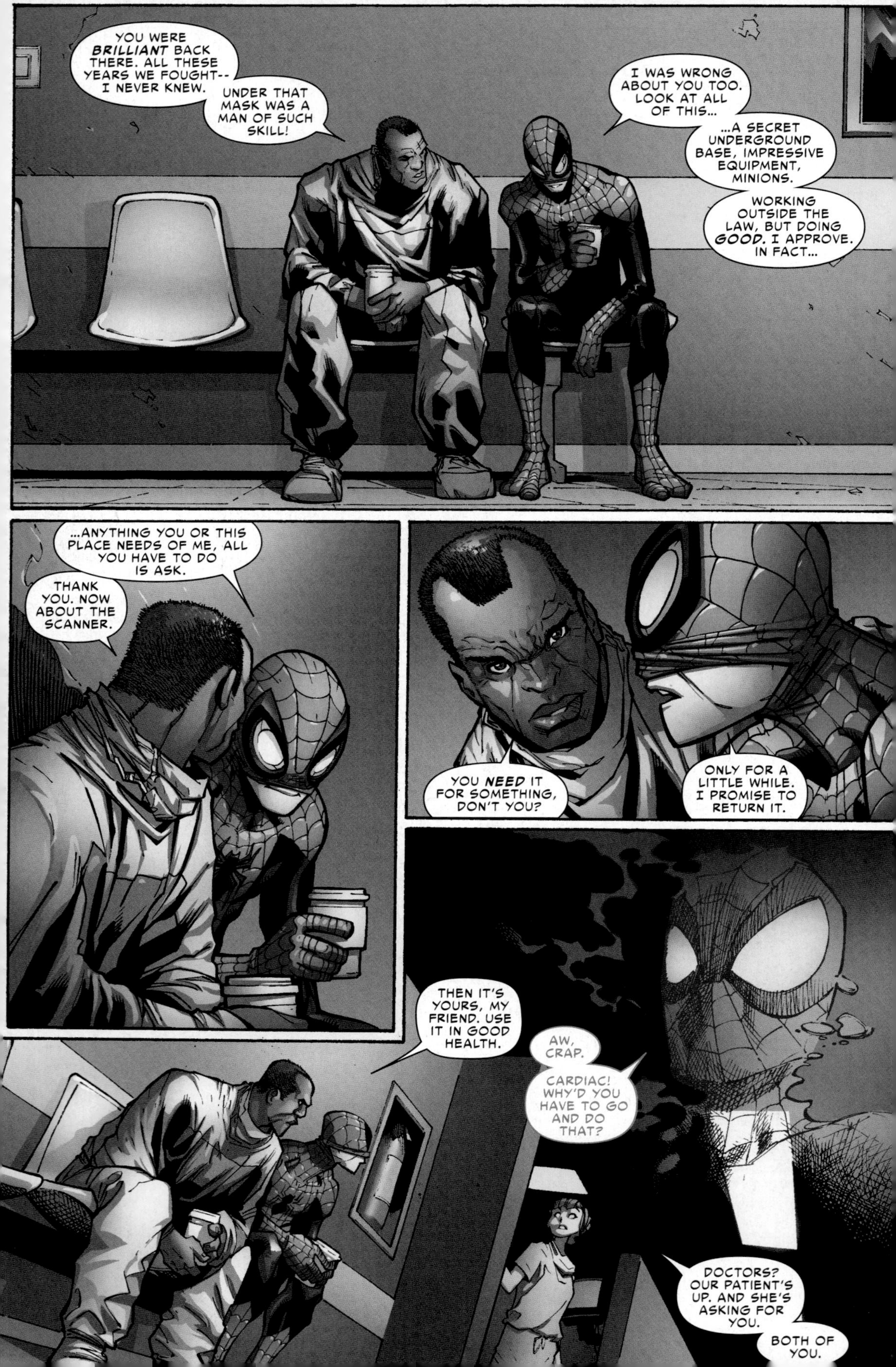

YOU WERE BRILLIANT BACK THERE. ALL THESE YEARS WE FOUGHT-- I NEVER KNEW.
UNDER THAT MASK WAS A MAN OF SUCH SKILL!
I WAS WRONG ABOUT YOU TOO. LOOK AT ALL OF THIS...
...A SECRET UNDERGROUND BASE, IMPRESSIVE EQUIPMENT, MINIONS.
WORKING OUTSIDE THE LAW, BUT DOING GOOD. I APPROVE. IN FACT...
...ANYTHING YOU OR THIS PLACE NEEDS OF ME, ALL YOU HAVE TO DO IS ASK.
THANK YOU. NOW ABOUT THE SCANNER.
YOU NEED IT FOR SOMETHING, DON'T YOU?
ONLY FOR A LITTLE WHILE. I PROMISE TO RETURN IT.
THEN IT'S YOURS, MY FRIEND. USE IT IN GOOD HEALTH.
AW, CRAP.
CARDIAC! WHY'D YOU HAVE TO GO AND DO THAT?
DOCTORS? OUR PATIENT'S UP. AND SHE'S ASKING FOR YOU.
BOTH OF YOU.

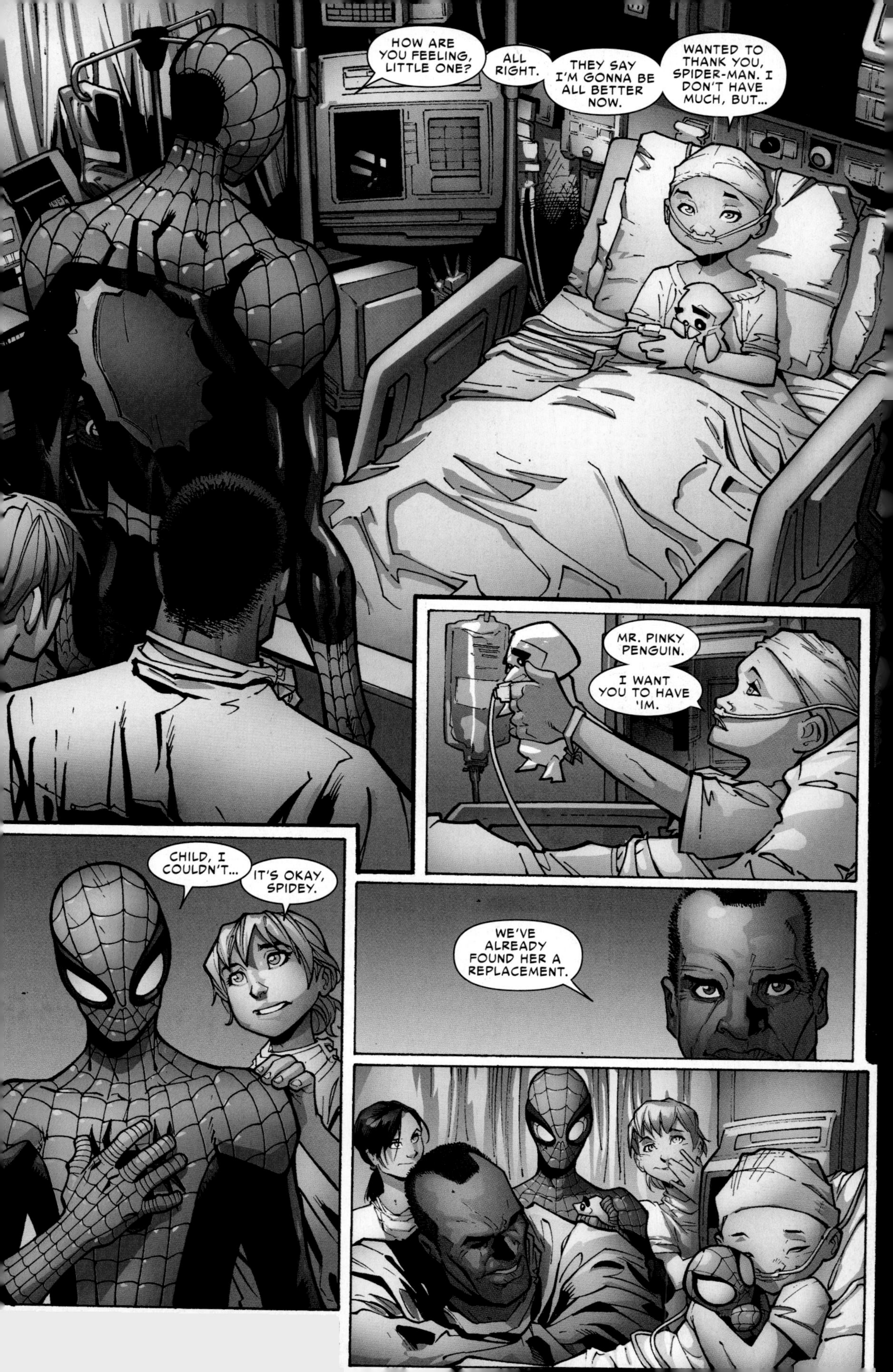
HOW ARE YOU FEELING, LITTLE ONE?
ALL RIGHT.
THEY SAY I'M GONNA BE ALL BETTER NOW.
WANTED TO THANK YOU, SPIDER-MAN. I DON'T HAVE MUCH, BUT...
MR. PINKY PENGUIN.
I WANT YOU TO HAVE 'IM.
CHILD, I COULDN'T...
IT'S OKAY, SPIDEY.
WE'VE ALREADY FOUND HER A REPLACEMENT.

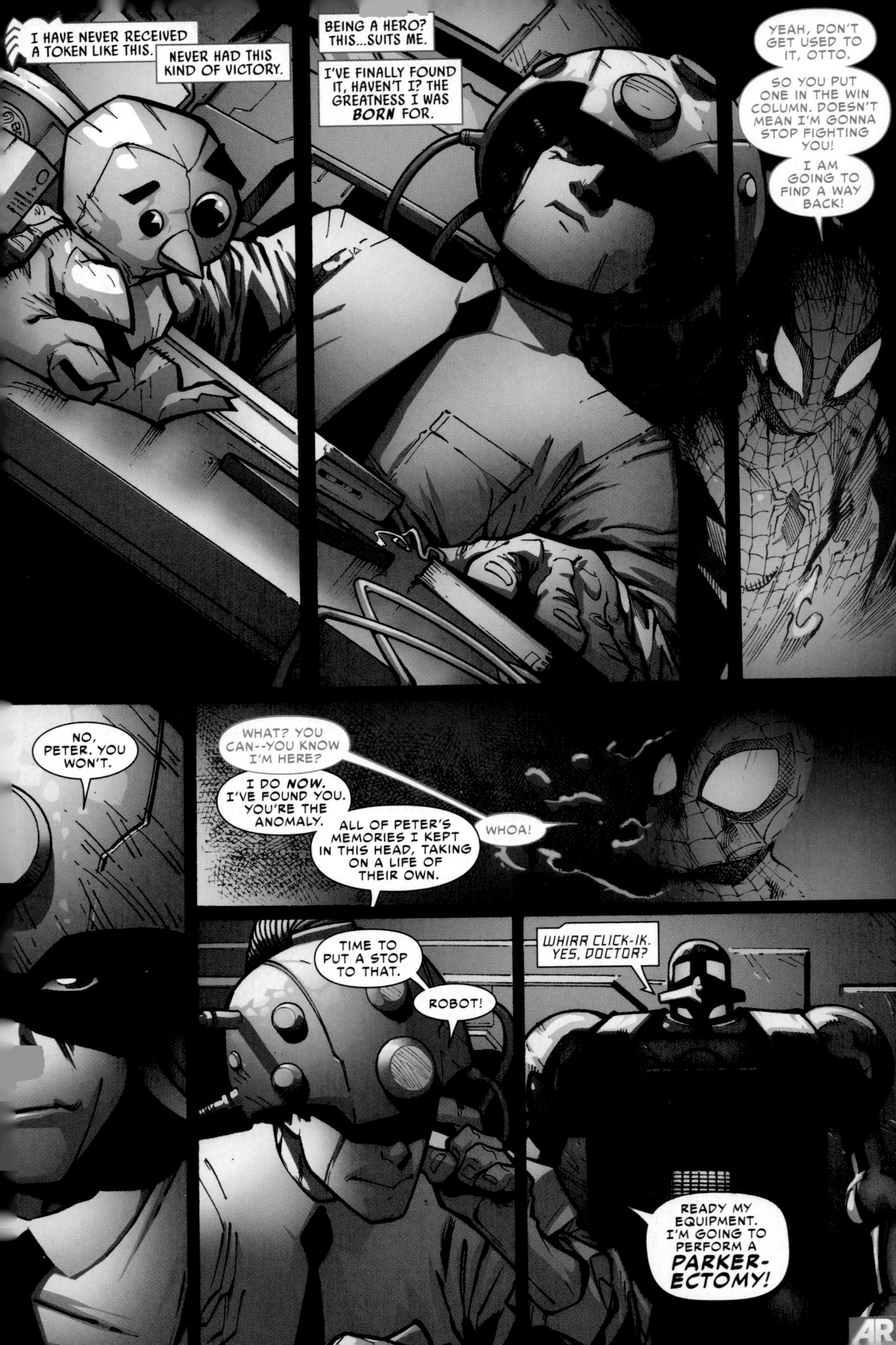
I HAVE NEVER RECEIVED A TOKEN LIKE THIS.
NEVER HAD THIS KIND OF VICTORY.
BEING A HERO? THIS...SUITS ME.
I'VE FINALLY FOUND IT, HAVEN'T I? THE GREATNESS I WAS BORN FOR.
YEAH, DON'T GET USED TO IT, OTTO.
SO YOU PUT ONE IN THE WIN COLUMN. DOESN'T MEAN I'M GONNA STOP FIGHTING YOU!
I AM GOING TO FIND A WAY BACK!
NO, PETER. YOU WON'T.
WHAT? YOU CAN--YOU KNOW I'M HERE?
I DO NOW. I'VE FOUND YOU. YOU'RE THE ANOMALY.
ALL OF PETER'S MEMORIES I KEPT IN THIS HEAD, TAKING ON A LIFE OF THEIR OWN.
WHOA!
TIME TO PUT A STOP TO THAT.
ROBOT!
WHIRR CLICK-IK. YES, DOCTOR?
READY MY EQUIPMENT. I'M GOING TO PERFORM A PARKER-ECTOMY!

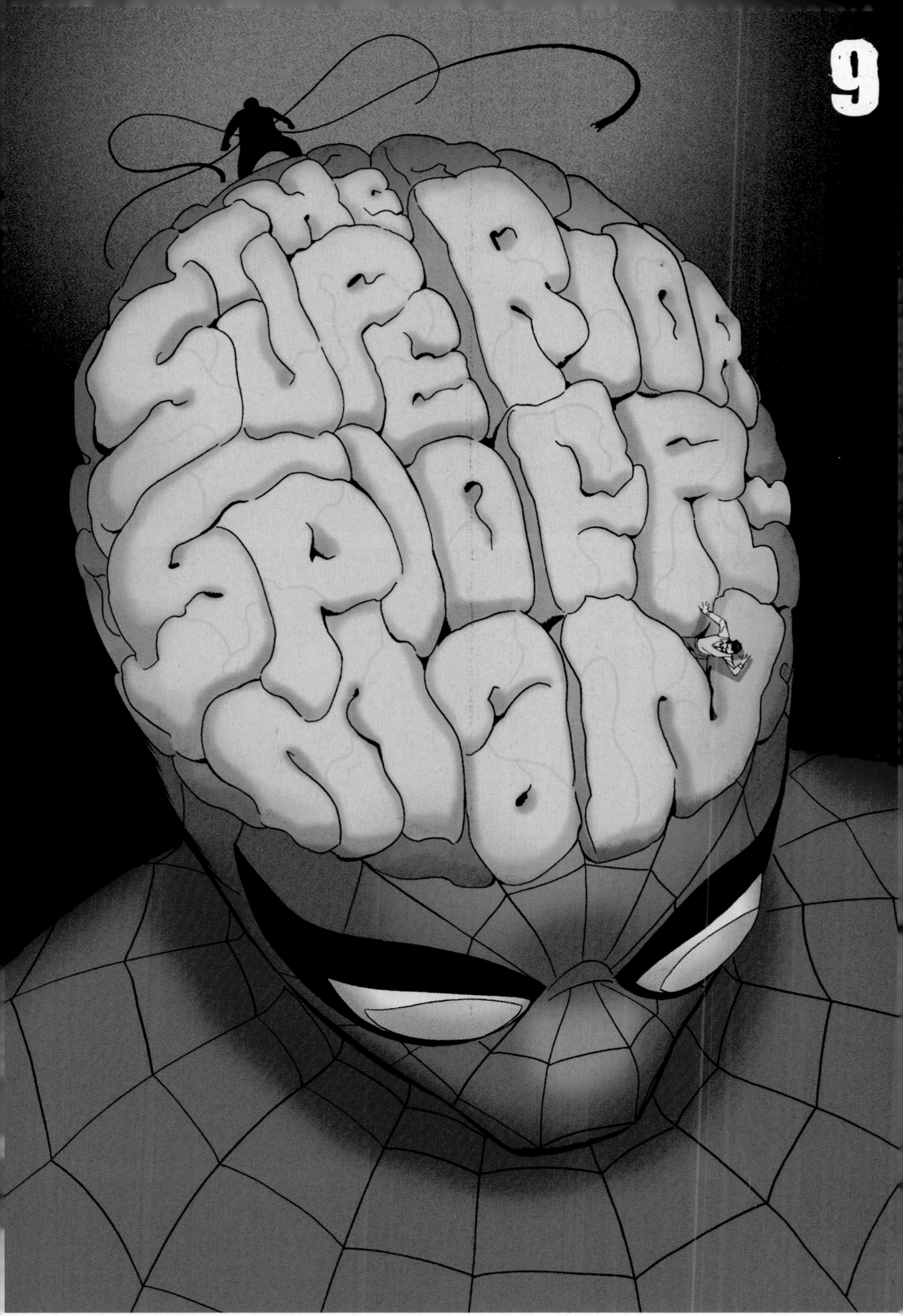
9
THE SUPERIOR SPIDER-MAN

TROUBLED MIND PART THREE: GRAY MATTERS

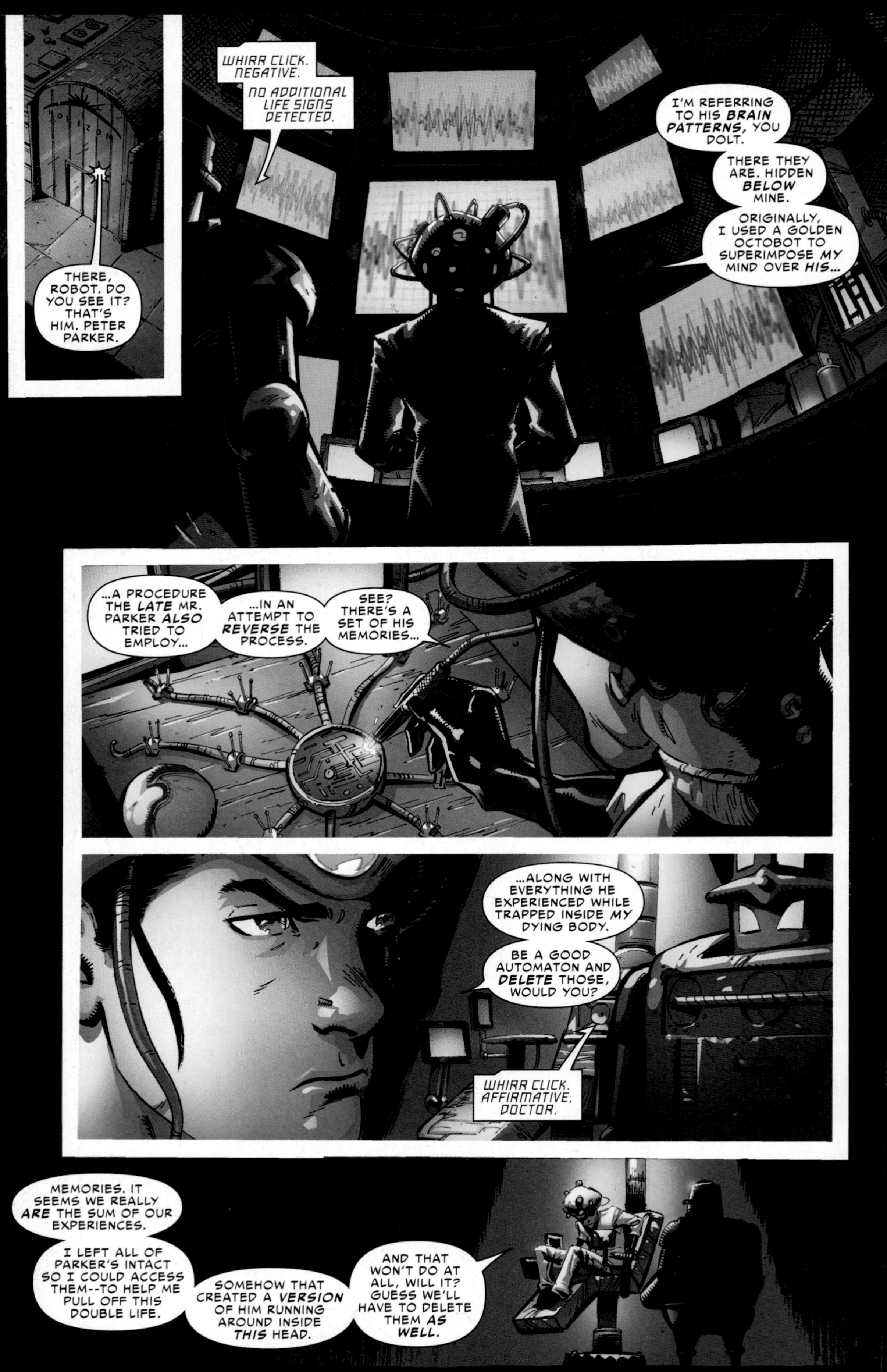
THERE, ROBOT. DO YOU SEE IT? THAT'S HIM. PETER PARKER.
WHIRR CLICK. NEGATIVE.
NO ADDITIONAL LIFE SIGNS DETECTED.
I'M REFERRING TO HIS BRAIN PATTERNS, YOU DOLT.
THERE THEY ARE. HIDDEN BELOW MINE.
ORIGINALLY, I USED A GOLDEN OCTOBOT TO SUPERIMPOSE MY MIND OVER HIS...
...A PROCEDURE THE LATE MR. PARKER ALSO TRIED TO EMPLOY...
...IN AN ATTEMPT TO REVERSE THE PROCESS.
SEE? THERE'S A SET OF HIS MEMORIES...
...ALONG WITH EVERYTHING HE EXPERIENCED WHILE TRAPPED INSIDE MY DYING BODY.
BE A GOOD AUTOMATON AND DELETE THOSE, WOULD YOU?
WHIRR CLICK. AFFIRMATIVE, DOCTOR.
MEMORIES. IT SEEMS WE REALLY ARE THE SUM OF OUR EXPERIENCES.
I LEFT ALL OF PARKER'S INTACT SO I COULD ACCESS THEM--TO HELP ME PULL OFF THIS DOUBLE LIFE.
SOMEHOW THAT CREATED A VERSION OF HIM RUNNING AROUND INSIDE THIS HEAD.
AND THAT WON'T DO AT ALL, WILL IT? GUESS WE'LL HAVE TO DELETE THEM AS WELL.

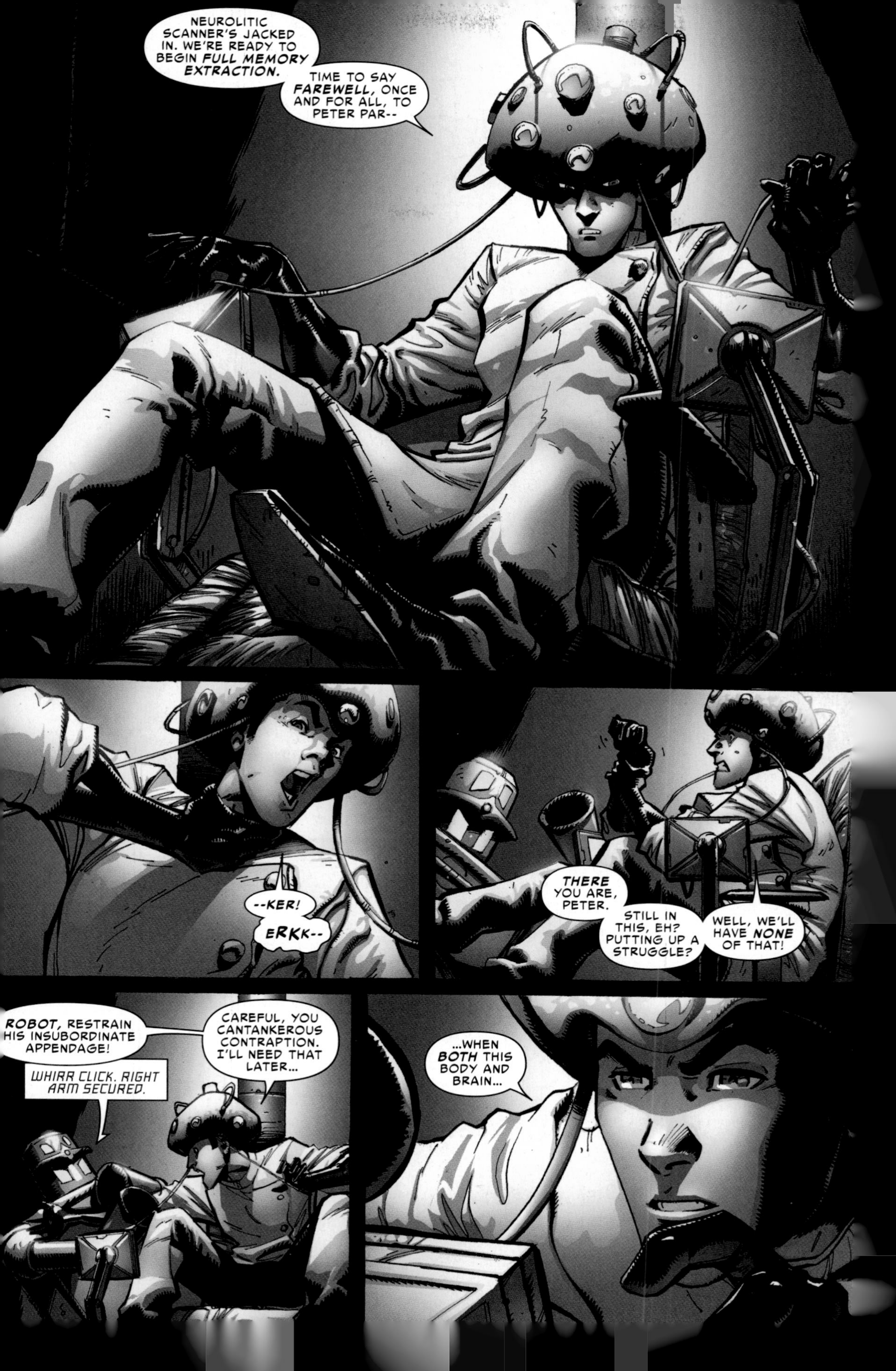
NEUROLITIC SCANNER'S JACKED IN. WE'RE READY TO BEGIN FULL MEMORY EXTRACTION.
TIME TO SAY FAREWELL, ONCE AND FOR ALL, TO PETER PAR--
--KER!
ERKk--
THERE YOU ARE, PETER.
STILL IN THIS, EH? PUTTING UP A STRUGGLE?
WELL, WE'LL HAVE NONE OF THAT!
ROBOT, RESTRAIN HIS INSUBORDINATE APPENDAGE!
WHIRR CLICK. RIGHT ARM SECURED.
CAREFUL, YOU CANTANKEROUS CONTRAPTION. I'LL NEED THAT LATER...
...WHEN BOTH THIS BODY AND BRAIN...

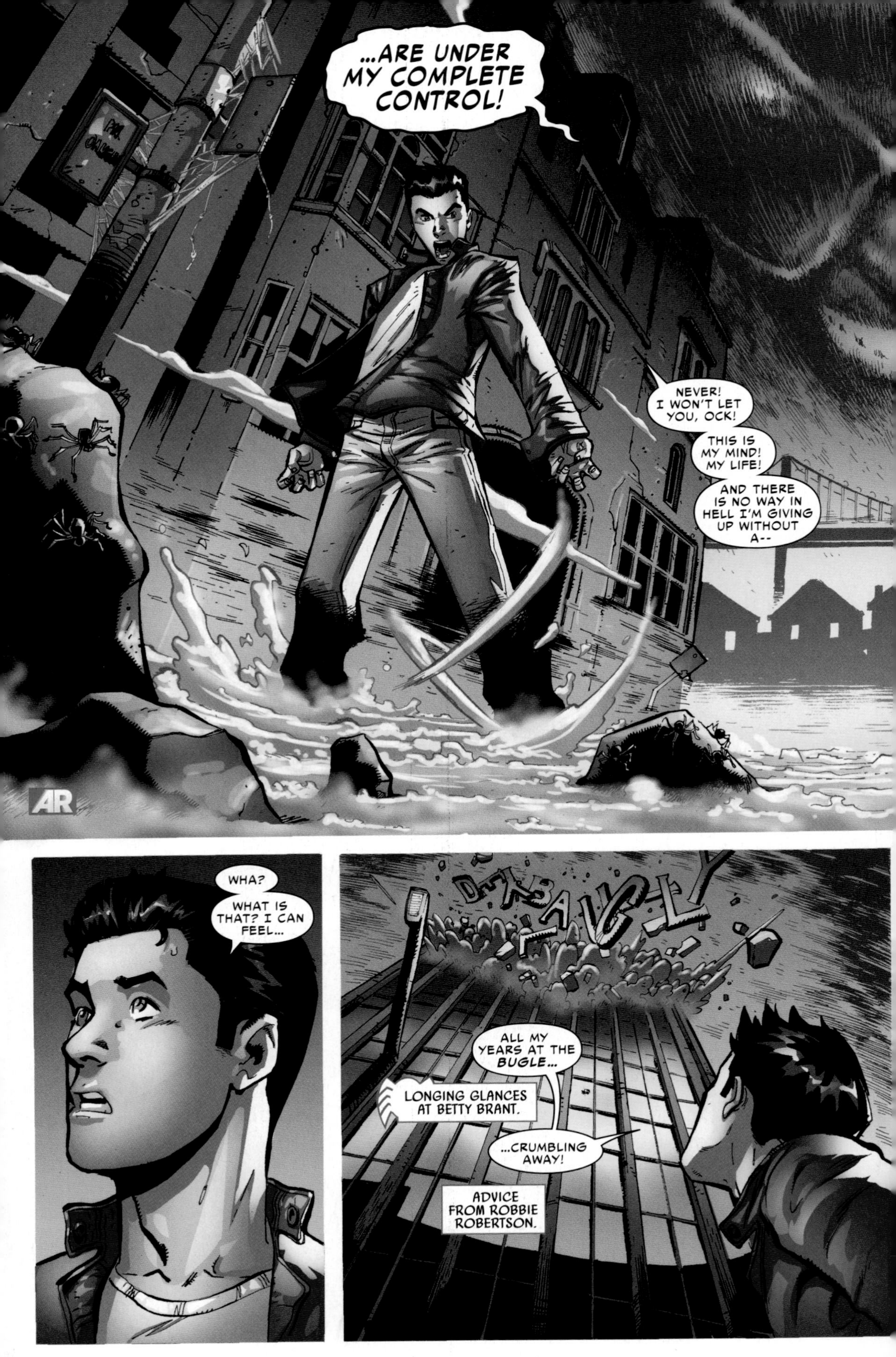

...ARE UNDER MY COMPLETE CONTROL!
NEVER! I WON'T LET YOU, OCK!
THIS IS MY MIND! MY LIFE!
AND THERE IS NO WAY IN HELL I'M GIVING UP WITHOUT A--
WHA?
WHAT IS THAT? I CAN FEEL...
ALL MY YEARS AT THE *BUGLE*...
LONGING GLANCES AT BETTY BRANT.
...CRUMBLING AWAY!
ADVICE FROM ROBBIE ROBERTSON.

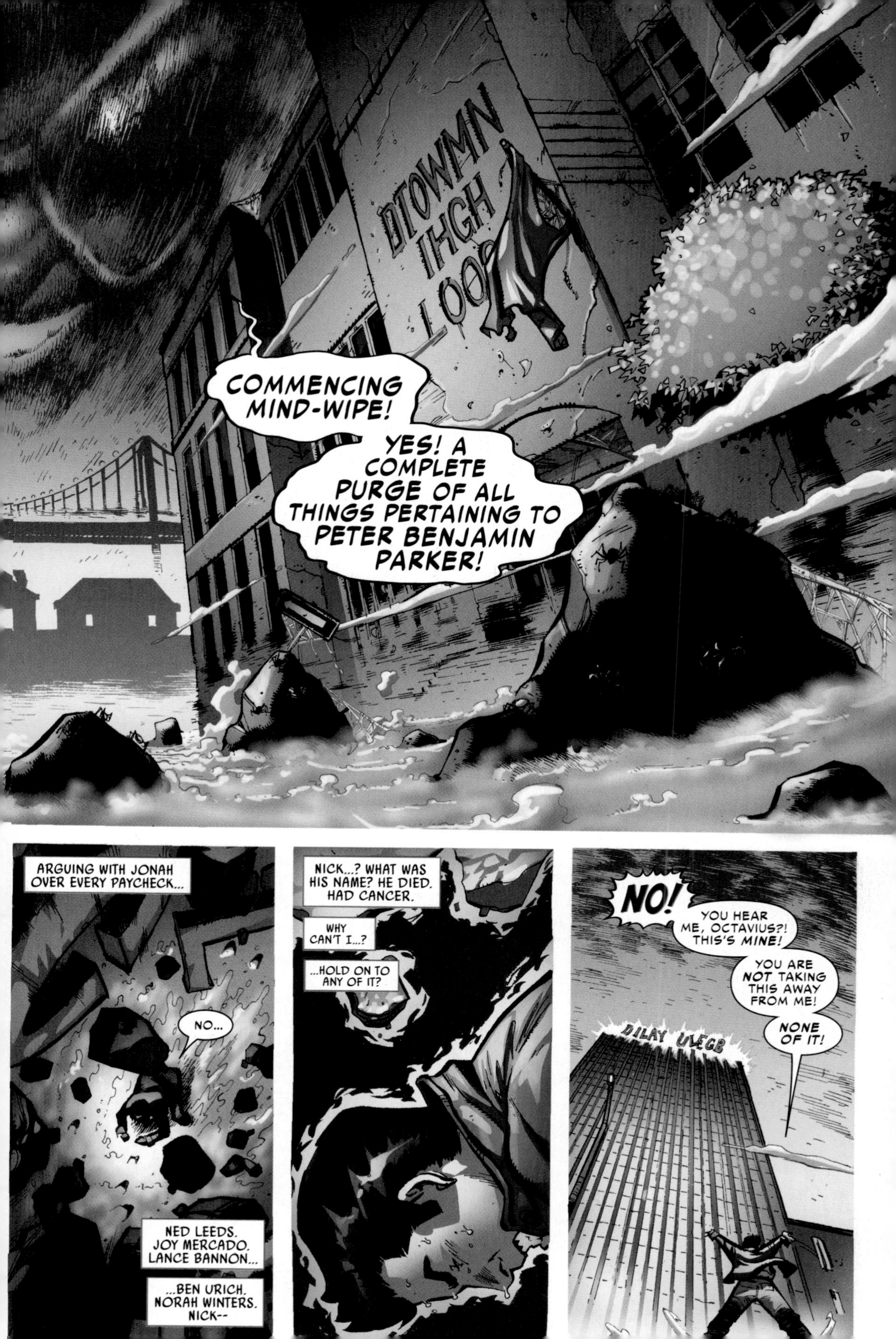
DTOWMN
IHGH
LOOP
COMMENCING MIND-WIPE!
YES! A COMPLETE PURGE OF ALL THINGS PERTAINING TO PETER BENJAMIN PARKER!
ARGUING WITH JONAH OVER EVERY PAYCHECK...
NO...
NED LEEDS. JOY MERCADO. LANCE BANNON...
...BEN URICH. NORAH WINTERS. NICK--
NICK...? WHAT WAS HIS NAME? HE DIED. HAD CANCER.
WHY CAN'T I...?
...HOLD ON TO ANY OF IT?
NO!
YOU HEAR ME, OCTAVIUS?! THIS'S MINE!
YOU ARE NOT TAKING THIS AWAY FROM ME!
NONE OF IT!
DILAY UVEGB

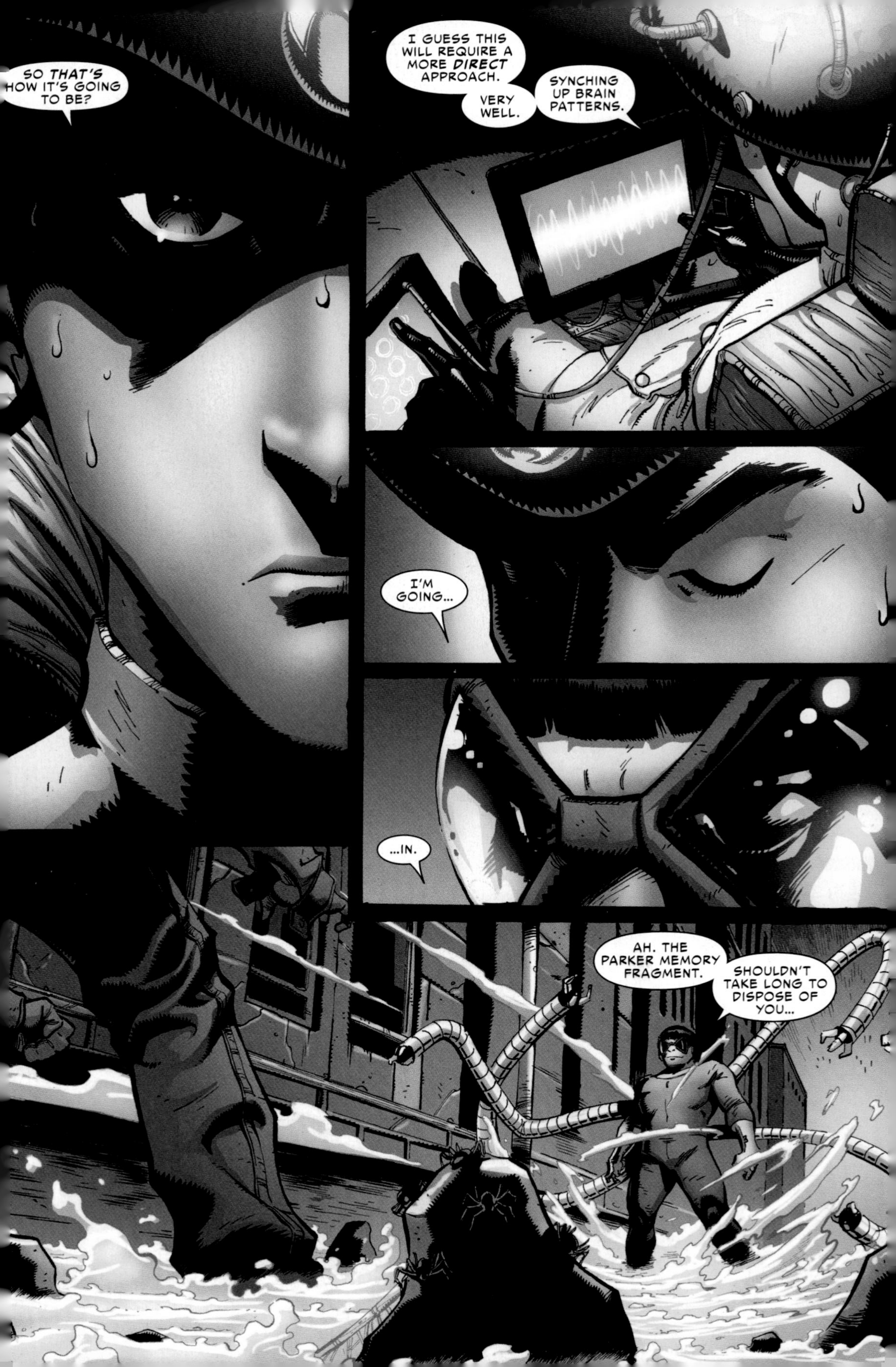
SO THAT'S HOW IT'S GOING TO BE?
I GUESS THIS WILL REQUIRE A MORE DIRECT APPROACH.
VERY WELL.
SYNCHING UP BRAIN PATTERNS.
I'M GOING...
...IN.
AH. THE PARKER MEMORY FRAGMENT.
SHOULDN'T TAKE LONG TO DISPOSE OF YOU...

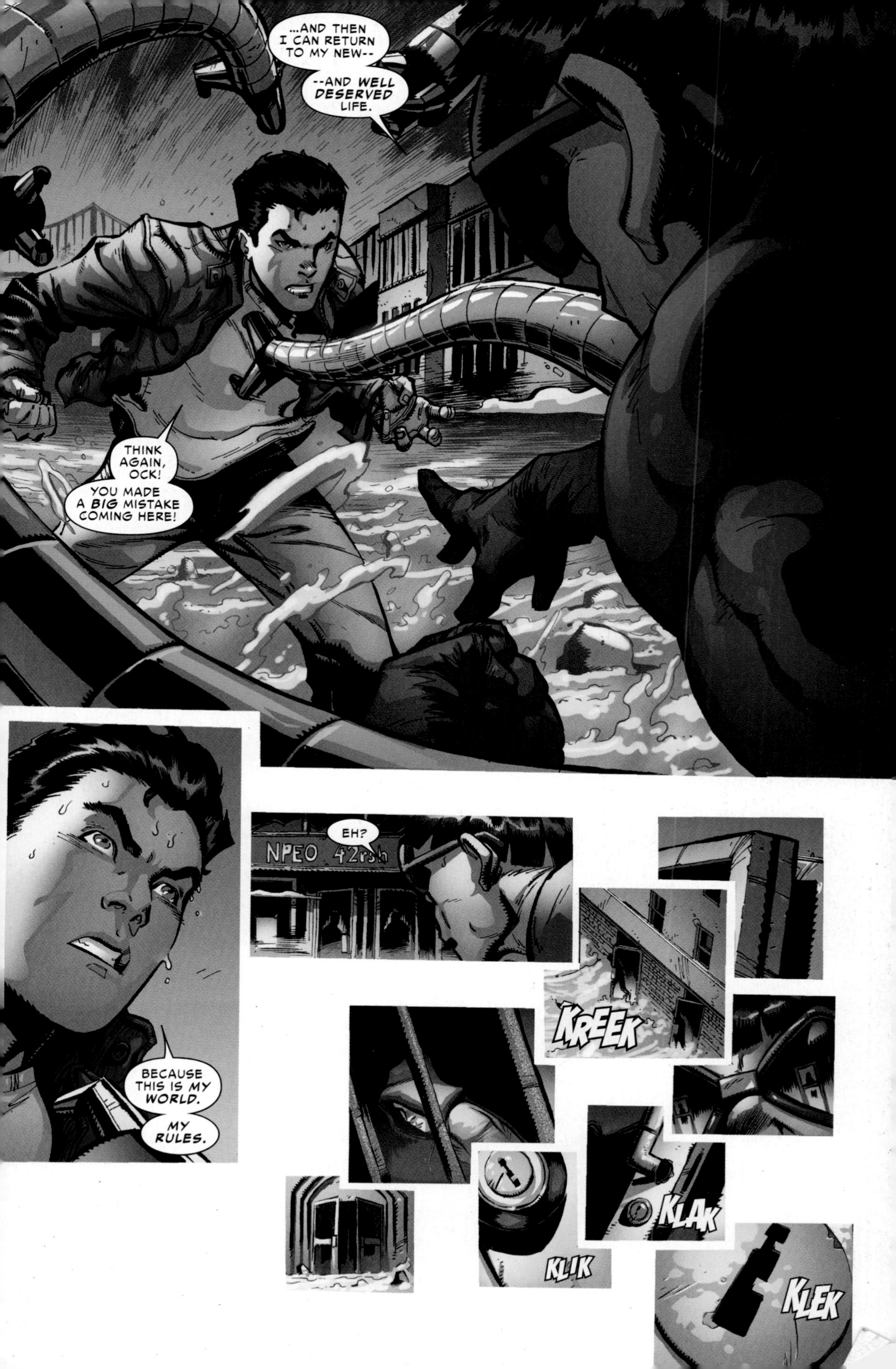
...AND THEN I CAN RETURN TO MY NEW--
--AND WELL DESERVED LIFE.
THINK AGAIN, OCK! YOU MADE A BIG MISTAKE COMING HERE!
BECAUSE THIS IS MY WORLD.
MY RULES.
EH?
NPEO 42rsh
KREEK
KLAK
KLIK
KLEK

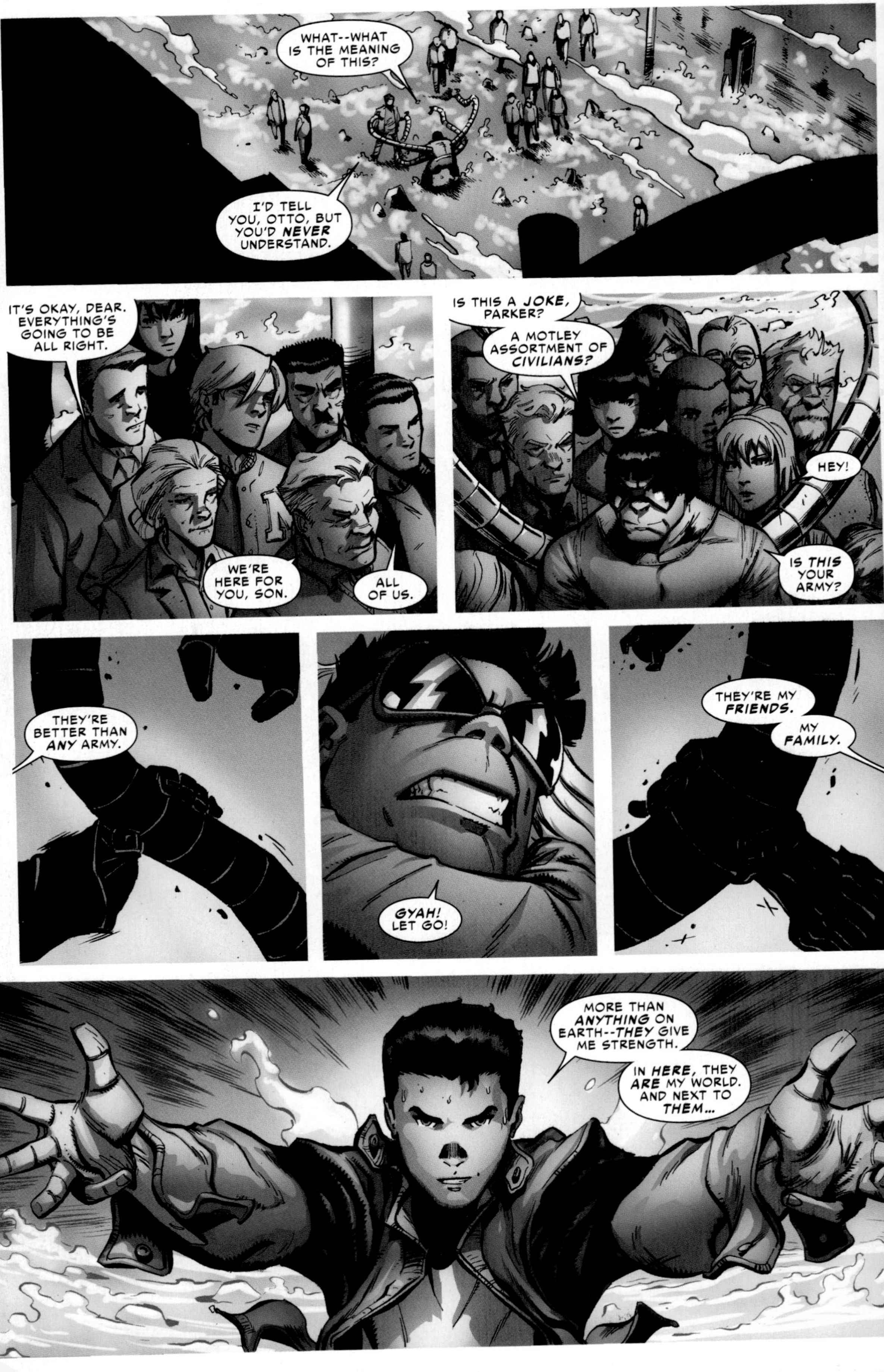
WHAT--WHAT IS THE MEANING OF THIS?
I'D TELL YOU, OTTO, BUT YOU'D NEVER UNDERSTAND.
IT'S OKAY, DEAR. EVERYTHING'S GOING TO BE ALL RIGHT.
WE'RE HERE FOR YOU, SON.
ALL OF US.
IS THIS A JOKE, PARKER?
A MOTLEY ASSORTMENT OF CIVILIANS?
HEY!
IS THIS YOUR ARMY?
THEY'RE BETTER THAN ANY ARMY.
GYAH! LET GO!
THEY'RE MY FRIENDS.
MY FAMILY.
MORE THAN ANYTHING ON EARTH--THEY GIVE ME STRENGTH.
IN HERE, THEY ARE MY WORLD. AND NEXT TO THEM...

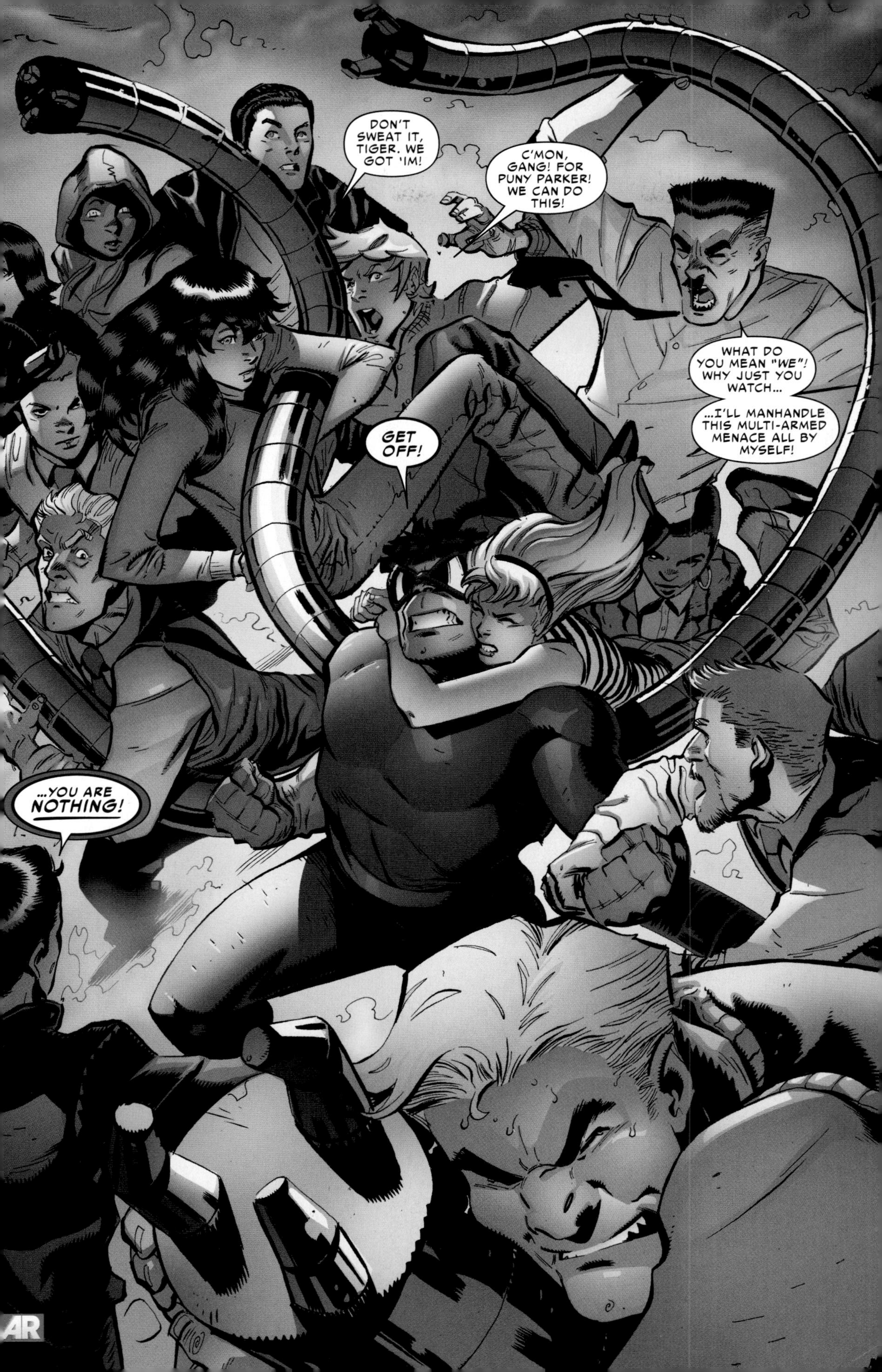
DON'T SWEAT IT, TIGER. WE GOT 'IM!
C'MON, GANG! FOR PUNY PARKER! WE CAN DO THIS!
WHAT DO YOU MEAN "WE"! WHY JUST YOU WATCH...
...I'LL MANHANDLE THIS MULTI-ARMED MENACE ALL BY MYSELF!
GET OFF!
...YOU ARE NOTHING!

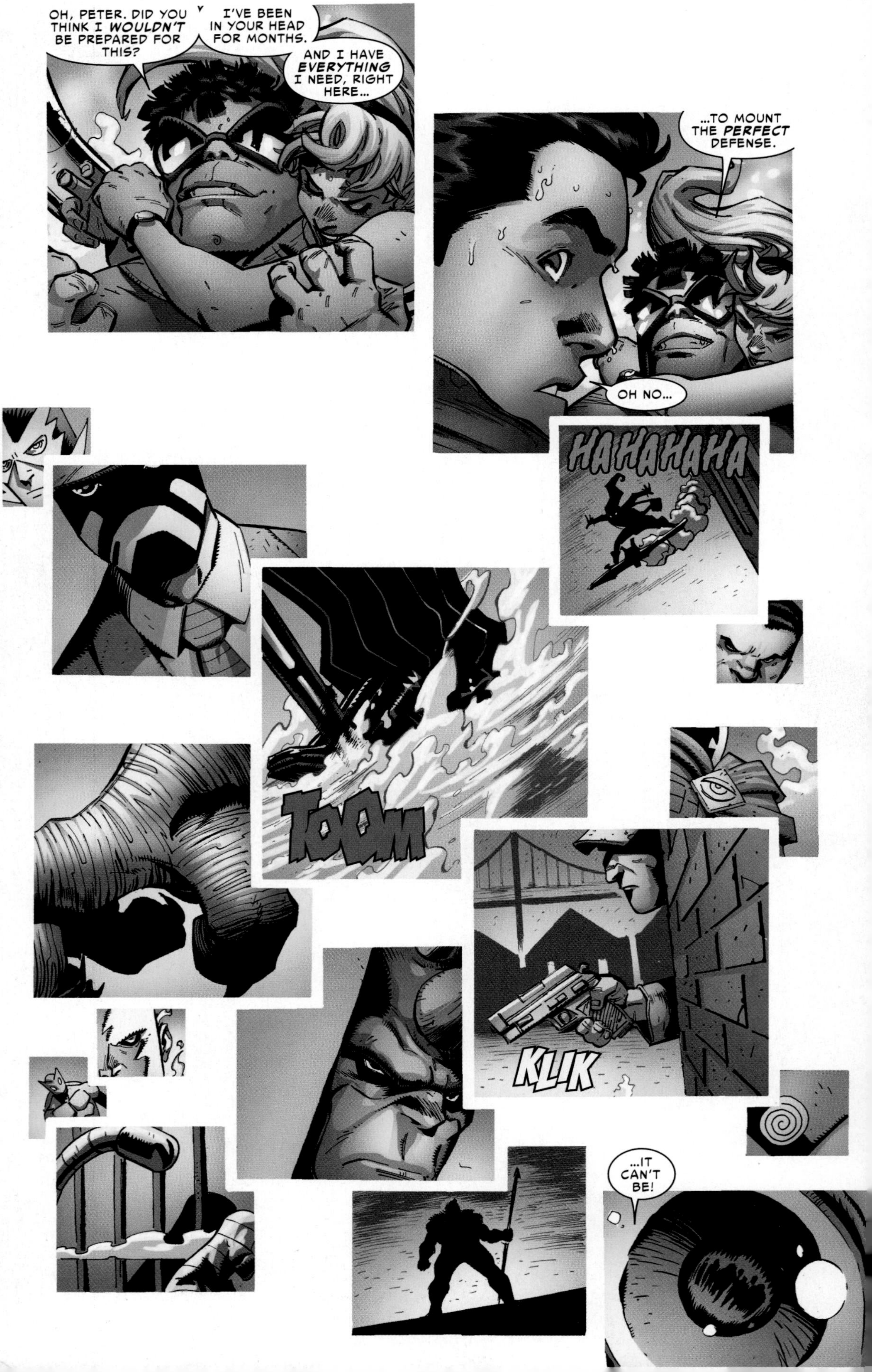
OH, PETER. DID YOU THINK I *WOULDN'T* BE PREPARED FOR THIS?
I'VE BEEN IN YOUR HEAD FOR MONTHS.
AND I HAVE *EVERYTHING* I NEED, RIGHT HERE...
...TO MOUNT THE *PERFECT* DEFENSE.
OH NO...
HAHAHAHAHA
TOOM
KLIK
...IT CAN'T BE!

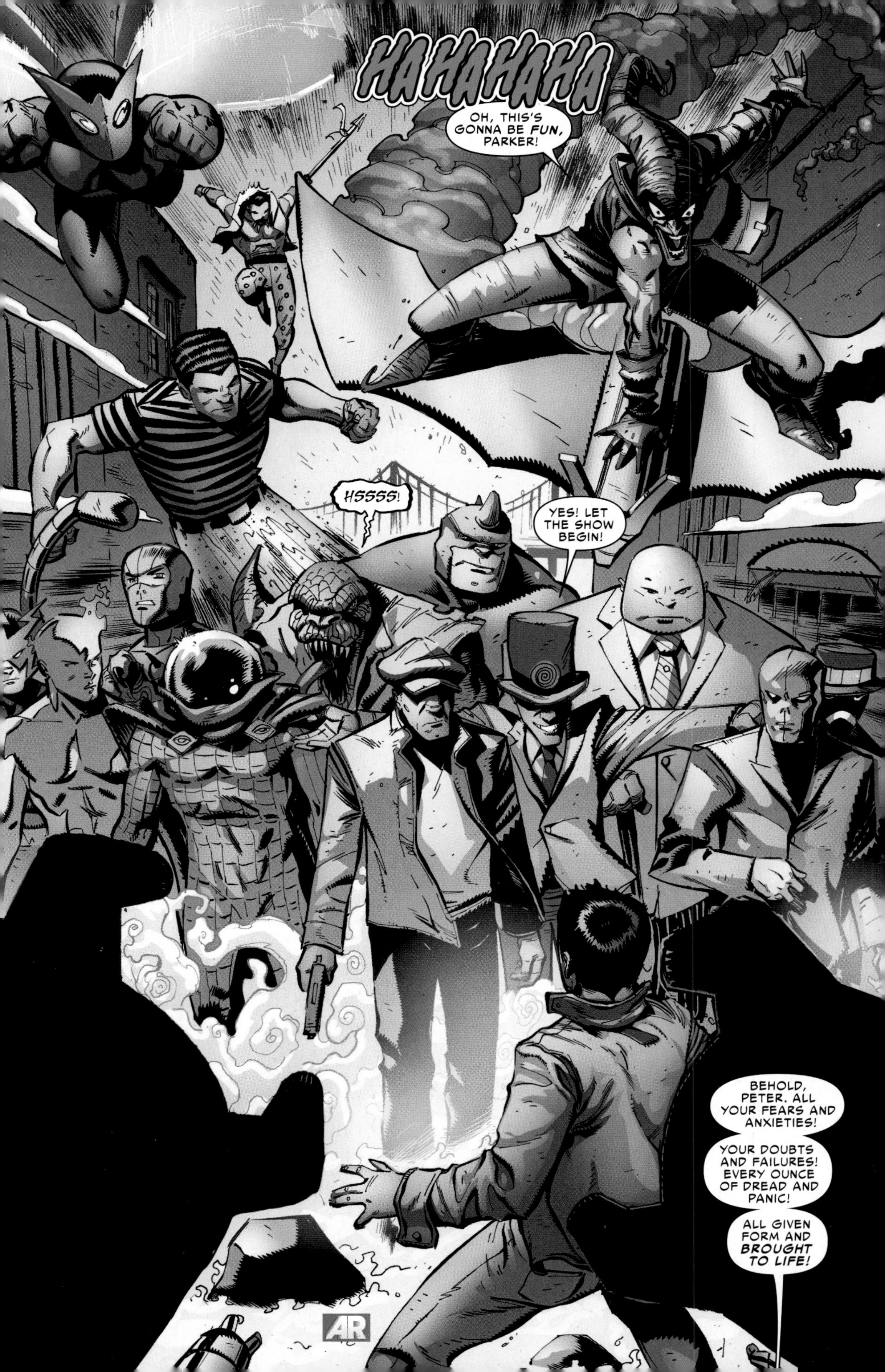
HAHAHAHAHA
OH, THIS'S GONNA BE FUN, PARKER!
HSSSS!
YES! LET THE SHOW BEGIN!
BEHOLD, PETER. ALL YOUR FEARS AND ANXIETIES!
YOUR DOUBTS AND FAILURES! EVERY OUNCE OF DREAD AND PANIC!
ALL GIVEN FORM AND BROUGHT TO LIFE!

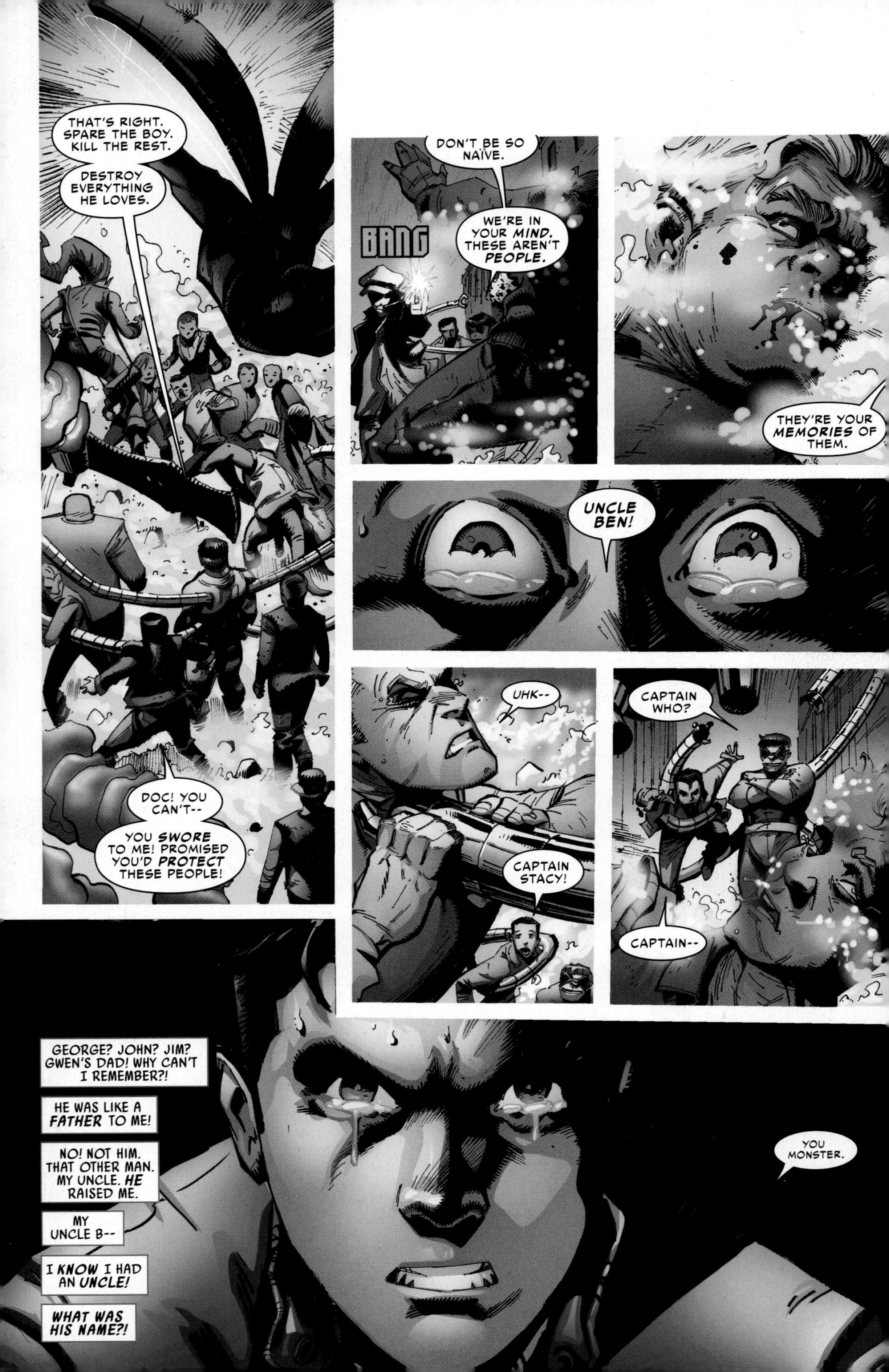
THAT'S RIGHT. SPARE THE BOY. KILL THE REST.
DESTROY EVERYTHING HE LOVES.
DOC! YOU CAN'T--
YOU SWORE TO ME! PROMISED YOU'D PROTECT THESE PEOPLE!
DON'T BE SO NAÏVE.
BANG
WE'RE IN YOUR MIND. THESE AREN'T PEOPLE.
THEY'RE YOUR MEMORIES OF THEM.
UNCLE BEN!
UHK--
CAPTAIN STACY!
CAPTAIN WHO?
CAPTAIN--
GEORGE? JOHN? JIM? GWEN'S DAD! WHY CAN'T I REMEMBER?!
HE WAS LIKE A FATHER TO ME!
NO! NOT HIM. THAT OTHER MAN. MY UNCLE. HE RAISED ME.
MY UNCLE B--
I KNOW I HAD AN UNCLE!
WHAT WAS HIS NAME?!
YOU MONSTER.

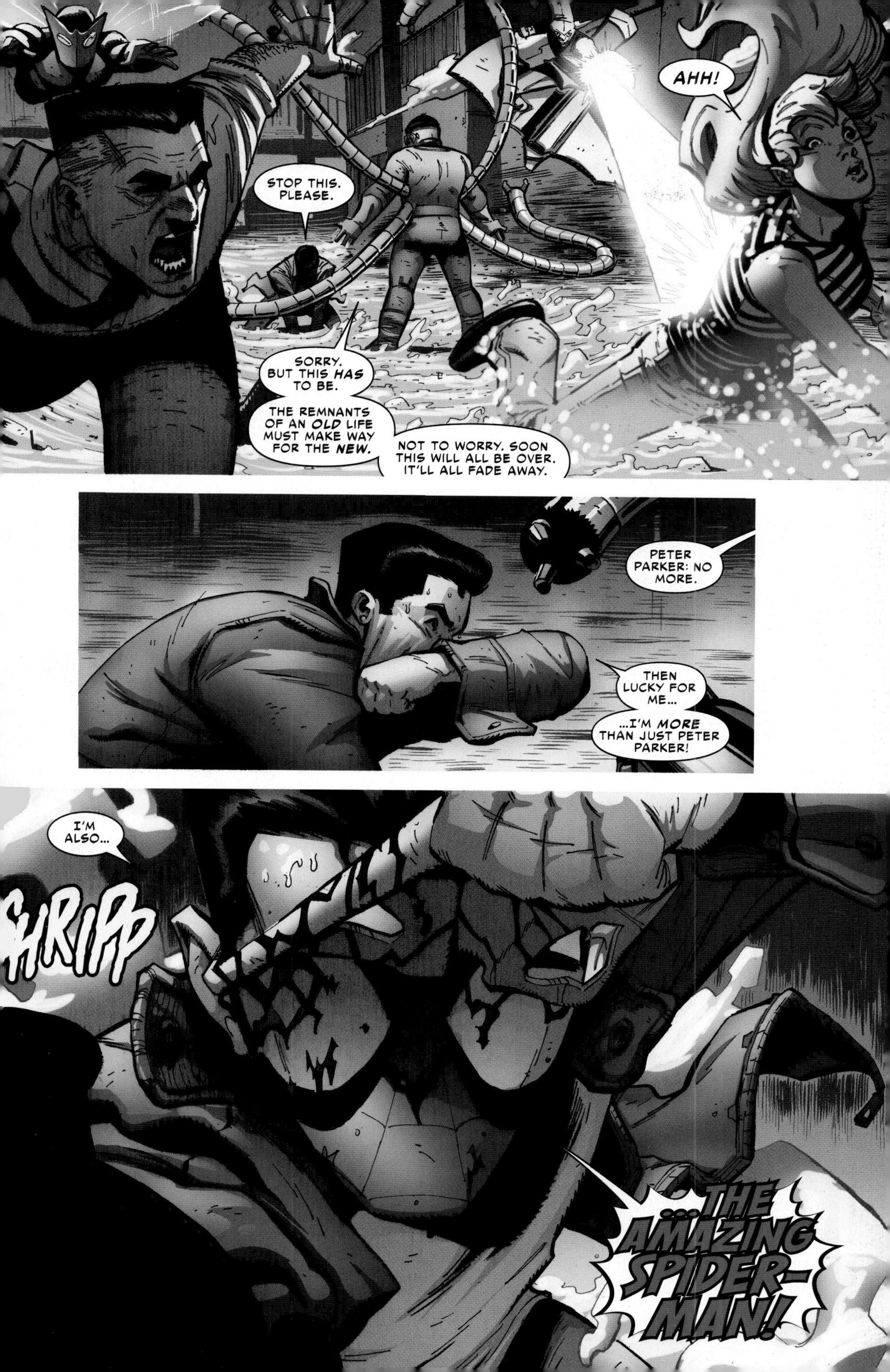
AHH!
STOP THIS. PLEASE.
SORRY. BUT THIS HAS TO BE.
THE REMNANTS OF AN OLD LIFE MUST MAKE WAY FOR THE NEW.
NOT TO WORRY. SOON THIS WILL ALL BE OVER. IT'LL ALL FADE AWAY.
PETER PARKER: NO MORE.
THEN LUCKY FOR ME...
...I'M MORE THAN JUST PETER PARKER!
I'M ALSO...
SHRIPP
...THE AMAZING SPIDER-MAN!

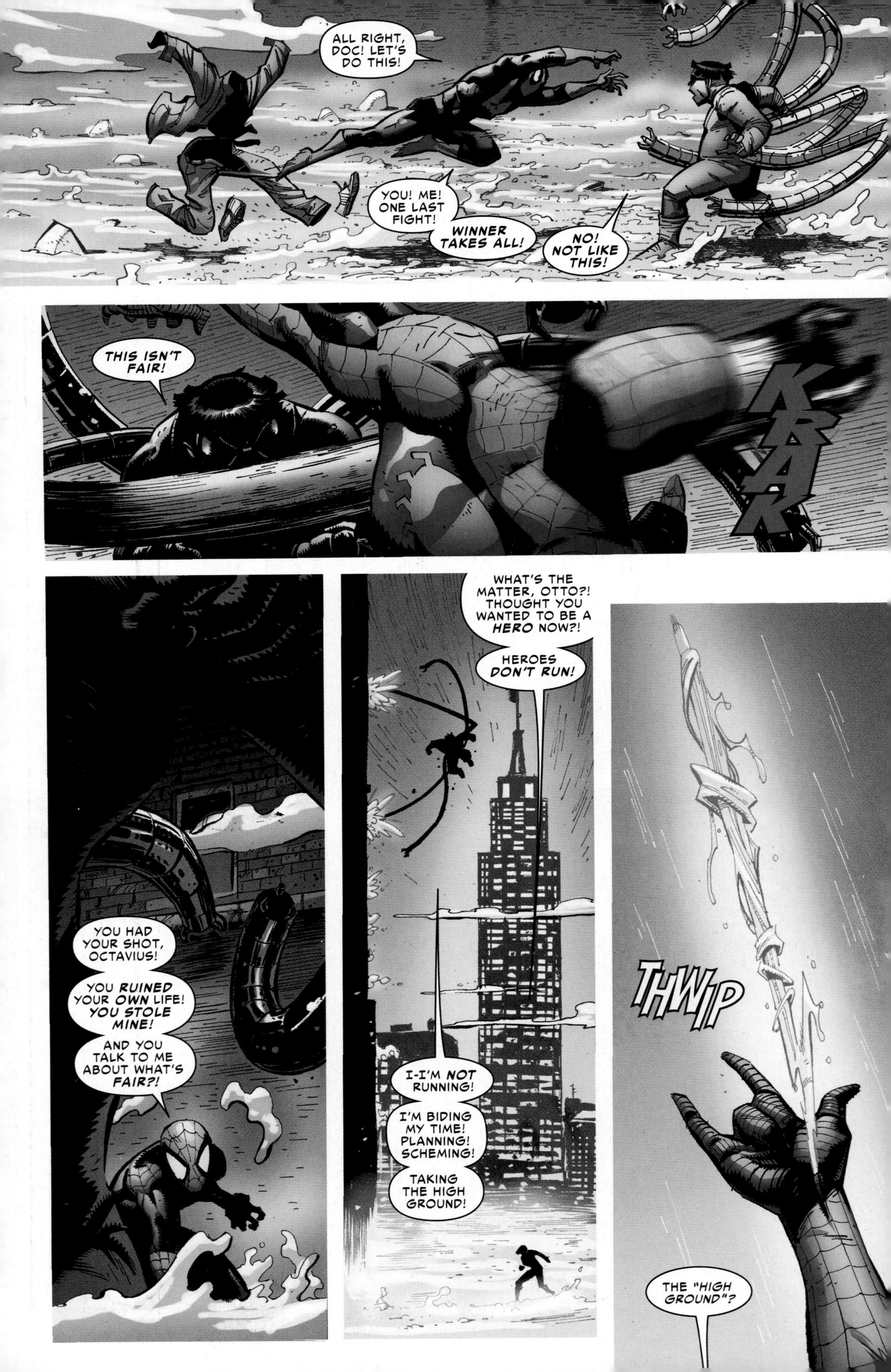
ALL RIGHT, DOC! LET'S DO THIS!
YOU! ME! ONE LAST FIGHT!
WINNER TAKES ALL!
NO! NOT LIKE THIS!
THIS ISN'T FAIR!
KRAK
YOU HAD YOUR SHOT, OCTAVIUS!
YOU RUINED YOUR OWN LIFE! YOU STOLE MINE!
AND YOU TALK TO ME ABOUT WHAT'S FAIR?!
WHAT'S THE MATTER, OTTO?! THOUGHT YOU WANTED TO BE A HERO NOW?!
HEROES DON'T RUN!
I-I'M NOT RUNNING!
I'M BIDING MY TIME! PLANNING! SCHEMING!
TAKING THE HIGH GROUND!
THWIP
THE "HIGH GROUND"?

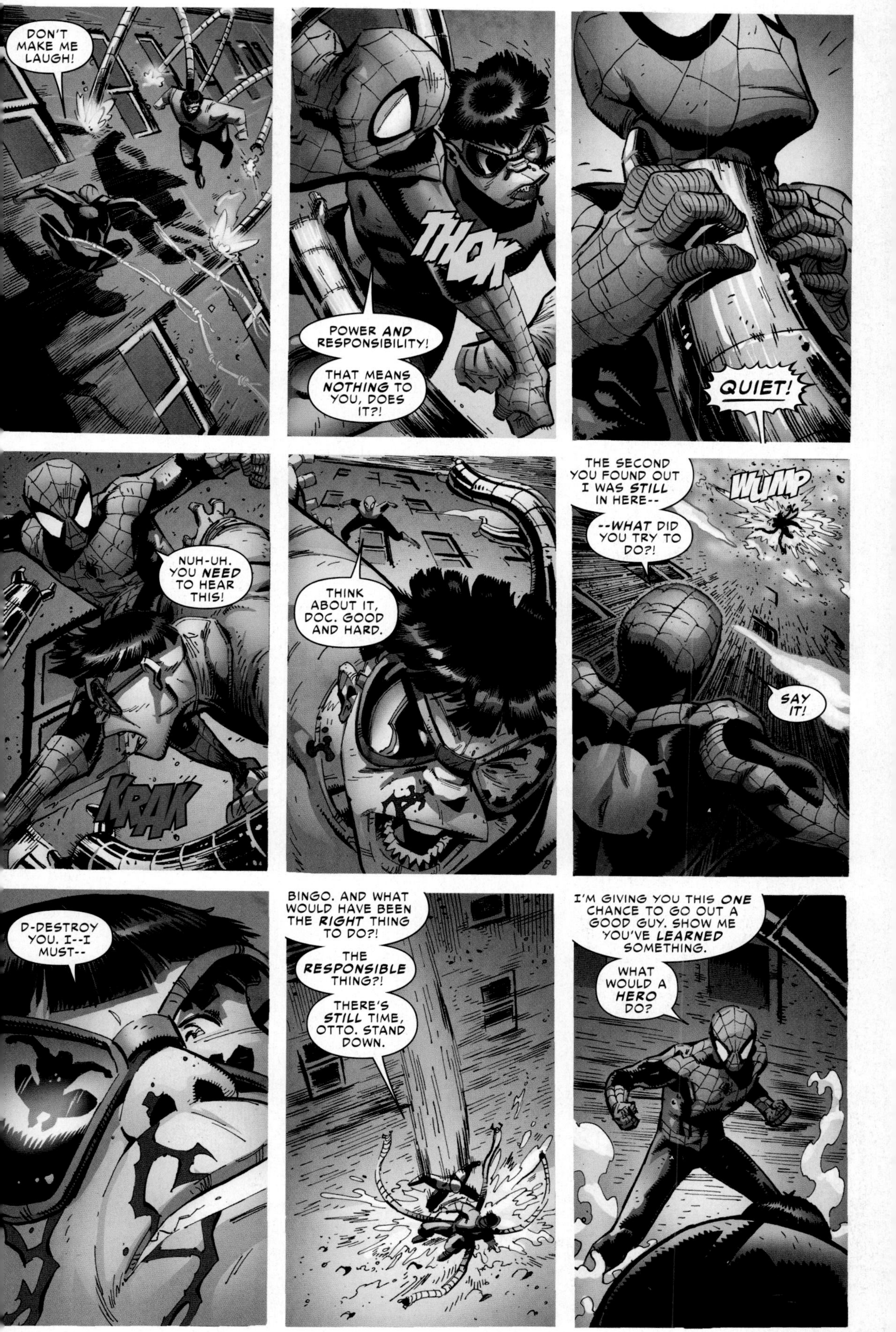
DON'T MAKE ME LAUGH!
THOK
POWER AND RESPONSIBILITY!
THAT MEANS NOTHING TO YOU, DOES IT?!
QUIET!
NUH-UH. YOU NEED TO HEAR THIS!
KRAK
THINK ABOUT IT, DOC. GOOD AND HARD.
THE SECOND YOU FOUND OUT I WAS STILL IN HERE--
--WHAT DID YOU TRY TO DO?!
WUMP
SAY IT!
D-DESTROY YOU. I--I MUST--
BINGO. AND WHAT WOULD HAVE BEEN THE RIGHT THING TO DO?!
THE RESPONSIBLE THING?!
THERE'S STILL TIME, OTTO. STAND DOWN.
I'M GIVING YOU THIS ONE CHANCE TO GO OUT A GOOD GUY. SHOW ME YOU'VE LEARNED SOMETHING.
WHAT WOULD A HERO DO?

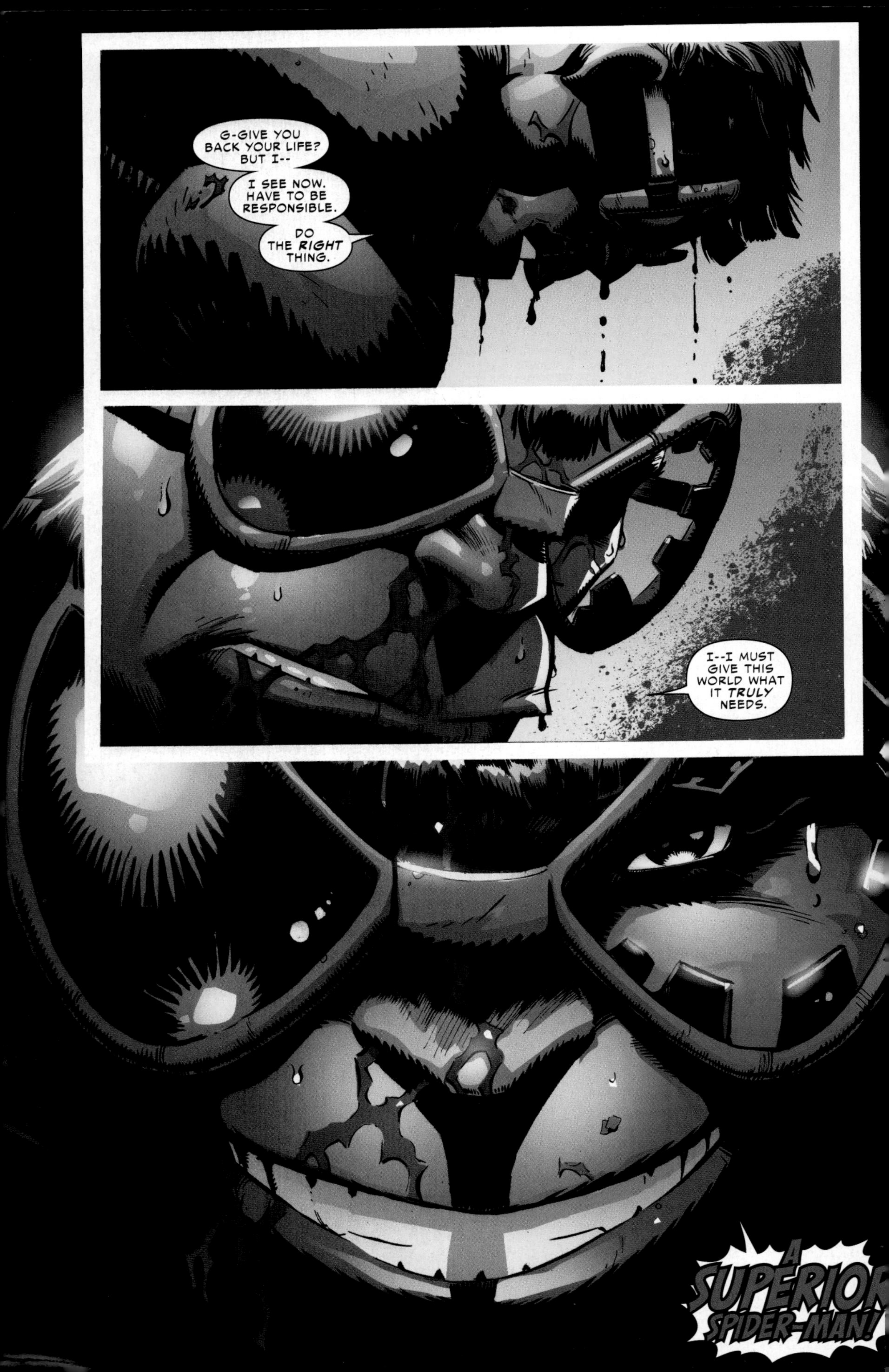
G-GIVE YOU BACK YOUR LIFE? BUT I--
I SEE NOW. HAVE TO BE RESPONSIBLE.
DO THE RIGHT THING.
I--I MUST GIVE THIS WORLD WHAT IT TRULY NEEDS.
A SUPERIOR SPIDER-MAN!

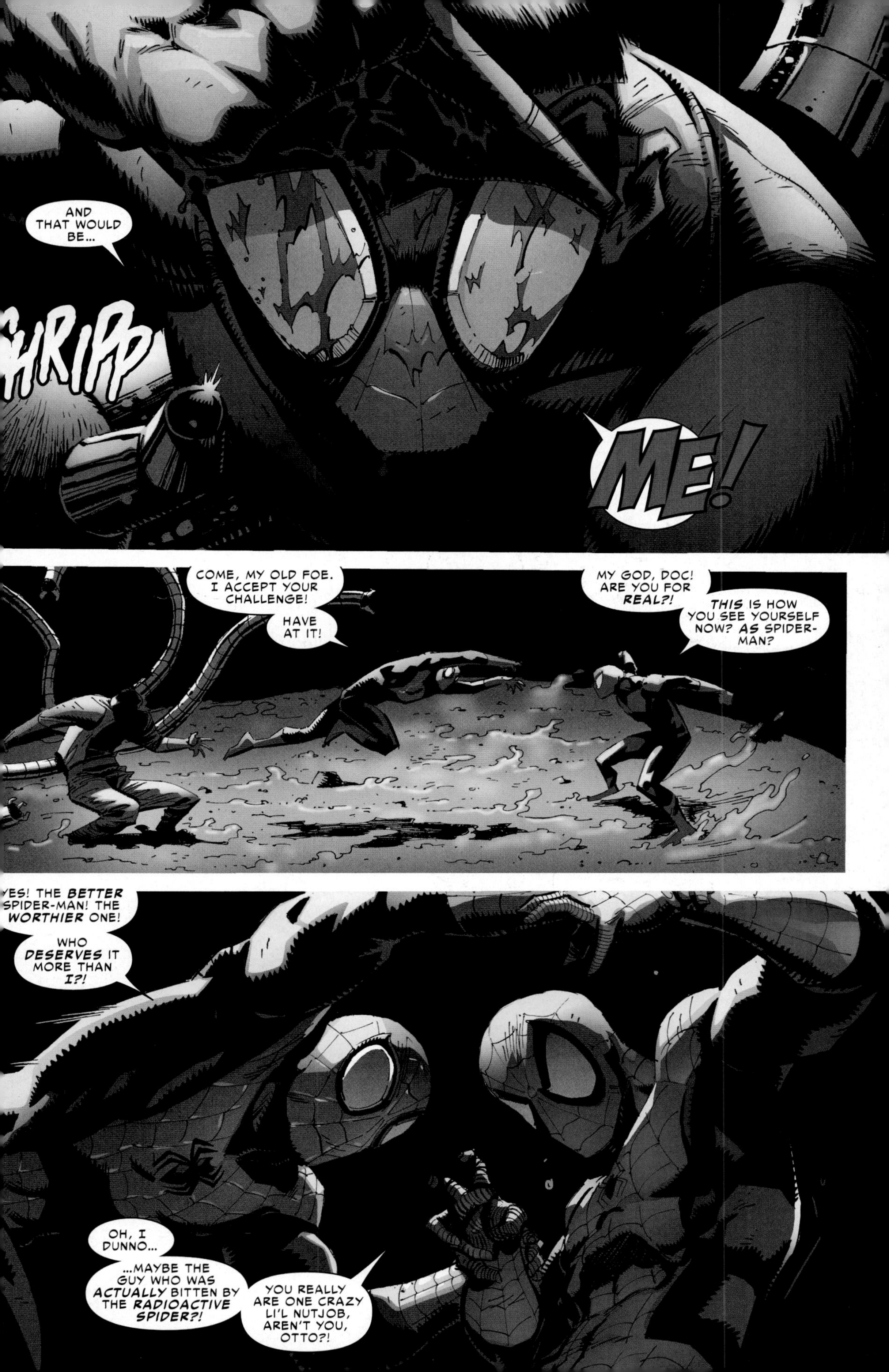
AND THAT WOULD BE...
SHRIPP
ME!
COME, MY OLD FOE. I ACCEPT YOUR CHALLENGE!
HAVE AT IT!
MY GOD, DOC! ARE YOU FOR REAL?!
THIS IS HOW YOU SEE YOURSELF NOW? AS SPIDER-MAN?
YES! THE BETTER SPIDER-MAN! THE WORTHIER ONE!
WHO DESERVES IT MORE THAN I?!
OH, I DUNNO...
...MAYBE THE GUY WHO WAS ACTUALLY BITTEN BY THE RADIOACTIVE SPIDER?!
YOU REALLY ARE ONE CRAZY LI'L NUTJOB, AREN'T YOU, OTTO?!

CRAZY?! DO YOU HAVE *ANY* IDEA WHAT I'VE ACCOMPLISHED AS SPIDER-MAN?

CRIME IS *DOWN* IN THIS CITY *BECAUSE* OF ME!

THE MAYOR *AND* THE POLIC SUPPORT ME LIK *NEVER* BEFORE

WHAT ABOUT THE *AVENGERS*, OCK?!

BECAUSE OF *YOU*, THEY'RE READY TO KICK ME OFF THE TEAM!

NOBODY *TRUSTS* ME ANYMORE!

NOT EVEN THE MAN ON THE STREET!

AND WHY *WOULD* THEY? AFTER YOU BEAT THE HELL OUT OF ALL MY ENEMIES!

YOU EVEN *KILLED* ONE OF THEM! THAT'S SOMETHING I'D *NEVER* DO, OTTO! *EVER!*

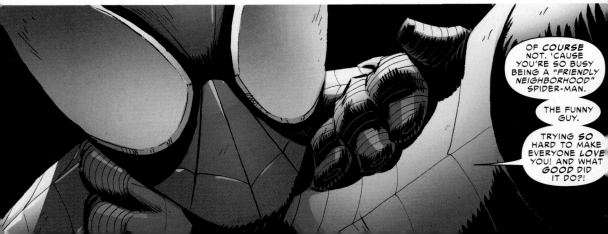

OF *COURSE* NOT. 'CAUSE YOU'RE SO BUSY BEING A *"FRIENDLY NEIGHBORHOOD"* SPIDER-MAN.

THE FUNNY GUY.

TRYING *SO* HARD TO MAKE EVERYONE *LOVE* YOU! AND WHAT *GOOD* DID IT DO?!

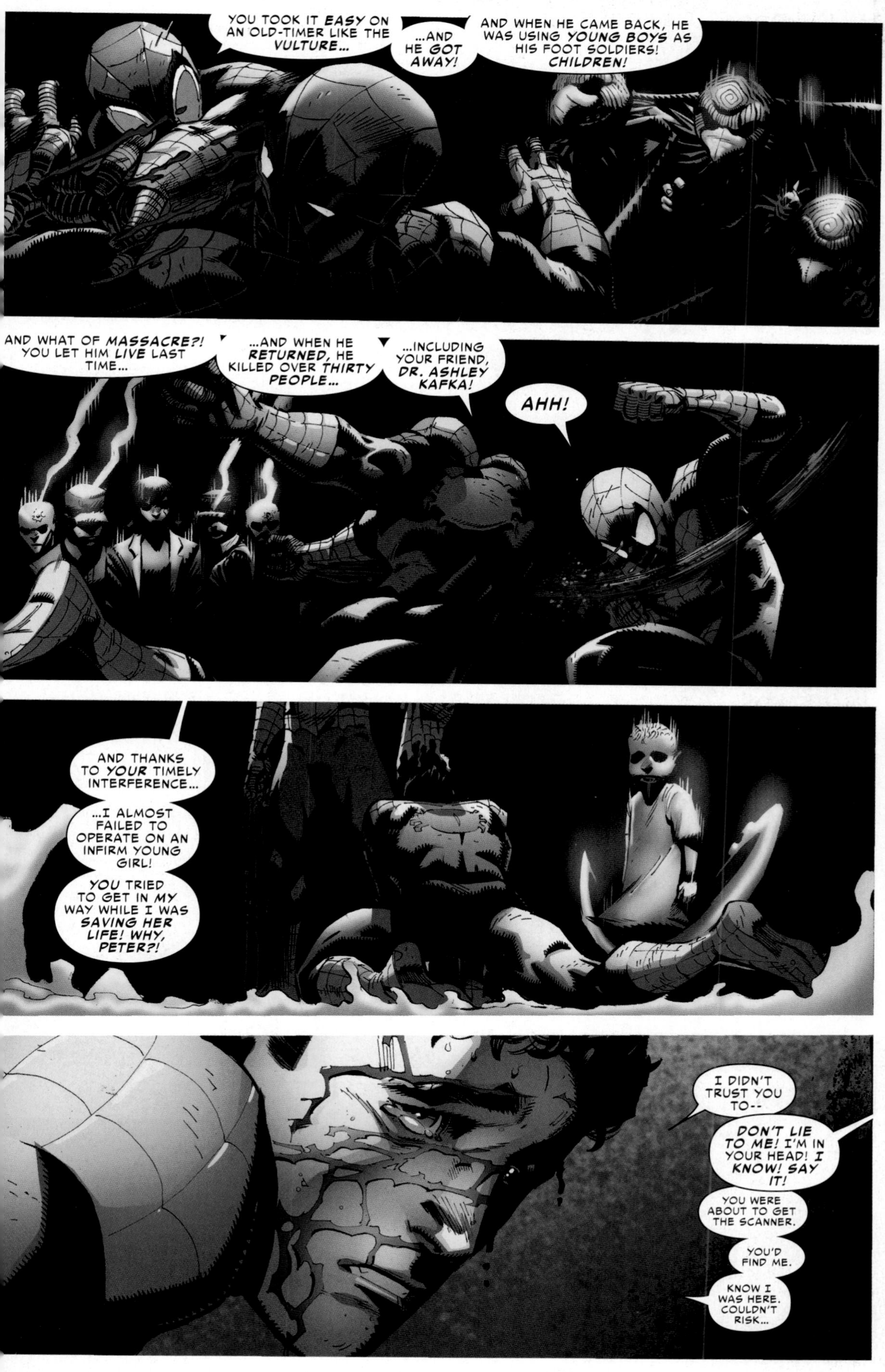
YOU TOOK IT EASY ON AN OLD-TIMER LIKE THE VULTURE...
...AND HE GOT AWAY!
AND WHEN HE CAME BACK, HE WAS USING YOUNG BOYS AS HIS FOOT SOLDIERS! CHILDREN!
AND WHAT OF MASSACRE?! YOU LET HIM LIVE LAST TIME...
...AND WHEN HE RETURNED, HE KILLED OVER THIRTY PEOPLE...
...INCLUDING YOUR FRIEND, DR. ASHLEY KAFKA!
AHH!
AND THANKS TO YOUR TIMELY INTERFERENCE...
...I ALMOST FAILED TO OPERATE ON AN INFIRM YOUNG GIRL!
YOU TRIED TO GET IN MY WAY WHILE I WAS SAVING HER LIFE! WHY, PETER?!
I DIDN'T TRUST YOU TO--
DON'T LIE TO ME! I'M IN YOUR HEAD! I KNOW! SAY IT!
YOU WERE ABOUT TO GET THE SCANNER.
YOU'D FIND ME.
KNOW I WAS HERE. COULDN'T RISK...

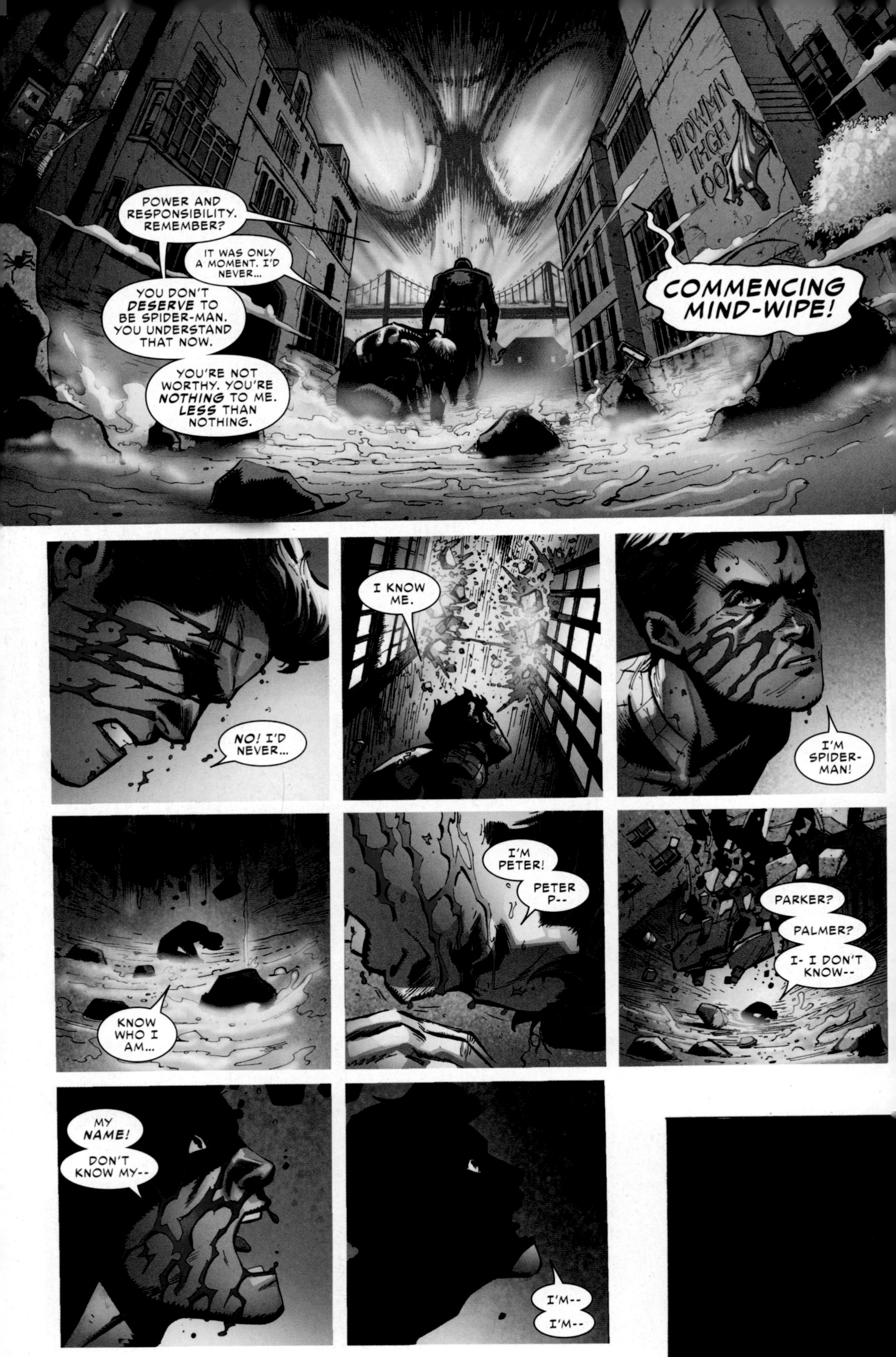
POWER AND RESPONSIBILITY. REMEMBER?
IT WAS ONLY A MOMENT. I'D NEVER...
YOU DON'T DESERVE TO BE SPIDER-MAN. YOU UNDERSTAND THAT NOW.
YOU'RE NOT WORTHY. YOU'RE NOTHING TO ME. LESS THAN NOTHING.
COMMENCING MIND-WIPE!
NO! I'D NEVER...
I KNOW ME.
I'M SPIDER-MAN!
KNOW WHO I AM...
I'M PETER!
PETER P--
PARKER?
PALMER?
I- I DON'T KNOW--
MY NAME!
DON'T KNOW MY--
I'M--
I'M--

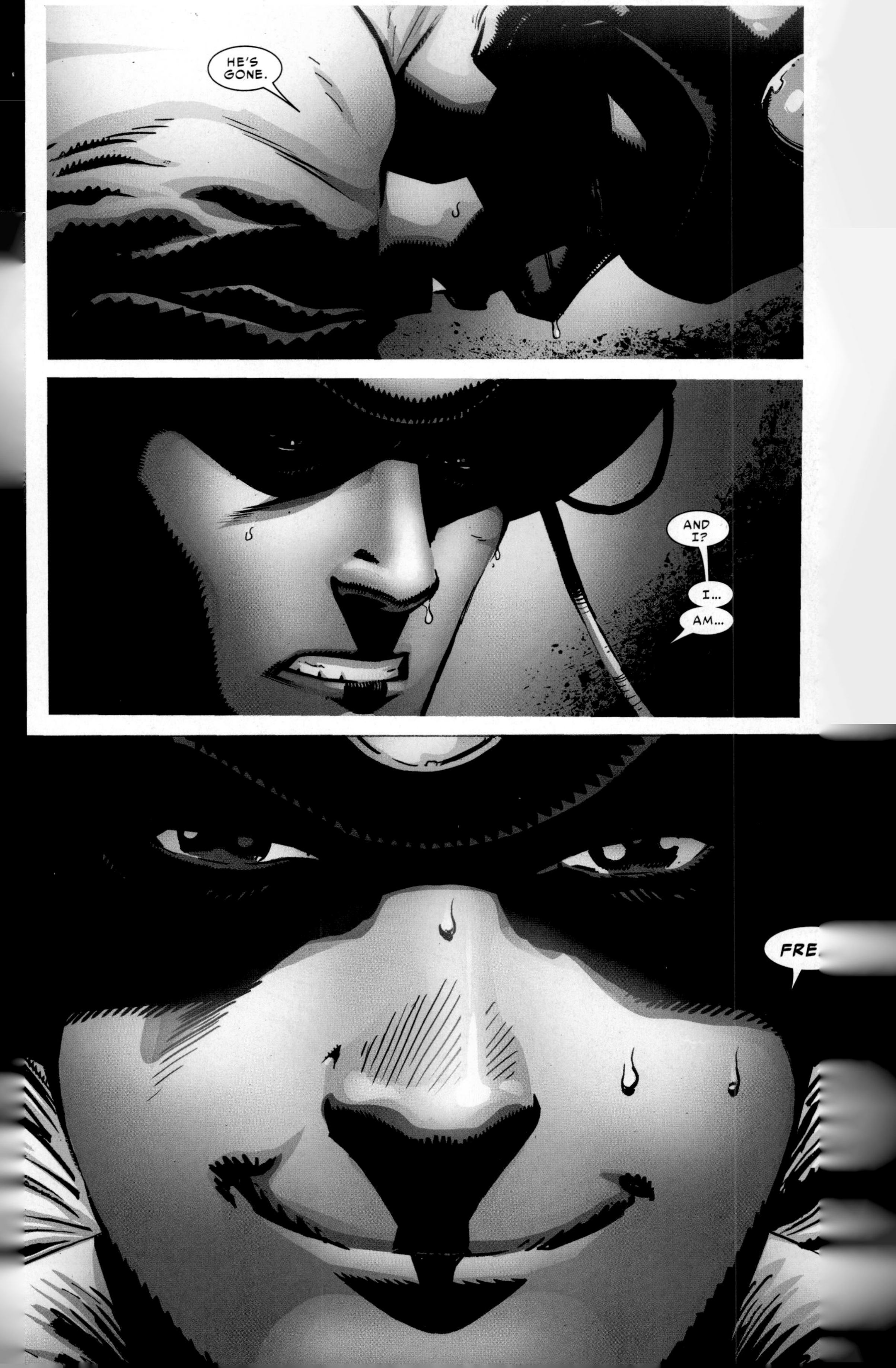
HE'S GONE.
AND I?
I...
AM...
FRE

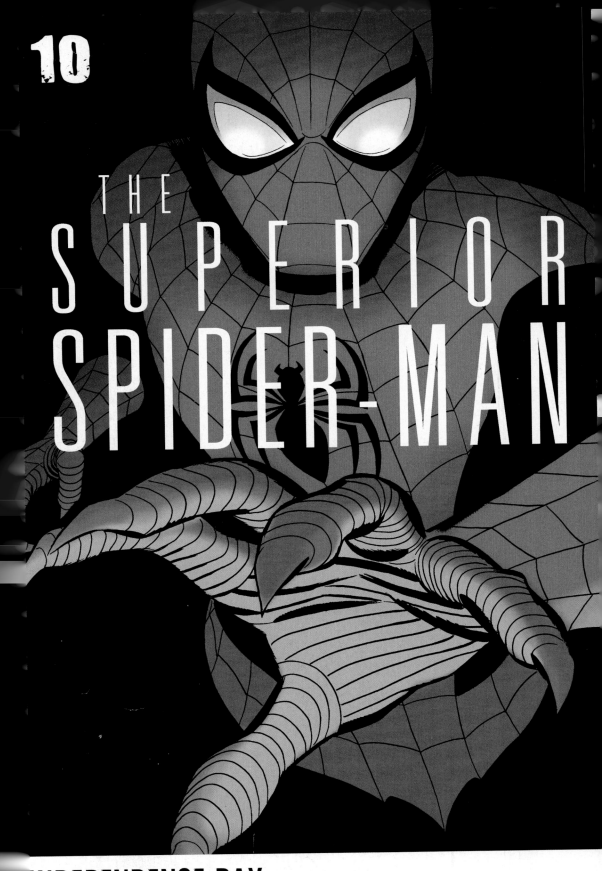

THE SUPERIOR SPIDER-MAN

10

INDEPENDENCE DAY

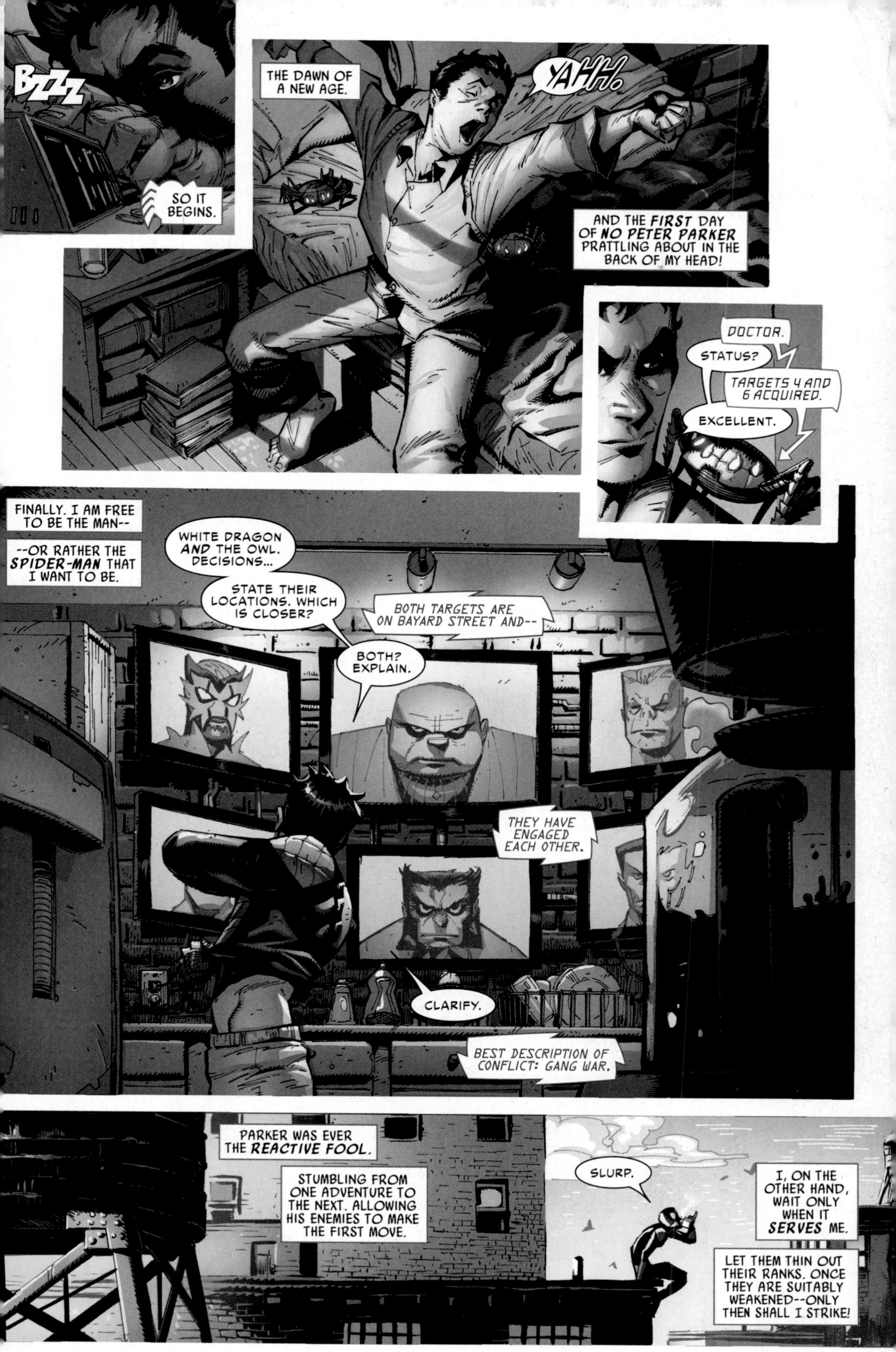
BZZZ
SO IT BEGINS.
THE DAWN OF A NEW AGE.
YAHH.
AND THE FIRST DAY OF NO PETER PARKER PRATTLING ABOUT IN THE BACK OF MY HEAD!
DOCTOR.
STATUS?
TARGETS 4 AND 6 ACQUIRED.
EXCELLENT.
FINALLY. I AM FREE TO BE THE MAN--
--OR RATHER THE SPIDER-MAN THAT I WANT TO BE.
WHITE DRAGON AND THE OWL. DECISIONS...
STATE THEIR LOCATIONS. WHICH IS CLOSER?
BOTH TARGETS ARE ON BAYARD STREET AND--
BOTH? EXPLAIN.
THEY HAVE ENGAGED EACH OTHER.
CLARIFY.
BEST DESCRIPTION OF CONFLICT: GANG WAR.
PARKER WAS EVER THE REACTIVE FOOL.
STUMBLING FROM ONE ADVENTURE TO THE NEXT. ALLOWING HIS ENEMIES TO MAKE THE FIRST MOVE.
SLURP.
I, ON THE OTHER HAND, WAIT ONLY WHEN IT SERVES ME.
LET THEM THIN OUT THEIR RANKS. ONCE THEY ARE SUITABLY WEAKENED--ONLY THEN SHALL I STRIKE!

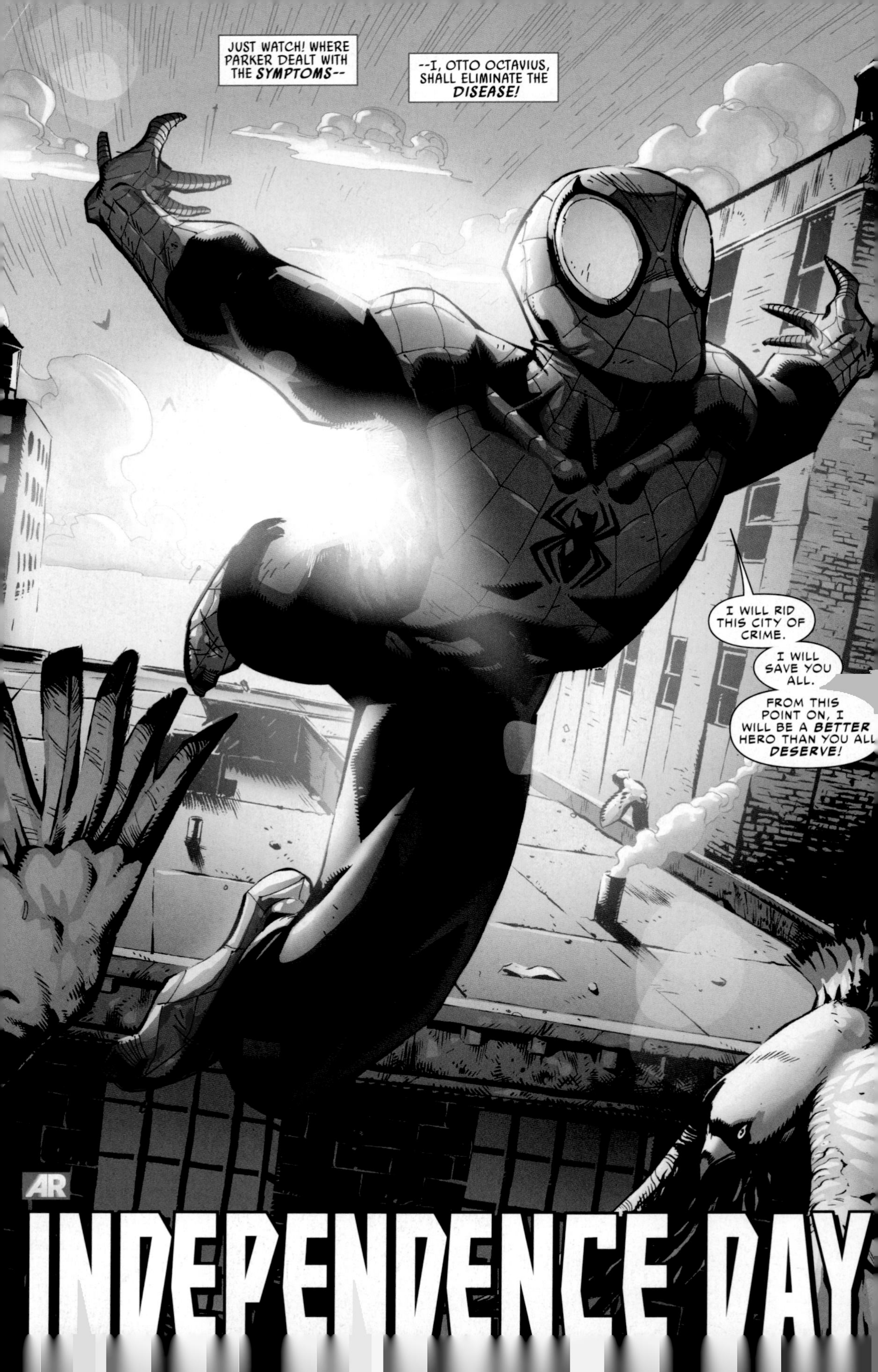
JUST WATCH! WHERE PARKER DEALT WITH THE *SYMPTOMS*--
--I, OTTO OCTAVIUS, SHALL ELIMINATE THE *DISEASE!*
I WILL RID THIS CITY OF CRIME.
I WILL SAVE YOU ALL.
FROM THIS POINT ON, I WILL BE A *BETTER* HERO THAN YOU ALL *DESERVE!*
AR
INDEPENDENCE DAY

YOU'VE OVERREACHED, OWLSLEY!

MOVING YOUR CHEAP NARCOTICS IN *MY* TERRITORY?! THIS GOES AGAINST ALL OF THE--

SILENCE! YOU HAVE *NO* CLAIM HERE!

THE *REAL* WHITE DRAGON PERISHED MONTHS AGO!

WHO ARE YOU? ONE OF KINGSLEY'S STAND-INS?!™

THE ORIGINAL HOBGOBLIN'S BEEN SELLING UNUSED SUPER VILLAIN IDENTITIES TO THE HIGHEST BIDDERS. SEE ASM #697 -STEVE.

IMPOSTER!

COME DOWN HERE, OWL.

I'LL SHOW YOU SOMETHING REAL.

WAK

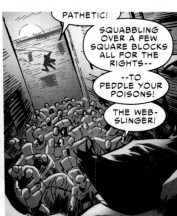

PATHETIC!

SQUABBLING OVER A FEW SQUARE BLOCKS ALL FOR THE RIGHTS--

--TO PEDDLE YOUR POISONS!

THE WEB-SLINGER!

I'LL HAVE *NONE* OF THAT!

KTAM

LET THIS SERVE AS A REMINDER...

SHK

...AND A WARNING...

SLSH

...FOR ANYONE STUPID ENOUGH...

SHRK

...TO BRING *THEIR* WARS...

FWSH

...TO MY *STREETS!*

TWOK

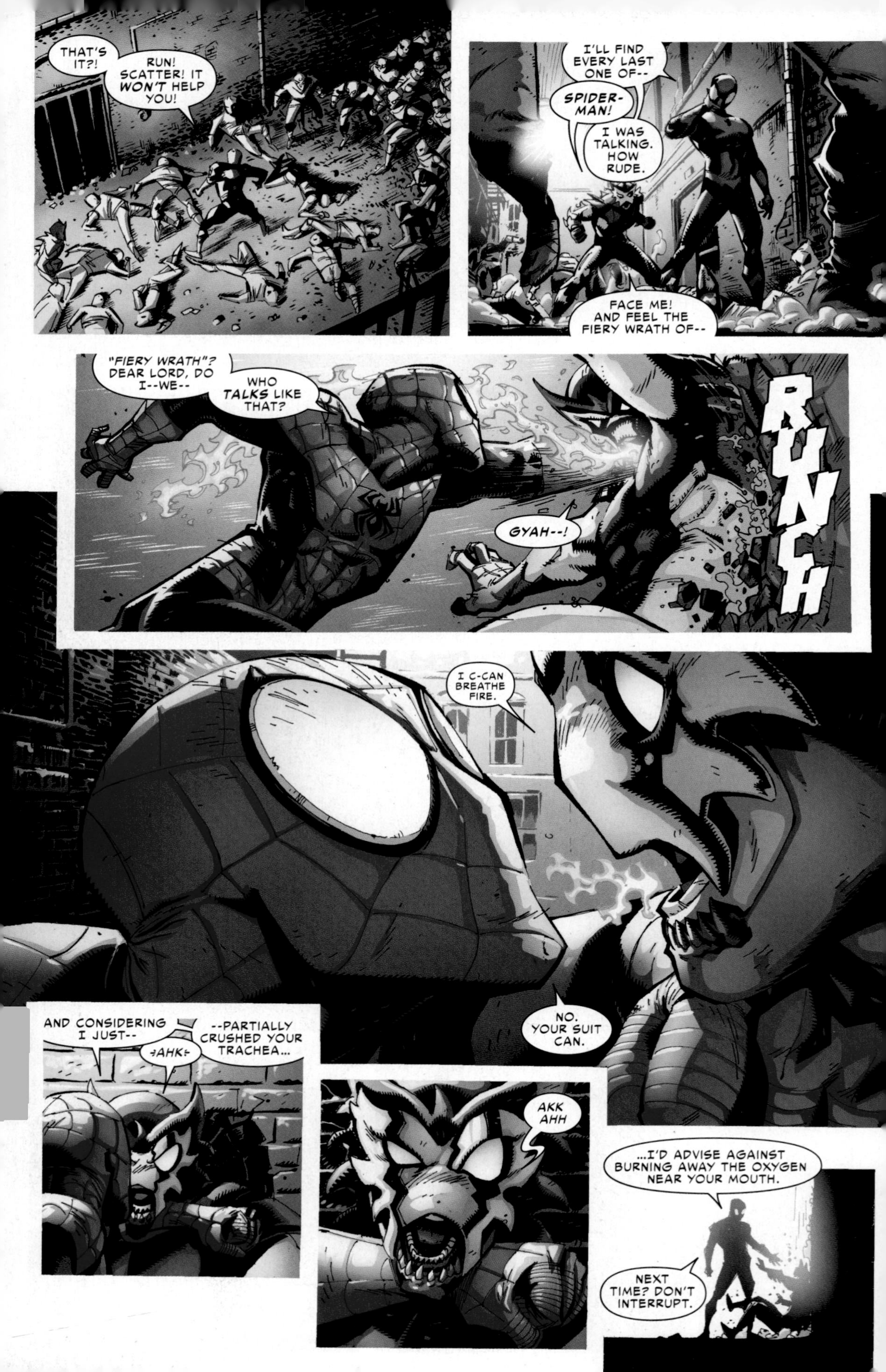
THAT'S IT?!
RUN! SCATTER! IT WON'T HELP YOU!
I'LL FIND EVERY LAST ONE OF--
SPIDER-MAN!
I WAS TALKING. HOW RUDE.
FACE ME! AND FEEL THE FIERY WRATH OF--
"FIERY WRATH"? DEAR LORD, DO I--WE--
WHO TALKS LIKE THAT?
GYAH--!
RUNCH
I C-CAN BREATHE FIRE.
NO. YOUR SUIT CAN.
AND CONSIDERING I JUST--
‹AHK›
--PARTIALLY CRUSHED YOUR TRACHEA...
AKK AHH
...I'D ADVISE AGAINST BURNING AWAY THE OXYGEN NEAR YOUR MOUTH.
NEXT TIME? DON'T INTERRUPT.

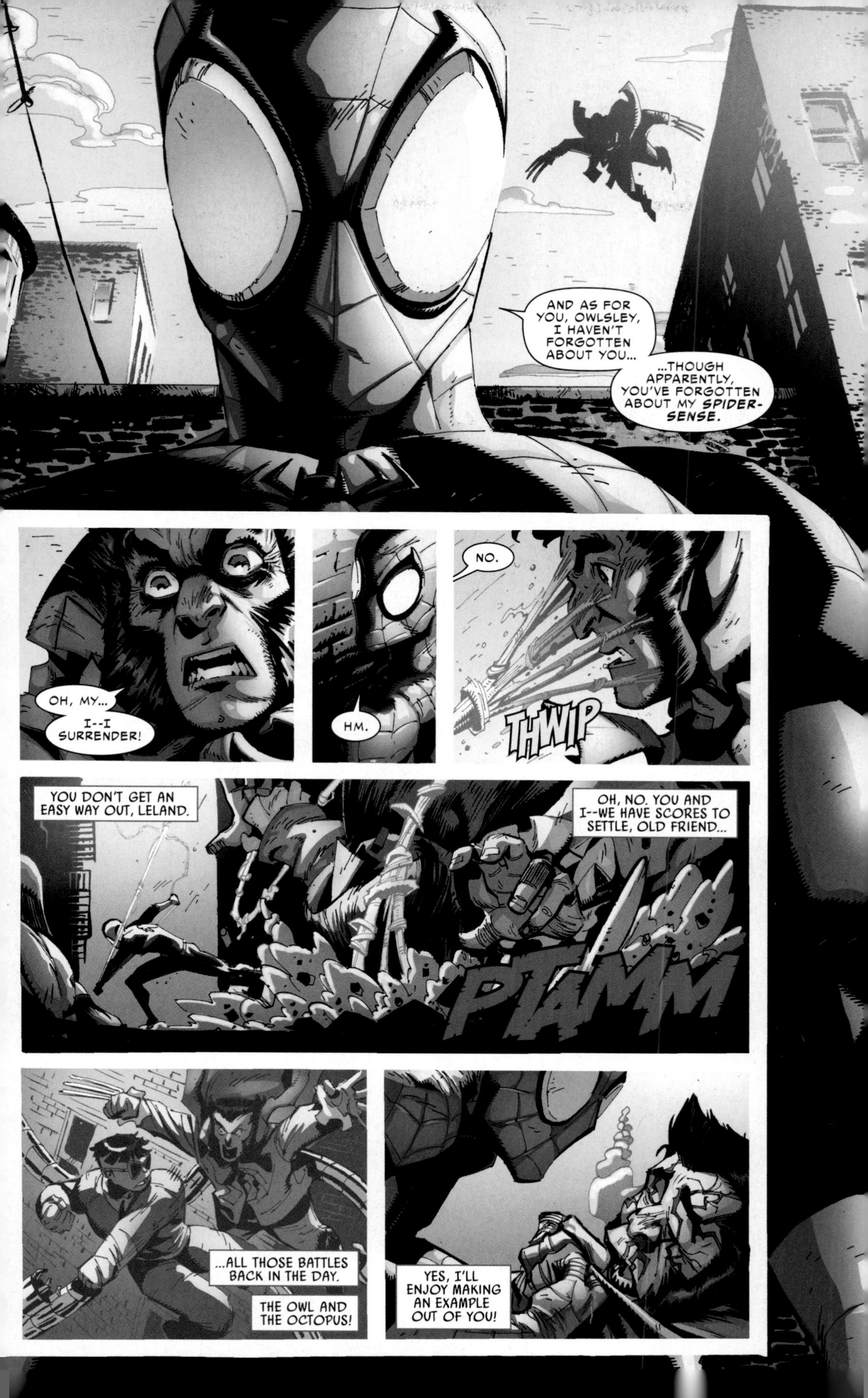

AND AS FOR YOU, OWLSLEY, I HAVEN'T FORGOTTEN ABOUT YOU...
...THOUGH APPARENTLY, YOU'VE FORGOTTEN ABOUT MY SPIDER-SENSE.
OH, MY... I--I SURRENDER!
HM.
NO.
THWIP
YOU DON'T GET AN EASY WAY OUT, LELAND.
OH, NO. YOU AND I--WE HAVE SCORES TO SETTLE, OLD FRIEND...
PTAMM
...ALL THOSE BATTLES BACK IN THE DAY.
THE OWL AND THE OCTOPUS!
YES, I'LL ENJOY MAKING AN EXAMPLE OUT OF YOU!

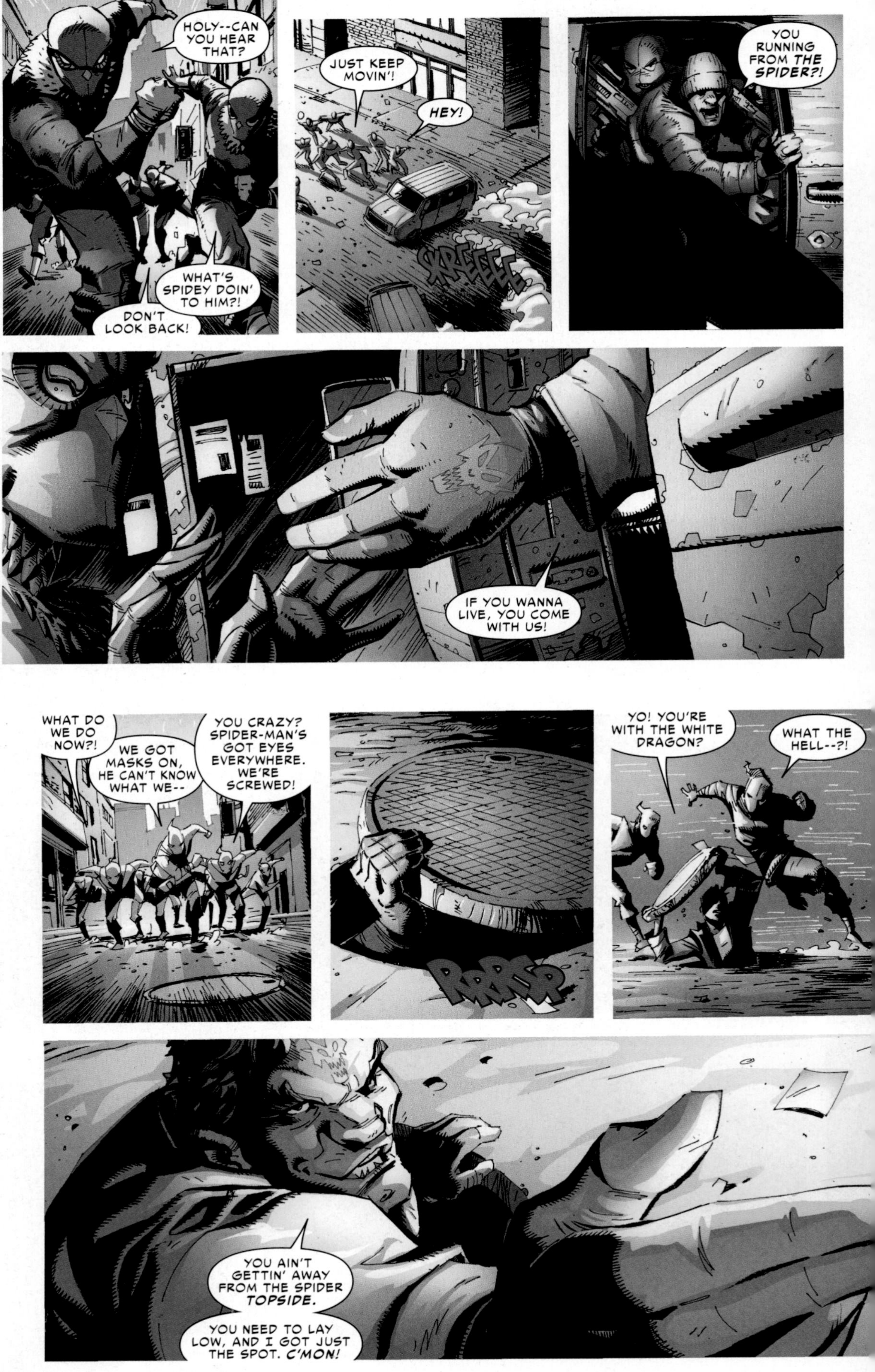
HOLY--CAN YOU HEAR THAT?
WHAT'S SPIDEY DOIN' TO HIM?!
DON'T LOOK BACK!
JUST KEEP MOVIN'!
HEY!
SKREEEEE
YOU RUNNING FROM *THE SPIDER?!*
IF YOU WANNA LIVE, YOU COME WITH US!
WHAT DO WE DO NOW?!
WE GOT MASKS ON, HE CAN'T KNOW WHAT WE--
YOU CRAZY? SPIDER-MAN'S GOT EYES EVERYWHERE. WE'RE SCREWED!
RRRSP
YO! YOU'RE WITH THE WHITE DRAGON?
WHAT THE HELL--?!
YOU AIN'T GETTIN' AWAY FROM THE SPIDER *TOPSIDE.*
YOU NEED TO LAY LOW, AND I GOT JUST THE SPOT. *C'MON!*

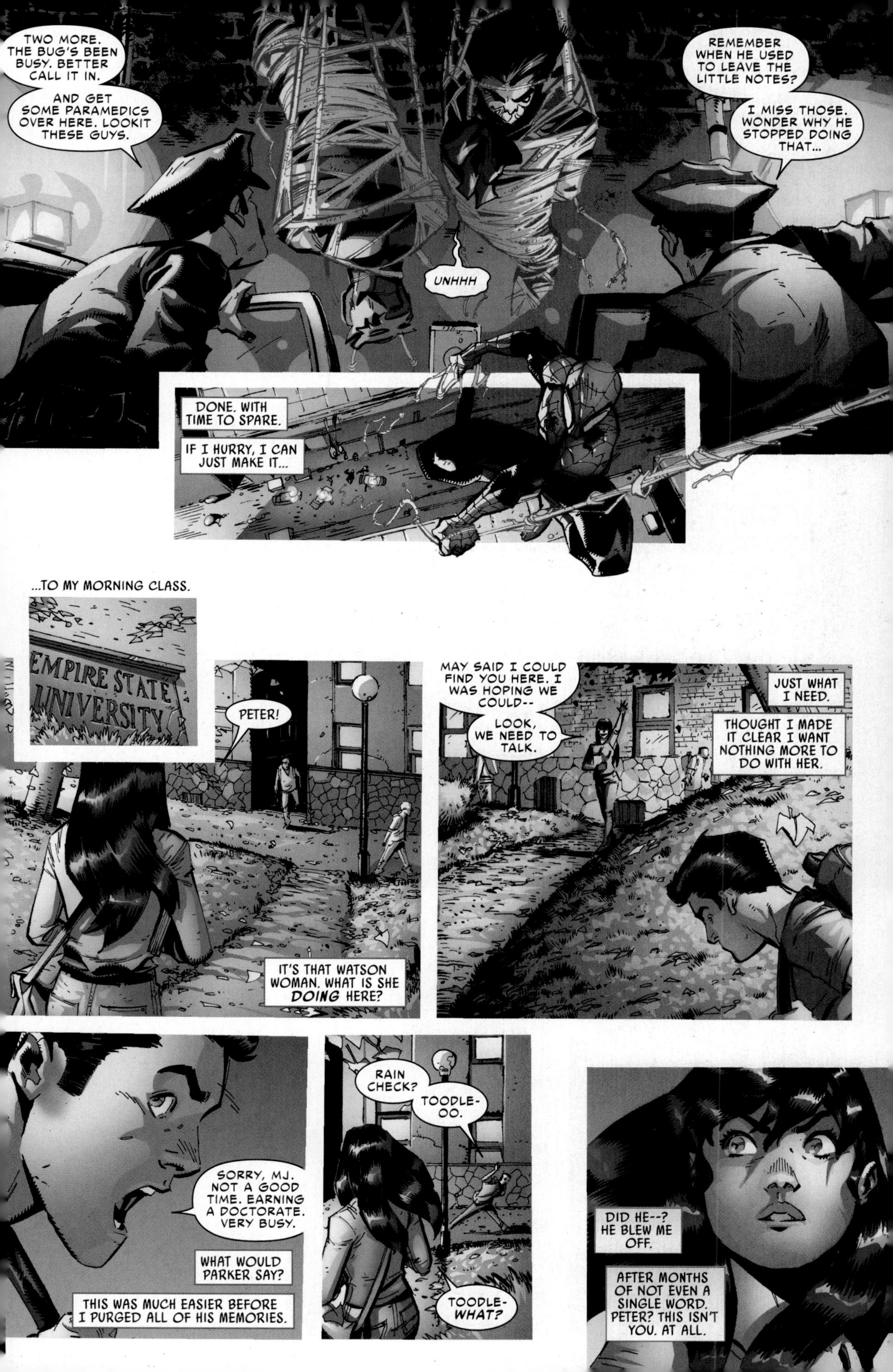

TWO MORE. THE BUG'S BEEN BUSY. BETTER CALL IT IN.
AND GET SOME PARAMEDICS OVER HERE. LOOKIT THESE GUYS.
REMEMBER WHEN HE USED TO LEAVE THE LITTLE NOTES?
I MISS THOSE. WONDER WHY HE STOPPED DOING THAT...
UNHHH
DONE. WITH TIME TO SPARE.
IF I HURRY, I CAN JUST MAKE IT...
...TO MY MORNING CLASS.
EMPIRE STATE UNIVERSITY
PETER!
IT'S THAT WATSON WOMAN. WHAT IS SHE DOING HERE?
MAY SAID I COULD FIND YOU HERE. I WAS HOPING WE COULD--
LOOK, WE NEED TO TALK.
JUST WHAT I NEED.
THOUGHT I MADE IT CLEAR I WANT NOTHING MORE TO DO WITH HER.
SORRY, MJ. NOT A GOOD TIME. EARNING A DOCTORATE. VERY BUSY.
WHAT WOULD PARKER SAY?
THIS WAS MUCH EASIER BEFORE I PURGED ALL OF HIS MEMORIES.
RAIN CHECK?
TOODLE-OO.
TOODLE-WHAT?
DID HE--? HE BLEW ME OFF.
AFTER MONTHS OF NOT EVEN A SINGLE WORD. PETER? THIS ISN'T YOU. AT ALL.

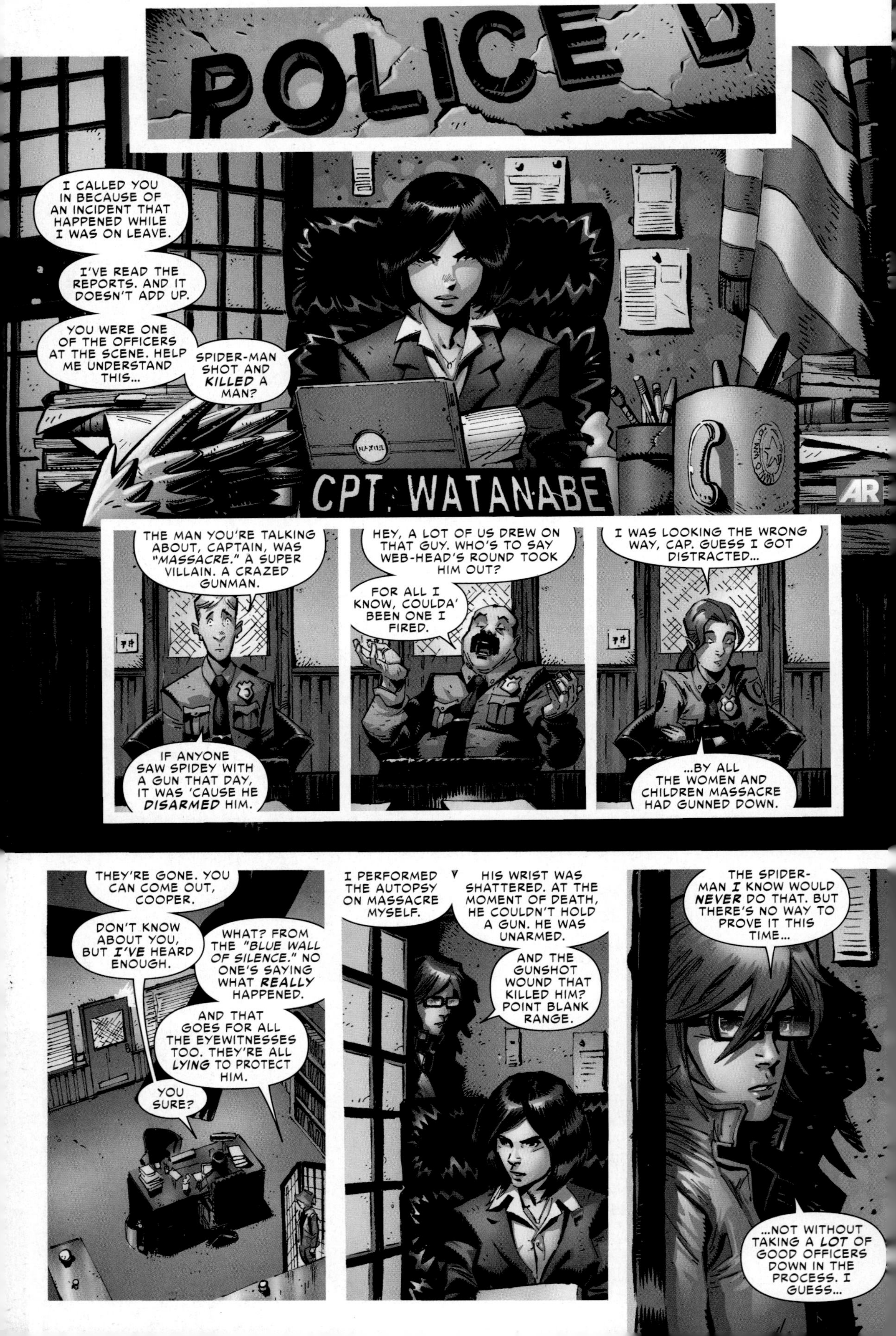
POLICE D
I CALLED YOU IN BECAUSE OF AN INCIDENT THAT HAPPENED WHILE I WAS ON LEAVE.
I'VE READ THE REPORTS. AND IT DOESN'T ADD UP.
YOU WERE ONE OF THE OFFICERS AT THE SCENE. HELP ME UNDERSTAND THIS...
SPIDER-MAN SHOT AND *KILLED* A MAN?
CPT. WATANABE
THE MAN YOU'RE TALKING ABOUT, CAPTAIN, WAS "*MASSACRE.*" A SUPER VILLAIN. A CRAZED GUNMAN.
IF ANYONE SAW SPIDEY WITH A GUN THAT DAY, IT WAS 'CAUSE HE *DISARMED* HIM.
HEY, A LOT OF US DREW ON THAT GUY. WHO'S TO SAY WEB-HEAD'S ROUND TOOK HIM OUT?
FOR ALL I KNOW, COULDA' BEEN ONE I FIRED.
I WAS LOOKING THE WRONG WAY, CAP. GUESS I GOT DISTRACTED...
...BY ALL THE WOMEN AND CHILDREN MASSACRE HAD GUNNED DOWN.
THEY'RE GONE. YOU CAN COME OUT, COOPER.
DON'T KNOW ABOUT YOU, BUT *I'VE* HEARD ENOUGH.
WHAT? FROM THE *"BLUE WALL OF SILENCE."* NO ONE'S SAYING WHAT *REALLY* HAPPENED.
AND THAT GOES FOR ALL THE EYEWITNESSES TOO. THEY'RE ALL *LYING* TO PROTECT HIM.
YOU SURE?
I PERFORMED THE AUTOPSY ON MASSACRE MYSELF.
HIS WRIST WAS SHATTERED. AT THE MOMENT OF DEATH, HE COULDN'T HOLD A GUN. HE WAS UNARMED.
AND THE GUNSHOT WOUND THAT KILLED HIM? POINT BLANK RANGE.
THE SPIDER-MAN *I* KNOW WOULD *NEVER* DO THAT. BUT THERE'S NO WAY TO PROVE IT THIS TIME...
...NOT WITHOUT TAKING A *LOT* OF GOOD OFFICERS DOWN IN THE PROCESS. I GUESS...

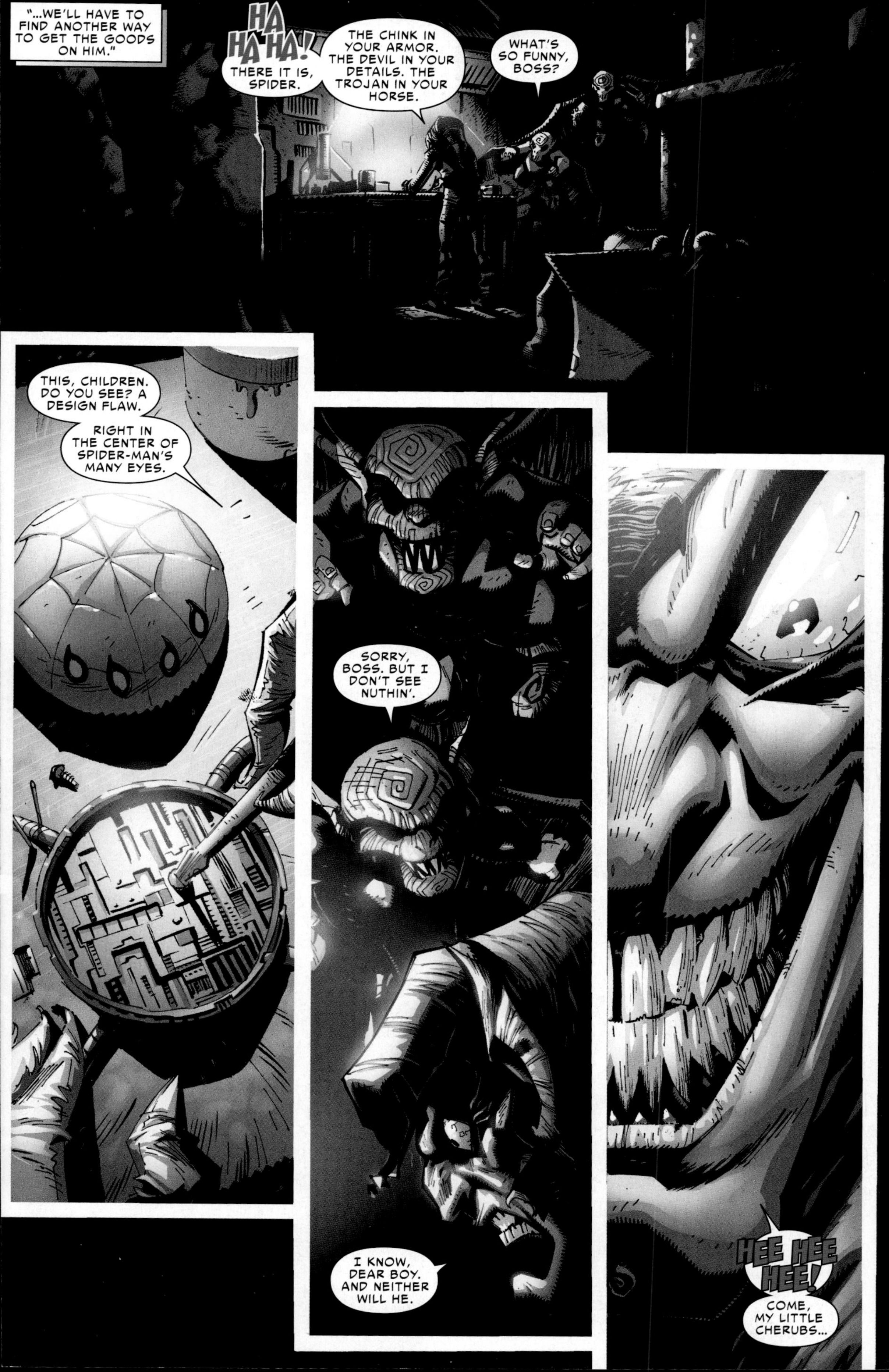
"...WE'LL HAVE TO FIND ANOTHER WAY TO GET THE GOODS ON HIM."
HA HA HA!
THERE IT IS, SPIDER.
THE CHINK IN YOUR ARMOR. THE DEVIL IN YOUR DETAILS. THE TROJAN IN YOUR HORSE.
WHAT'S SO FUNNY, BOSS?
THIS, CHILDREN. DO YOU SEE? A DESIGN FLAW.
RIGHT IN THE CENTER OF SPIDER-MAN'S MANY EYES.
SORRY, BOSS. BUT I DON'T SEE NUTHIN'.
I KNOW, DEAR BOY. AND NEITHER WILL HE.
HEE HEE HEE!
COME, MY LITTLE CHERUBS...

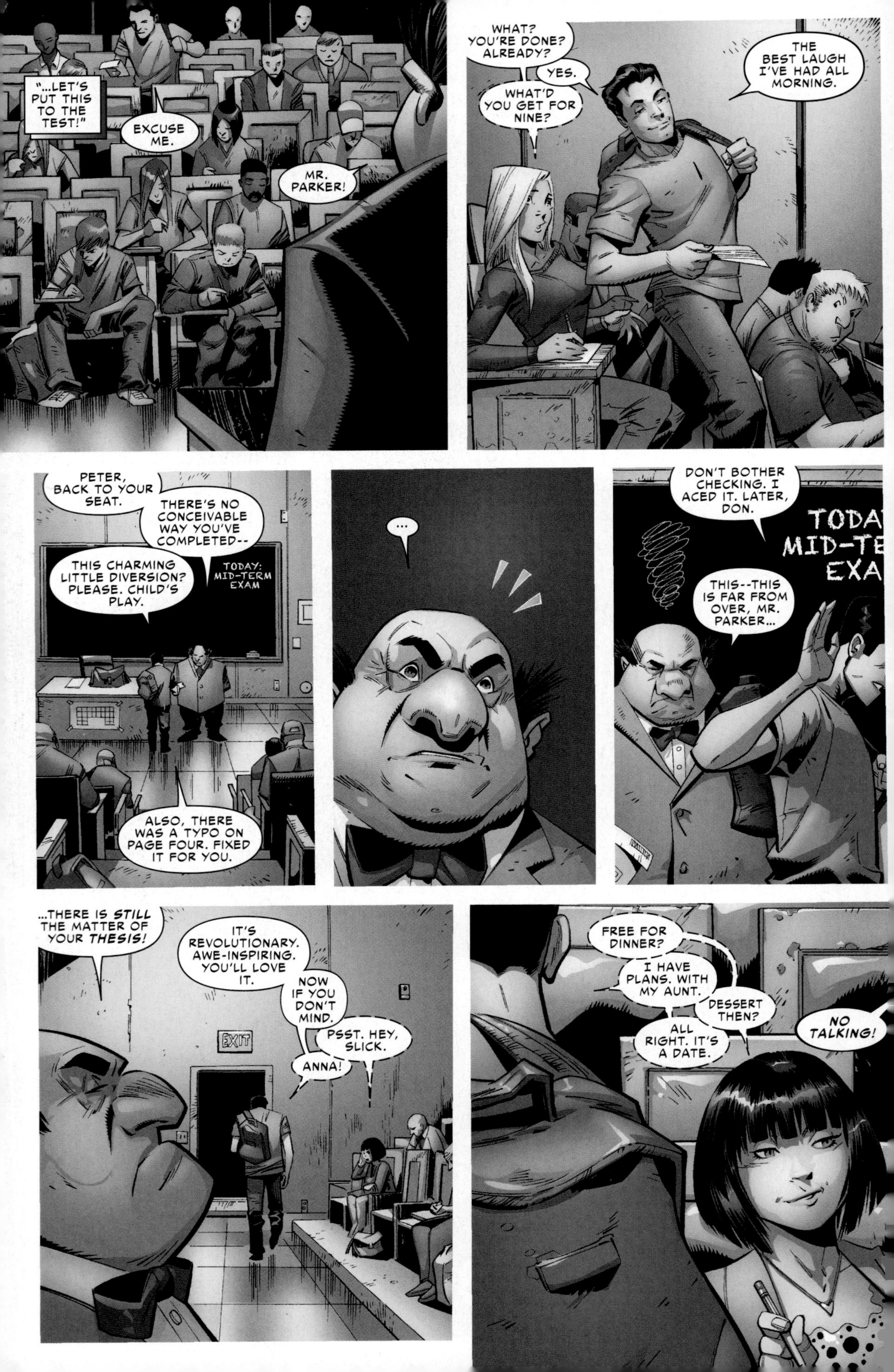
"...LET'S PUT THIS TO THE TEST!"
EXCUSE ME.
MR. PARKER!
WHAT? YOU'RE DONE? ALREADY?
YES.
WHAT'D YOU GET FOR NINE?
THE BEST LAUGH I'VE HAD ALL MORNING.
PETER, BACK TO YOUR SEAT.
THERE'S NO CONCEIVABLE WAY YOU'VE COMPLETED--
THIS CHARMING LITTLE DIVERSION? PLEASE. CHILD'S PLAY.
TODAY: MID-TERM EXAM
ALSO, THERE WAS A TYPO ON PAGE FOUR. FIXED IT FOR YOU.
...
DON'T BOTHER CHECKING. I ACED IT. LATER, DON.
THIS--THIS IS FAR FROM OVER, MR. PARKER...
...THERE IS STILL THE MATTER OF YOUR THESIS!
IT'S REVOLUTIONARY. AWE-INSPIRING. YOU'LL LOVE IT.
NOW IF YOU DON'T MIND.
PSST. HEY, SLICK.
ANNA!
EXIT
FREE FOR DINNER?
I HAVE PLANS. WITH MY AUNT.
DESSERT THEN?
ALL RIGHT. IT'S A DATE.
NO TALKING!

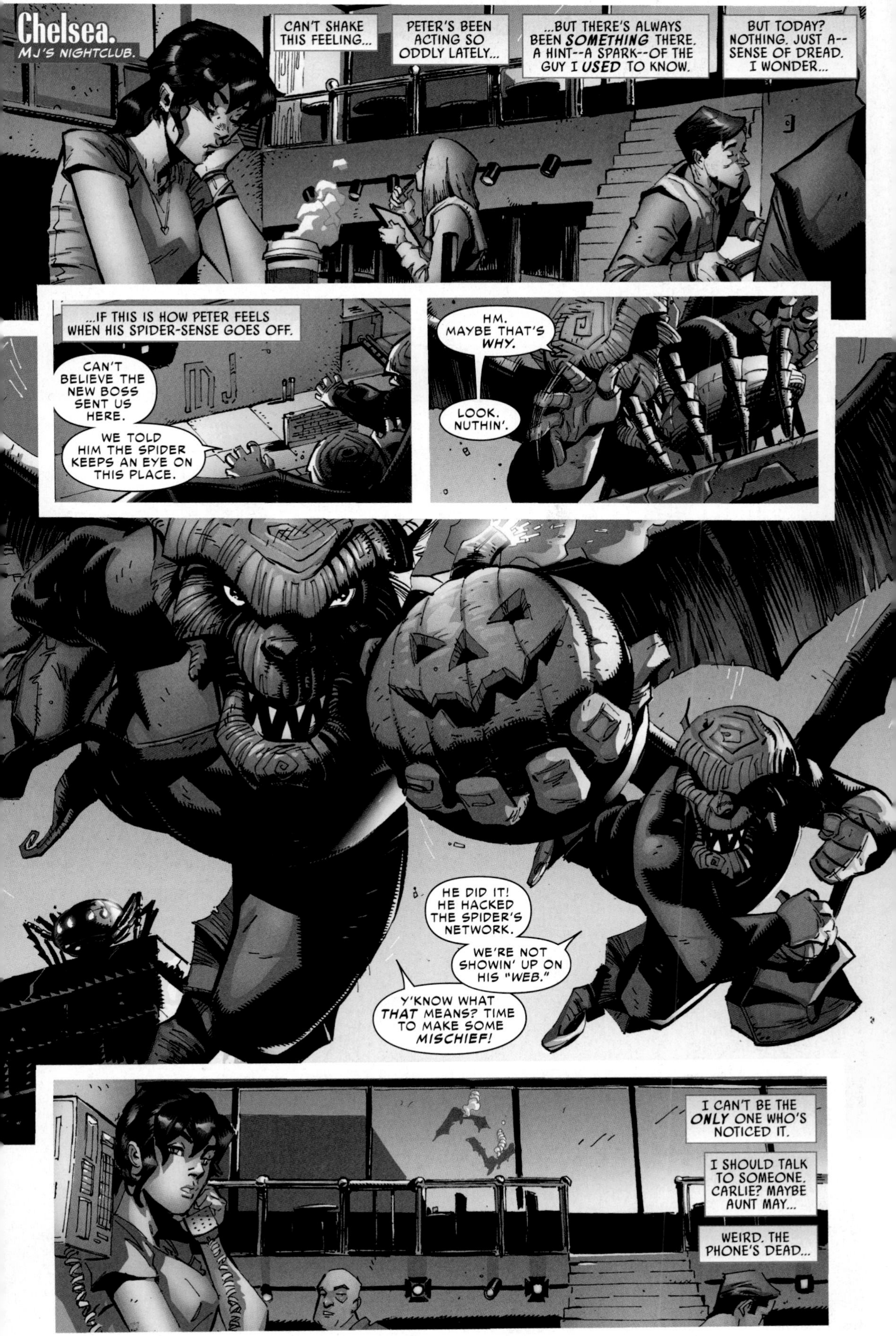
Chelsea.
MJ's NIGHTCLUB.
CAN'T SHAKE THIS FEELING...
PETER'S BEEN ACTING SO ODDLY LATELY...
...BUT THERE'S ALWAYS BEEN SOMETHING THERE. A HINT--A SPARK--OF THE GUY I USED TO KNOW.
BUT TODAY? NOTHING. JUST A-- SENSE OF DREAD. I WONDER...
...IF THIS IS HOW PETER FEELS WHEN HIS SPIDER-SENSE GOES OFF.
CAN'T BELIEVE THE NEW BOSS SENT US HERE.
WE TOLD HIM THE SPIDER KEEPS AN EYE ON THIS PLACE.
HM. MAYBE THAT'S WHY.
LOOK. NUTHIN'.
HE DID IT! HE HACKED THE SPIDER'S NETWORK.
WE'RE NOT SHOWIN' UP ON HIS "WEB."
Y'KNOW WHAT THAT MEANS? TIME TO MAKE SOME MISCHIEF!
I CAN'T BE THE ONLY ONE WHO'S NOTICED IT.
I SHOULD TALK TO SOMEONE. CARLIE? MAYBE AUNT MAY...
WEIRD. THE PHONE'S DEAD...

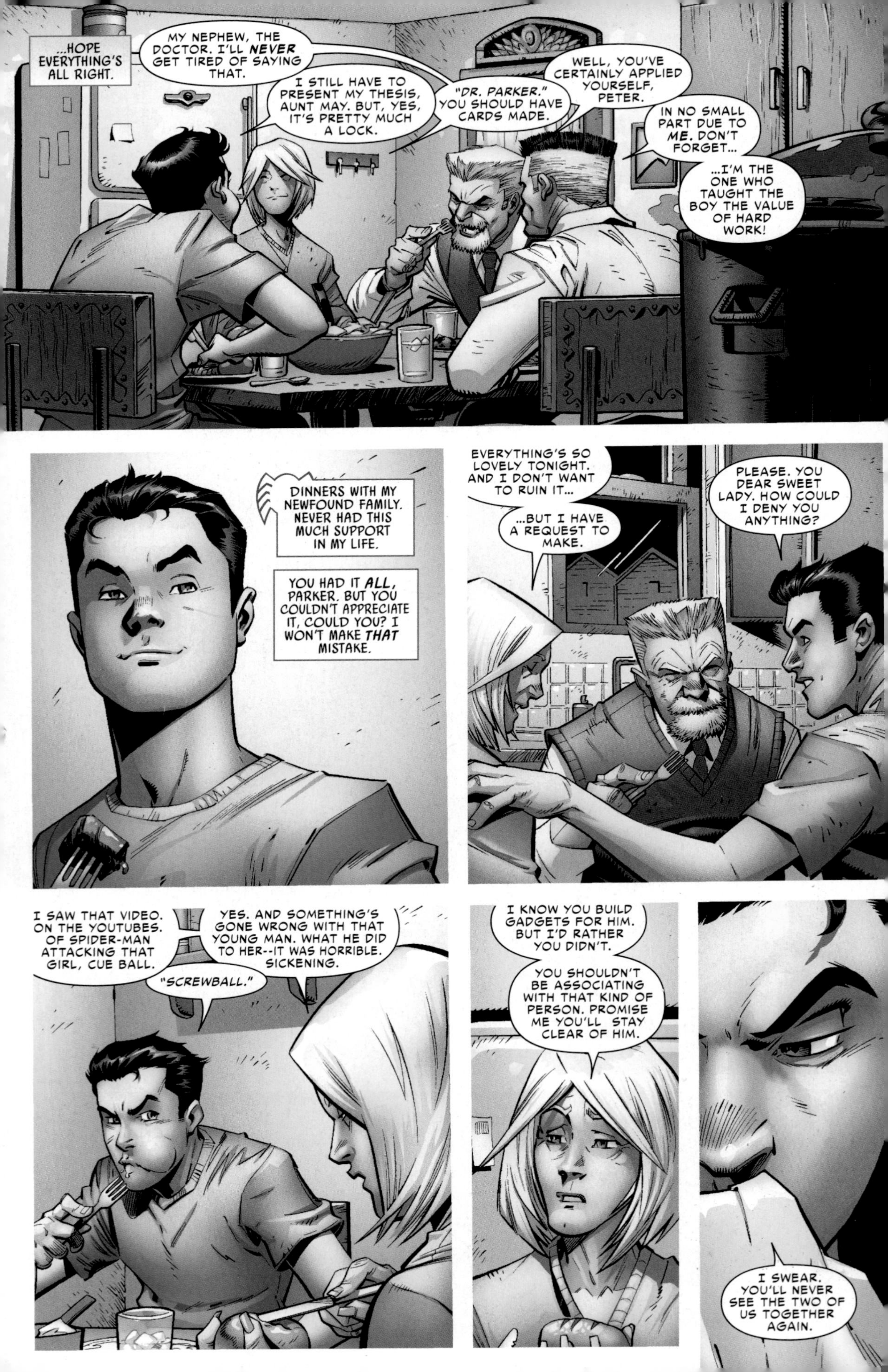
...HOPE EVERYTHING'S ALL RIGHT.
MY NEPHEW, THE DOCTOR. I'LL NEVER GET TIRED OF SAYING THAT.
I STILL HAVE TO PRESENT MY THESIS, AUNT MAY. BUT, YES, IT'S PRETTY MUCH A LOCK.
"DR. PARKER." YOU SHOULD HAVE CARDS MADE.
WELL, YOU'VE CERTAINLY APPLIED YOURSELF, PETER.
IN NO SMALL PART DUE TO ME. DON'T FORGET...
...I'M THE ONE WHO TAUGHT THE BOY THE VALUE OF HARD WORK!
DINNERS WITH MY NEWFOUND FAMILY. NEVER HAD THIS MUCH SUPPORT IN MY LIFE.
YOU HAD IT ALL, PARKER. BUT YOU COULDN'T APPRECIATE IT, COULD YOU? I WON'T MAKE THAT MISTAKE.
EVERYTHING'S SO LOVELY TONIGHT. AND I DON'T WANT TO RUIN IT...
...BUT I HAVE A REQUEST TO MAKE.
PLEASE. YOU DEAR SWEET LADY. HOW COULD I DENY YOU ANYTHING?
I SAW THAT VIDEO. ON THE YOUTUBES. OF SPIDER-MAN ATTACKING THAT GIRL, CUE BALL.
"SCREWBALL."
YES. AND SOMETHING'S GONE WRONG WITH THAT YOUNG MAN. WHAT HE DID TO HER--IT WAS HORRIBLE. SICKENING.
I KNOW YOU BUILD GADGETS FOR HIM. BUT I'D RATHER YOU DIDN'T.
YOU SHOULDN'T BE ASSOCIATING WITH THAT KIND OF PERSON. PROMISE ME YOU'LL STAY CLEAR OF HIM.
I SWEAR. YOU'LL NEVER SEE THE TWO OF US TOGETHER AGAIN.

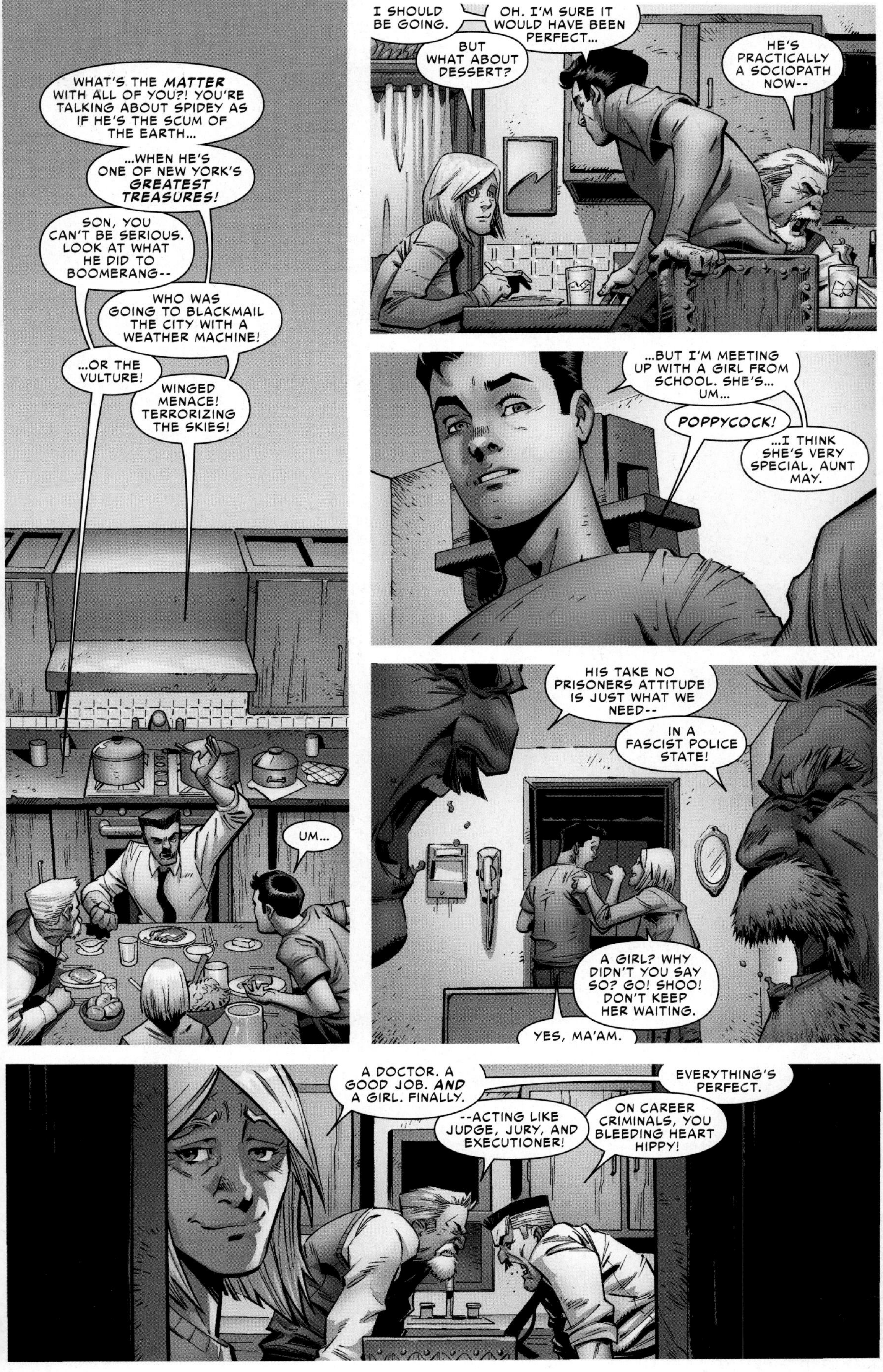
WHAT'S THE MATTER WITH ALL OF YOU?! YOU'RE TALKING ABOUT SPIDEY AS IF HE'S THE SCUM OF THE EARTH...
...WHEN HE'S ONE OF NEW YORK'S GREATEST TREASURES!
SON, YOU CAN'T BE SERIOUS. LOOK AT WHAT HE DID TO BOOMERANG--
WHO WAS GOING TO BLACKMAIL THE CITY WITH A WEATHER MACHINE!
...OR THE VULTURE!
WINGED MENACE! TERRORIZING THE SKIES!
UM...
I SHOULD BE GOING.
OH. I'M SURE IT WOULD HAVE BEEN PERFECT...
BUT WHAT ABOUT DESSERT?
HE'S PRACTICALLY A SOCIOPATH NOW--
...BUT I'M MEETING UP WITH A GIRL FROM SCHOOL. SHE'S... UM...
POPPYCOCK!
...I THINK SHE'S VERY SPECIAL, AUNT MAY.
HIS TAKE NO PRISONERS ATTITUDE IS JUST WHAT WE NEED--
IN A FASCIST POLICE STATE!
A GIRL? WHY DIDN'T YOU SAY SO? GO! SHOO! DON'T KEEP HER WAITING.
YES, MA'AM.
A DOCTOR. A GOOD JOB. AND A GIRL. FINALLY.
EVERYTHING'S PERFECT.
--ACTING LIKE JUDGE, JURY, AND EXECUTIONER!
ON CAREER CRIMINALS, YOU BLEEDING HEART HIPPY!

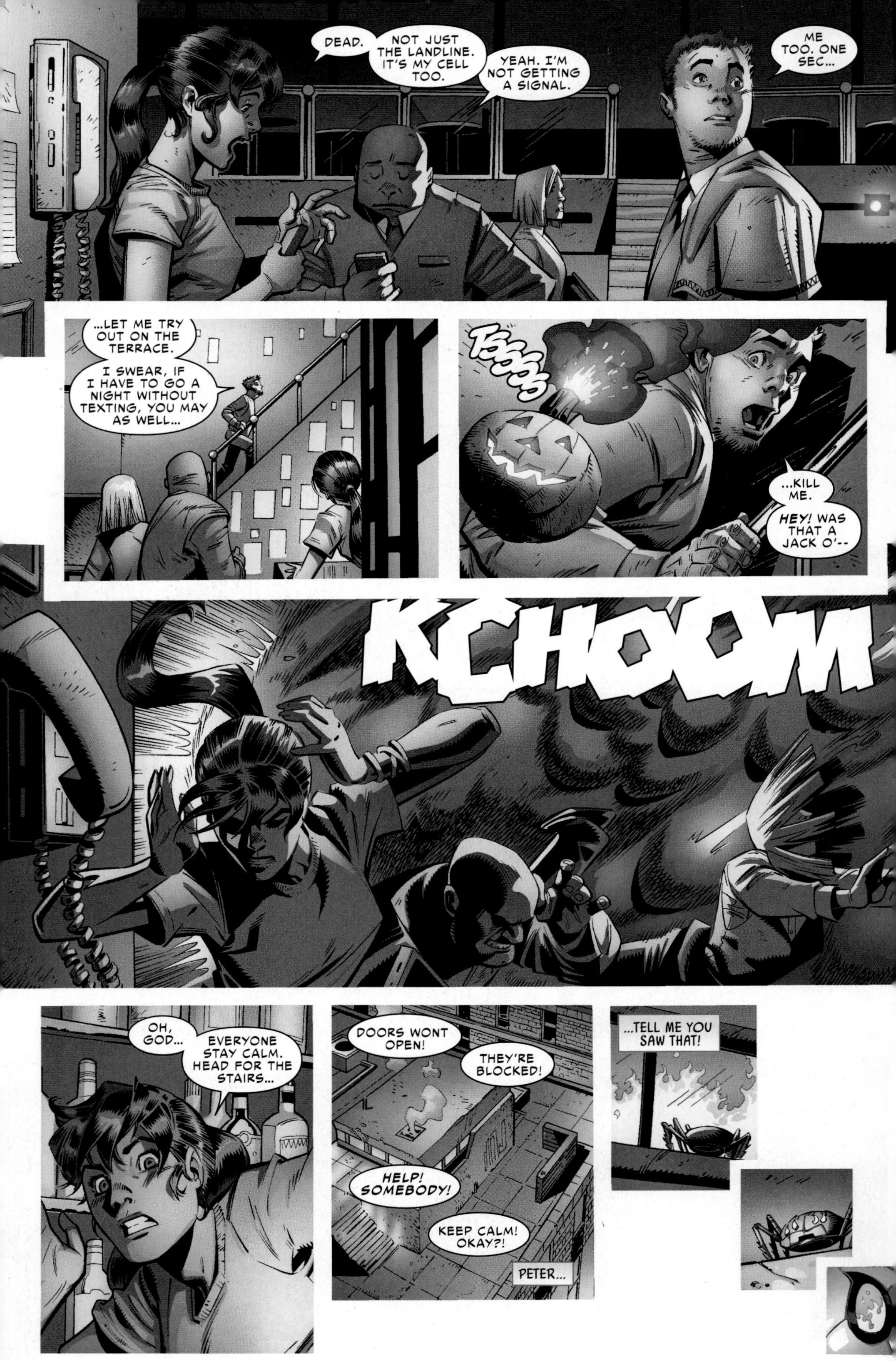
DEAD.
NOT JUST THE LANDLINE. IT'S MY CELL TOO.
YEAH. I'M NOT GETTING A SIGNAL.
ME TOO. ONE SEC...
...LET ME TRY OUT ON THE TERRACE.
I SWEAR, IF I HAVE TO GO A NIGHT WITHOUT TEXTING, YOU MAY AS WELL...
TSSSSS
...KILL ME.
HEY! WAS THAT A JACK O'--
KCHOOM
OH, GOD...
EVERYONE STAY CALM. HEAD FOR THE STAIRS...
DOORS WONT OPEN!
THEY'RE BLOCKED!
HELP! SOMEBODY!
KEEP CALM! OKAY?!
PETER...
...TELL ME YOU SAW THAT!

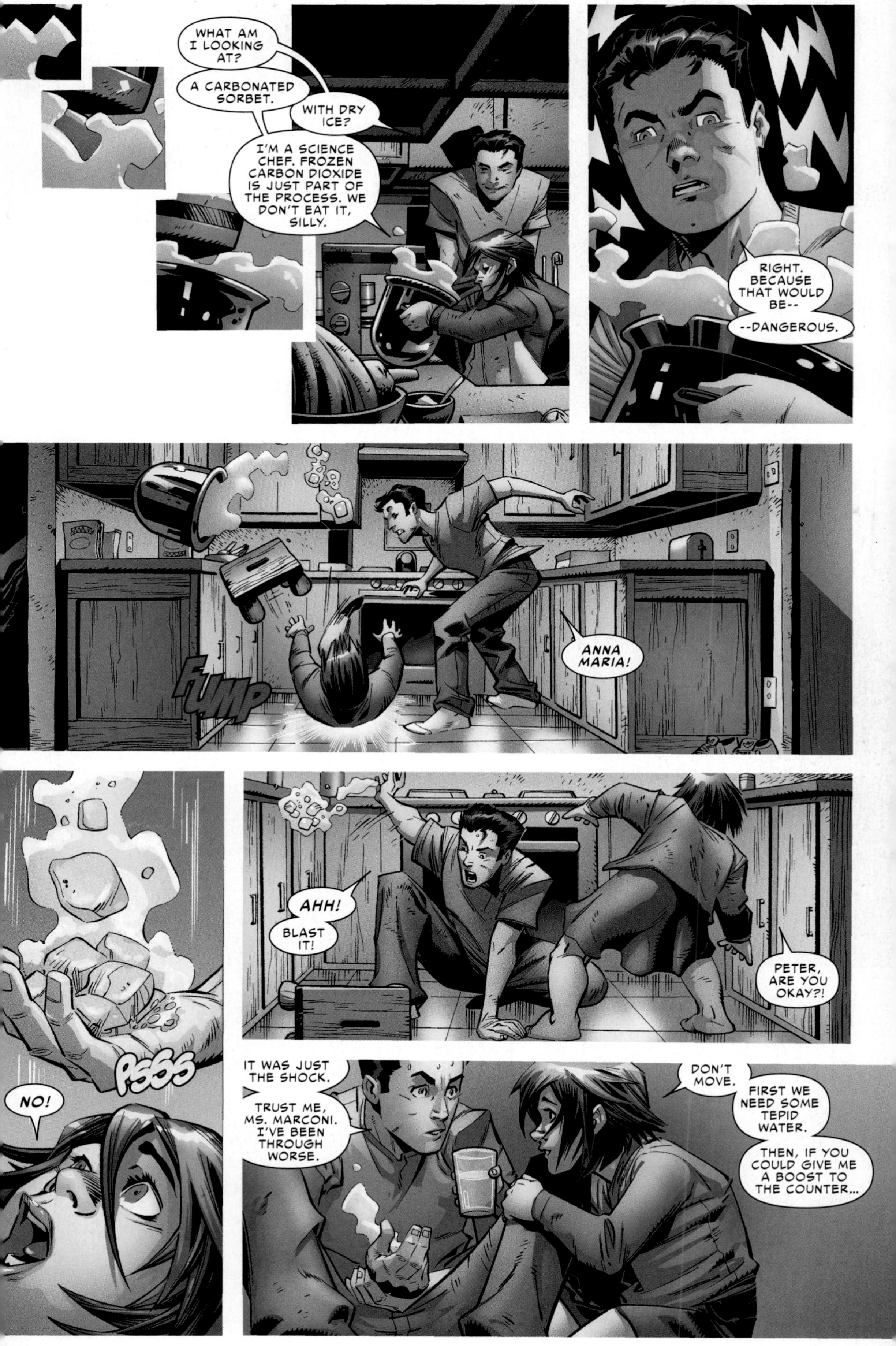
WHAT AM I LOOKING AT?
A CARBONATED SORBET.
WITH DRY ICE?
I'M A SCIENCE CHEF. FROZEN CARBON DIOXIDE IS JUST PART OF THE PROCESS. WE DON'T EAT IT, SILLY.
RIGHT. BECAUSE THAT WOULD BE--
--DANGEROUS.
FLUMP
ANNA MARIA!
PSSS
NO!
AHH!
BLAST IT!
PETER, ARE YOU OKAY?!
IT WAS JUST THE SHOCK.
TRUST ME, MS. MARCONI. I'VE BEEN THROUGH WORSE.
DON'T MOVE.
FIRST WE NEED SOME TEPID WATER.
THEN, IF YOU COULD GIVE ME A BOOST TO THE COUNTER...

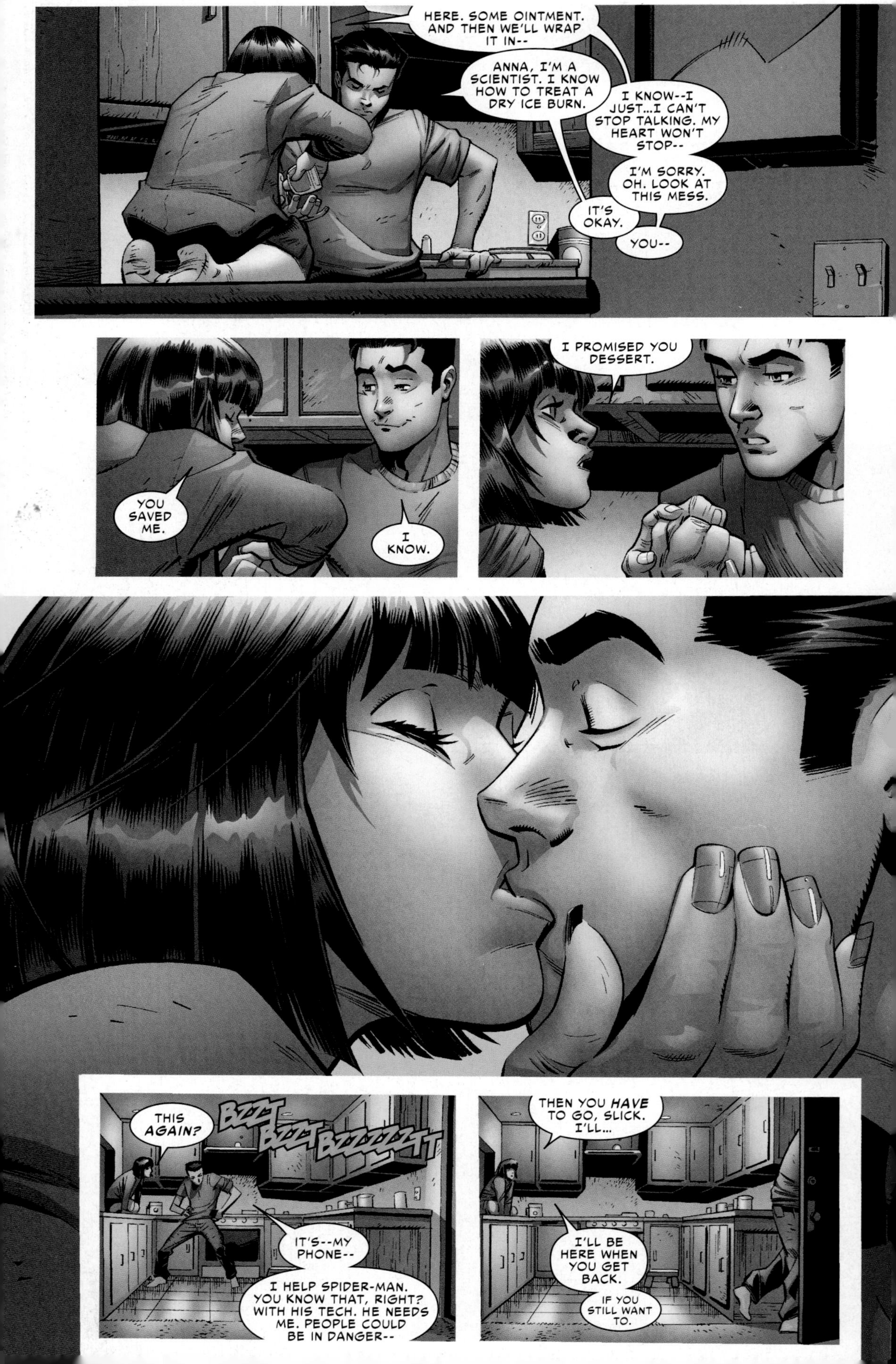
HERE. SOME OINTMENT. AND THEN WE'LL WRAP IT IN--
ANNA, I'M A SCIENTIST. I KNOW HOW TO TREAT A DRY ICE BURN.
I KNOW--I JUST...I CAN'T STOP TALKING. MY HEART WON'T STOP--
I'M SORRY. OH. LOOK AT THIS MESS.
IT'S OKAY.
YOU--
YOU SAVED ME.
I KNOW.
I PROMISED YOU DESSERT.
THIS AGAIN?
BZZZT BZZZT BZZZZZZZT
IT'S--MY PHONE--
I HELP SPIDER-MAN. YOU KNOW THAT, RIGHT? WITH HIS TECH. HE NEEDS ME. PEOPLE COULD BE IN DANGER--
THEN YOU HAVE TO GO, SLICK. I'LL...
I'LL BE HERE WHEN YOU GET BACK.
IF YOU STILL WANT TO.

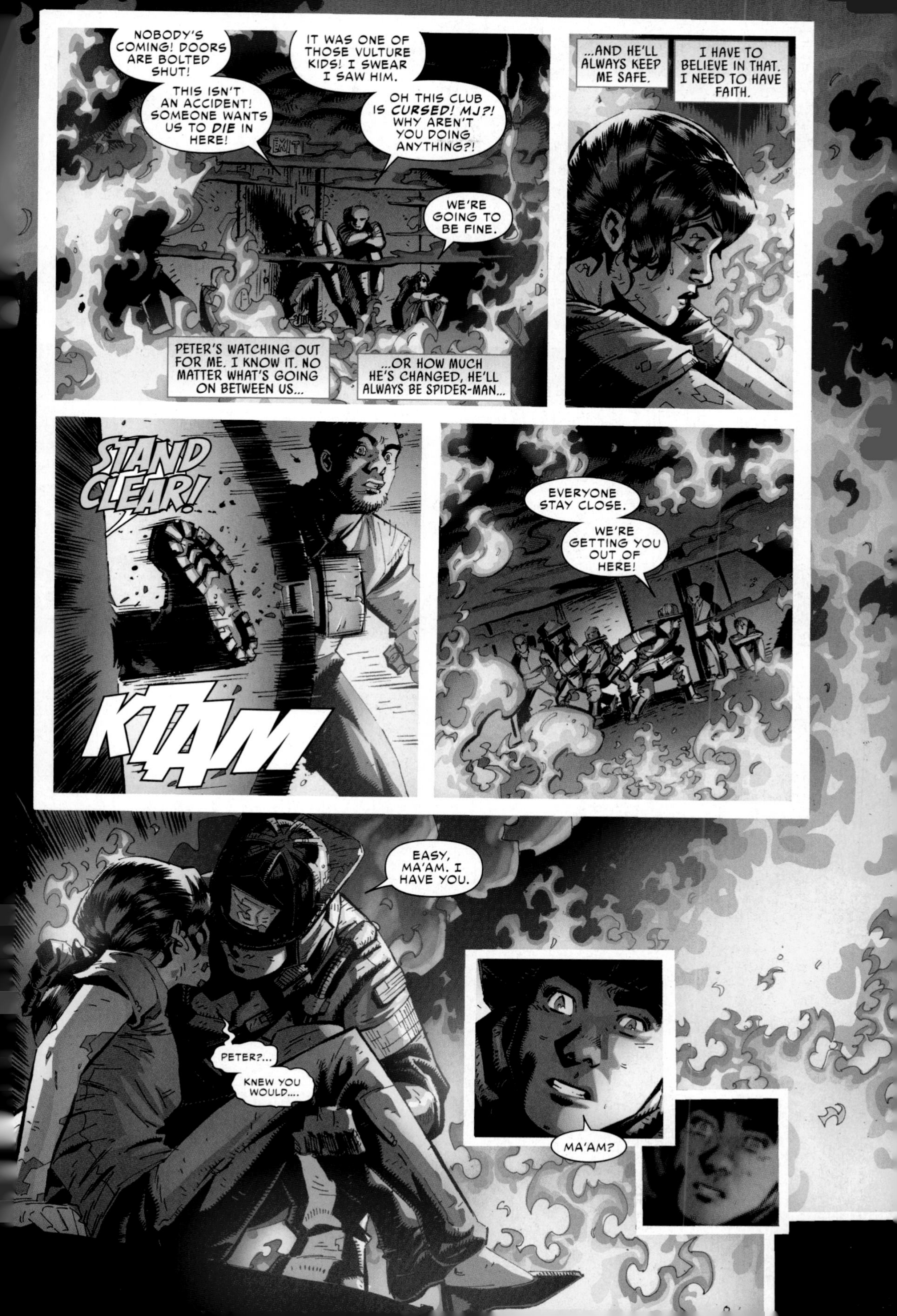
NOBODY'S COMING! DOORS ARE BOLTED SHUT!
THIS ISN'T AN ACCIDENT! SOMEONE WANTS US TO DIE IN HERE!
IT WAS ONE OF THOSE VULTURE KIDS! I SWEAR I SAW HIM.
OH THIS CLUB IS CURSED! MJ?! WHY AREN'T YOU DOING ANYTHING?!
WE'RE GOING TO BE FINE.
PETER'S WATCHING OUT FOR ME. I KNOW IT. NO MATTER WHAT'S GOING ON BETWEEN US...
...OR HOW MUCH HE'S CHANGED, HE'LL ALWAYS BE SPIDER-MAN...
...AND HE'LL ALWAYS KEEP ME SAFE.
I HAVE TO BELIEVE IN THAT. I NEED TO HAVE FAITH.
STAND CLEAR!
KTAM
EVERYONE STAY CLOSE.
WE'RE GETTING YOU OUT OF HERE!
EASY, MA'AM. I HAVE YOU.
PETER?...
KNEW YOU WOULD....
MA'AM?

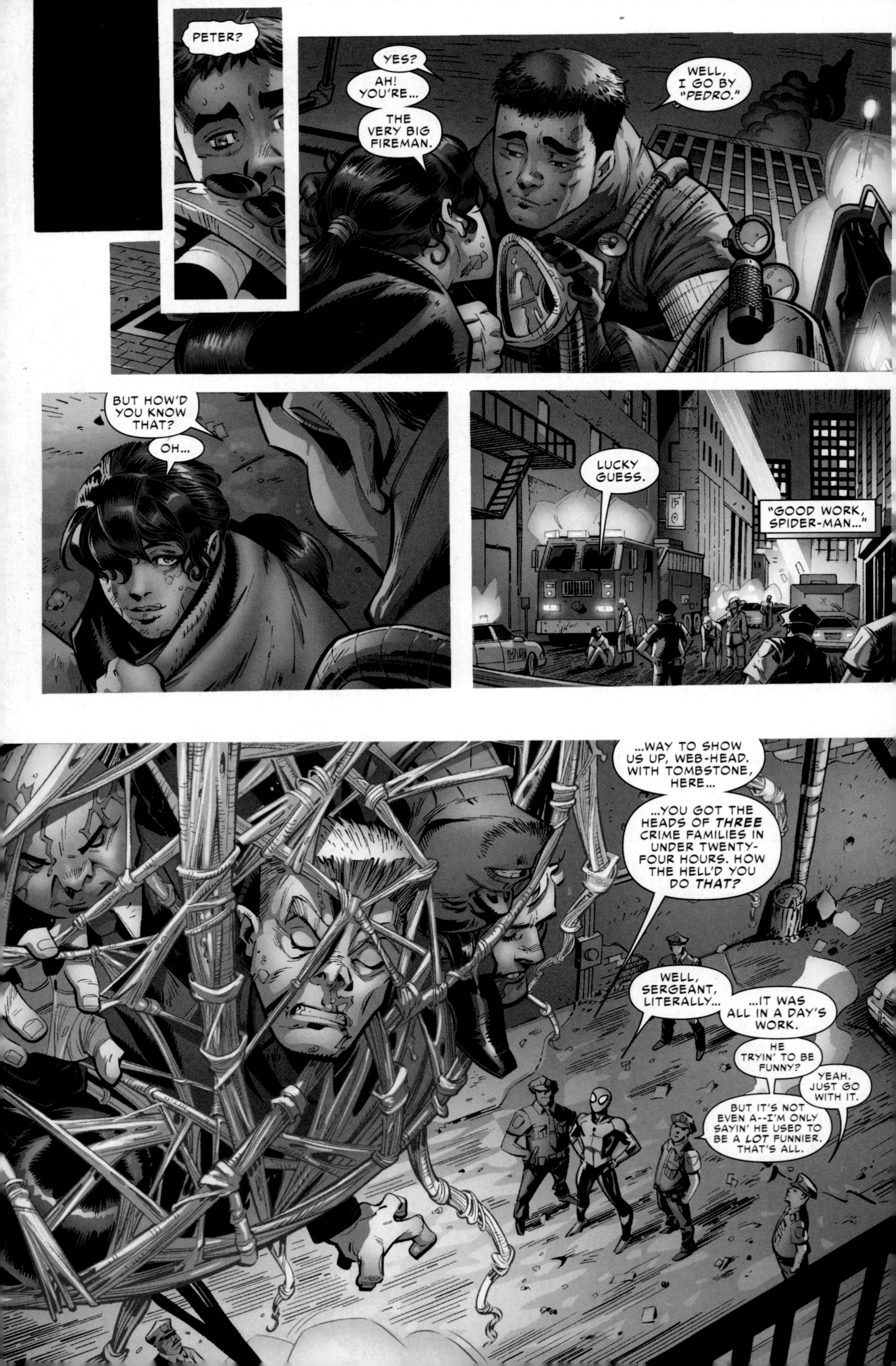
PETER?
YES?
AH! YOU'RE...
THE VERY BIG FIREMAN.
WELL, I GO BY "PEDRO."
BUT HOW'D YOU KNOW THAT?
OH...
LUCKY GUESS.
"GOOD WORK, SPIDER-MAN..."
...WAY TO SHOW US UP, WEB-HEAD. WITH TOMBSTONE, HERE...
...YOU GOT THE HEADS OF THREE CRIME FAMILIES IN UNDER TWENTY-FOUR HOURS. HOW THE HELL'D YOU DO THAT?
WELL, SERGEANT, LITERALLY...
...IT WAS ALL IN A DAY'S WORK.
HE TRYIN' TO BE FUNNY?
YEAH. JUST GO WITH IT.
BUT IT'S NOT EVEN A--I'M ONLY SAYIN' HE USED TO BE A LOT FUNNIER. THAT'S ALL.

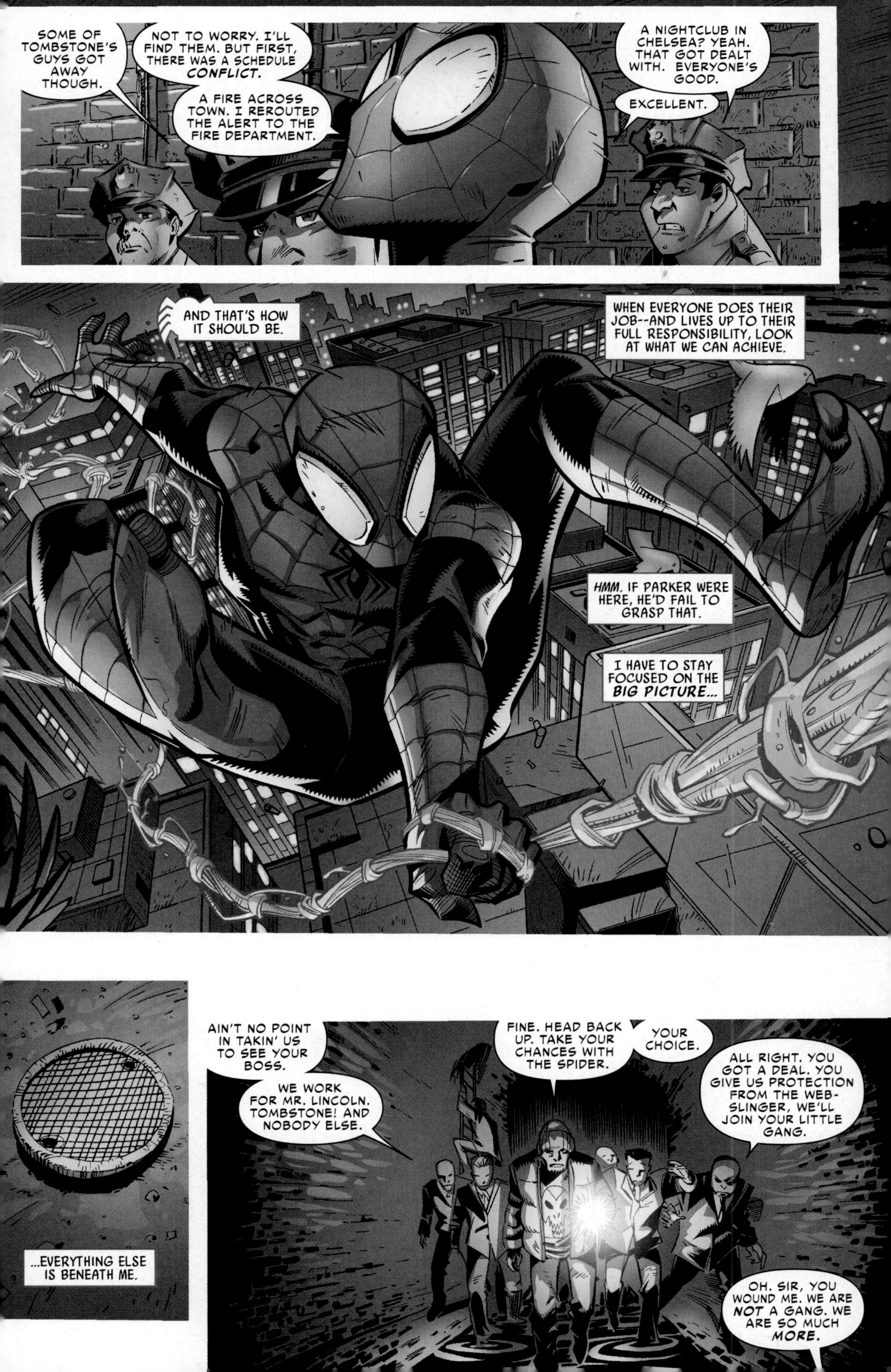

SOME OF TOMBSTONE'S GUYS GOT AWAY THOUGH.
NOT TO WORRY. I'LL FIND THEM. BUT FIRST, THERE WAS A SCHEDULE CONFLICT.
A FIRE ACROSS TOWN. I REROUTED THE ALERT TO THE FIRE DEPARTMENT.
A NIGHTCLUB IN CHELSEA? YEAH. THAT GOT DEALT WITH. EVERYONE'S GOOD.
EXCELLENT.
AND THAT'S HOW IT SHOULD BE.
WHEN EVERYONE DOES THEIR JOB--AND LIVES UP TO THEIR FULL RESPONSIBILITY, LOOK AT WHAT WE CAN ACHIEVE.
HMM. IF PARKER WERE HERE, HE'D FAIL TO GRASP THAT.
I HAVE TO STAY FOCUSED ON THE BIG PICTURE...
...EVERYTHING ELSE IS BENEATH ME.
AIN'T NO POINT IN TAKIN' US TO SEE YOUR BOSS.
WE WORK FOR MR. LINCOLN. TOMBSTONE! AND NOBODY ELSE.
FINE. HEAD BACK UP. TAKE YOUR CHANCES WITH THE SPIDER.
YOUR CHOICE.
ALL RIGHT. YOU GOT A DEAL. YOU GIVE US PROTECTION FROM THE WEB-SLINGER, WE'LL JOIN YOUR LITTLE GANG.
OH. SIR, YOU WOUND ME. WE ARE NOT A GANG. WE ARE SO MUCH MORE.

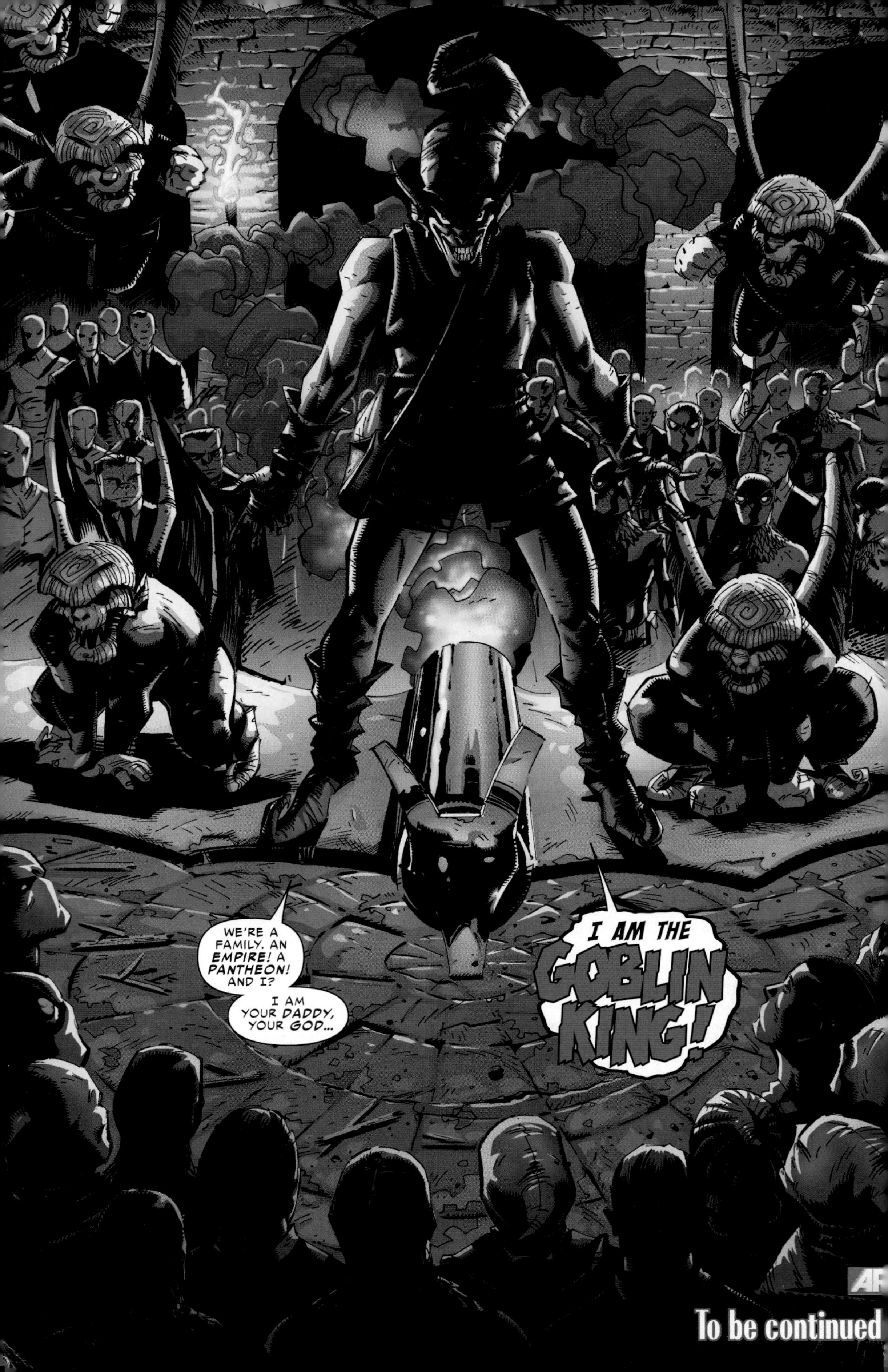
WE'RE A FAMILY. AN EMPIRE! A PANTHEON! AND I?
I AM YOUR DADDY, YOUR GOD...
I AM THE GOBLIN KING!
To be continued

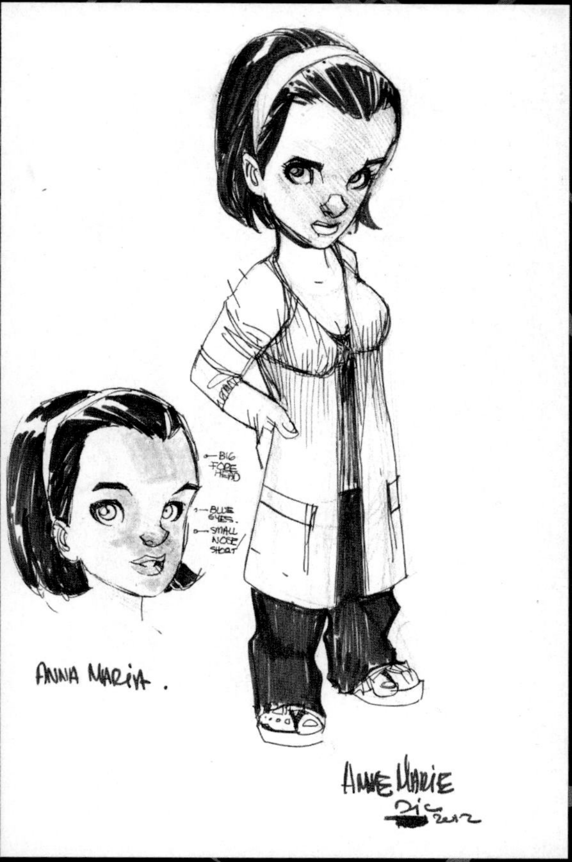
BIG FORE HEAD
BLUE EYES.
SMALL NOSE/ SHORT
ANNA MARIA.
ANNE MARIE
DIC 2012

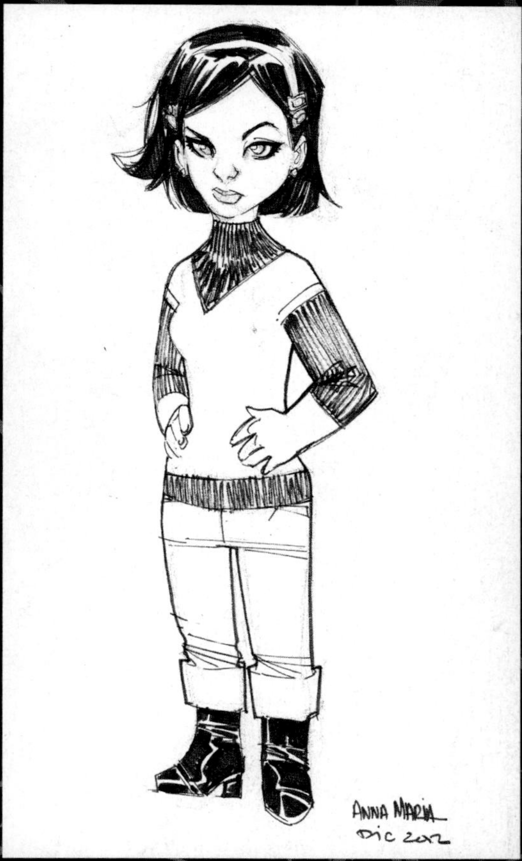
ANNA MARIA
DIC 2012

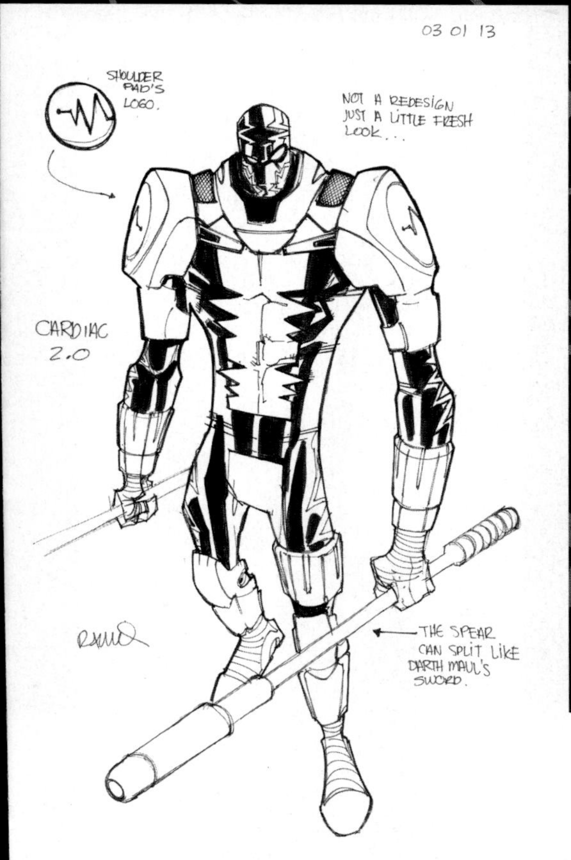
03 01 13
SHOULDER PAD'S LOGO.
NOT A REDESIGN JUST A LITTLE FRESH LOOK...
CARDIAC 2.0
RAMOS
THE SPEAR CAN SPLIT LIKE DARTH MAUL'S SWORD.

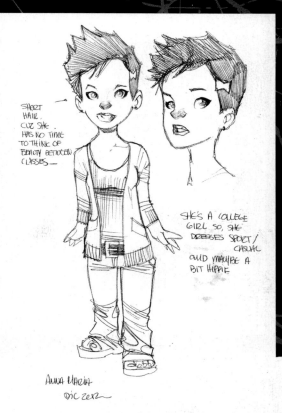

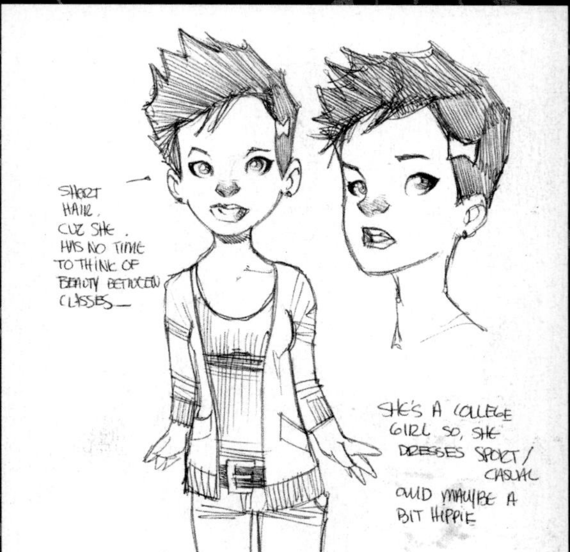
SHORT HAIR, CUZ SHE HAS NO TIME TO THINK OF BEAUTY BETWEEN CLASSES_
SHE'S A COLLEGE GIRL SO, SHE DRESSES SPORT/ CASUAL AND MAYBE A BIT HIPPIE
ANNA MARIA
DIC 2012

CHARACTER SKETCHES
BY HUMBERTO RAMOS

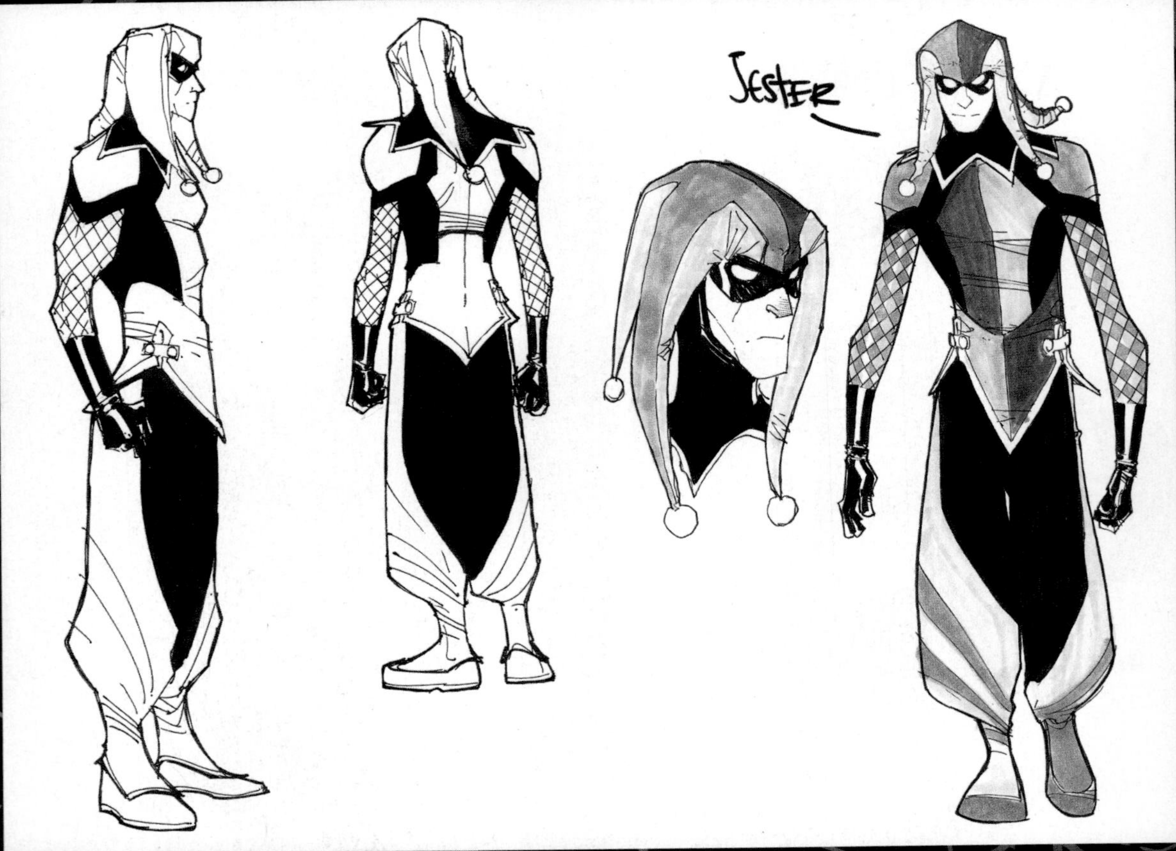
JESTER

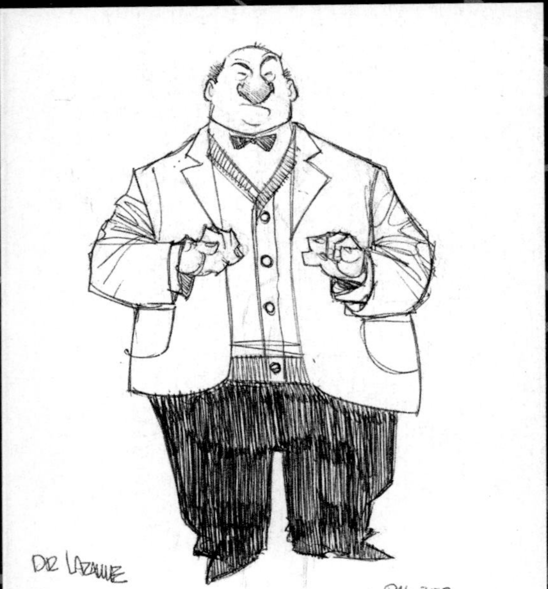
DR LAZALLE
DIC 2012

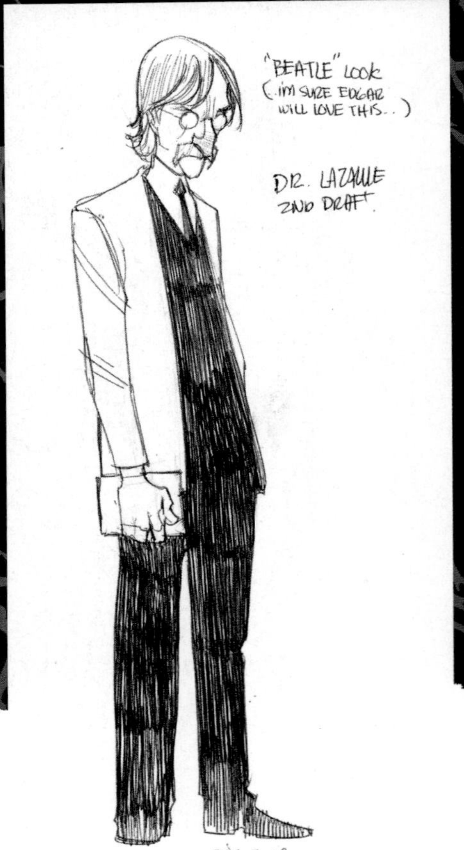
"BEATLE" LOOK
(..I'M SURE EDGAR WILL LOVE THIS...)
DR. LAZALLE
2ND DRAFT.
DIC 2012

CHARACTER SKETCHES
BY HUMBERTO RAMOS

"THIS STORY ALONE IS LIKELY TO MAKE IT ONE OF THE GREATS" – CBR.com

THE SUPERIOR SPIDER-MAN

"This is a great start to a new chapter of Spider-Man, and you're not going to want to miss a second of it."
— ComicVine.com

SLOTT **MARVEL NOW!** STEGMAN CAMUNCOLI

AR

MY OWN WORST ENEMY

SUPERIOR SPIDER-MAN VOL. 1: MY OWN WORST ENEMY TPB
978-0-7851-6704-4 • MAR130724

"...THE NEW STATUS QUO HAS GIVEN THIS BOOK A BOOST IN MOMENTUM." – AVClub.com

MARVEL NOW!

© 2013 MARVEL

TO ACCESS THE FREE *MARVEL AUGMENTED REALITY APP* THAT ENHANCES AND CHANGES THE WAY YOU EXPERIENCE COMICS:

1. Download the app for free via marvel.com/ARapp

2. Launch the app on your camera-enabled Apple iOS® or Android™ device*

3. Hold your mobile device's camera over any cover or panel with the **AR** graphic

4. Sit back and see the future of comics in action!

*Available on most camera-enabled Apple iOS® and Android™ devices. Content subject to change and availability.

THE SUPERIOR SPIDER-MAN AR INDEX